INTELLIGENCE, PSYCHOLOGY AND EDUCATION

INTELLIGENCE, PSYCHOLOGY AND EDUCATION

a Marxist Critique

BRIAN SIMON

Revised edition

LAWRENCE & WISHART
LONDON

Lawrence and Wishart Ltd.
39 Museum Street, WC1

Second, revised edition, 1978

Printed and bound in Great Britain at
The Camelot Press Ltd, Southampton

CONTENTS

AUTHOR'S NOTE

Thanks are due to the editor of the bulletin of the British Psychological Society for permission to reprint the paper "Some Contributions of Soviet Psychology"; to the Confederation for the Advancement of State Education for permission to reprint "Inequalities in Education"; to the editors of *Marxist Quarterly* and *Marxism Today* for permission to reprint "Psychology and Education", "Secondary School Selection", "Intelligence, Race, Class and Education" and "Contemporary Problems in Educational Theory".

As always, I am indebted to Joan Simon for many discussions of the material reproduced here. I am also glad to have an opportunity of acknowledging the preface contributed in 1953 to *Intelligence Testing and the Comprehensive School* by the late G. C. T. Giles, for years headmaster of Acton Grammar School and president of the National Union of Teachers in the year of the Education Act, 1944. It should also be underlined here that this book was written in 1952, for there has been no insertion of notes to indicate a now changed situation.

The other articles printed are, with one exception making for continuity, printed in the order they were written and reproduced as they were originally published except for the elimination of some unnecessary repetition and the correction of minor errors.

BRIAN SIMON
Leicester, December 1977

FOREWORD TO SECOND EDITION

The topics with which this collection of papers is concerned are still very relevant to controversies in the field of education and psychology. It has, therefore, been decided to publish a second edition but making one major change in the contents. In place of the original "Epilogue" on "Comprehensive School Organisation in the 1970s", a paper on "Contemporary Problems in Educational Theory", originally published in *Marxism Today* in June 1976, is included. As its title indicates, this paper tangles with some of the key ideological issues in education today.

Much of the material in this book deals with the vexed, and still highly controversial question of intelligence testing and its application to education. Arthur Jensen's attempt to rehabilitate the hereditarian thesis in his now famous *Harvard Educational Review* article (1969) forms the subject of a critical analysis in one of the papers in Part II. In this article Jensen relied very heavily on data on identical and fraternal twins reared apart and together accumulated by Cyril Burt over a long period and published in a series of articles in the 1950s and 1960s. After the publication of the first edition of this book it was revealed, as a result of close analysis of this data by Professor Kamin and others, that Burt consistently "fudged" his evidence to support the hereditarian hypothesis. Inevitably his material, cited frequently in this book, is now regarded as scientifically highly vulnerable.

The main charge against Burt is of *estimating* ("guestimating" might be a better word) the Intelligence Quotients of many of his subjects instead of giving them standardised tests, and even of "revising" results where he did administer such tests. In both cases the explanation suggested is that he was determined to ensure that his measurements were consistent with his theory that variation in "Intelligence" is the resultant 80 per cent of heredity (genetic endowment) and 20 per cent of environmental factors. He is further accused, by Kamin, of "frequent arithmetical inconsistencies and mutually contradictory descriptions". Kamin's full analysis needs to be studied to recognise the force of his criticisms, which are presented in detail in his book.[1] His conclusion

---

[1] Leon J. Kamin, *The Science and Politics of I.Q.*, Penguin Education, 1977, pp. 55–71, 202–207.

is of some significance; it is that Burt's data "are simply not worthy of our current scientific attention".

This conclusion applies to material gathered by Burt over a period of forty or fifty years—from the time he operated as educational psychologist to the London County Council in the early 1920s and before. To appreciate the full implications of these revelations it is necessary to recall that Cyril Burt was the leading psychologist whose evidence as to the nature of children's intellectual capacities was proffered to and consistently accepted by the Consultative Committee to theBoard of Education in the inter-war period. This "evidence" was reflected more or less precisely in important recommendations by the Committee in favour of developing a divided system of secondary education and, in particular, of imposing rigid forms of streaming in primary schools. It provided, in fact, the theoretical rationale for the selective and hierarchical system of public education as it was developed at that time.

This matter is dealt with at some length in the paper entitled "Classification and Streaming" in Part II of this volume. However, it is worth here recalling that the Consultative Committee's 1931 report on *The Primary School* followed Burt's specific advice on streaming, based on his analysis of the "mental characteristics of children" aged 7 to 11, which is printed as an appendix to the report. The section on streaming is taken almost word for word from Burt's appendix. Equally important, the crucial Spens report on *Secondary Education* (1938), which proposed the tripartite system, specifically acknowledges a similar memorandum by Burt on the age-group 11 to 16 (p. xvi). This, say the Committee, "forms the basis" of the chapter in which the Committee proposes the separation of children over 11 into different types of secondary school. Thus it was Burt's psychometric evidence that provided the rationale for this proposal, referred to specifically on pages 225–226 below.

It is precisely Burt's data "proving" his hereditarian thesis that is challenged by Kamin and others; but it was this thesis—in fact that of the *entire* dominance of heredity—that Burt presented as scientifically validated by data derived from mental testing, and it was *this* thesis that the Consultative Committee accepted. Not only did they accept the theory; they also accepted its educational implications as spelt out by Burt in terms of streaming and selection.[1] In view of this it now

[1] Burt's evidence was challenged within the Committee, but this was overridden. See Joan Simon, "The Shaping of the Spens Report on Secondary Education 1933–38: an inside view": Part II, *British Journal of Educational Studies*, XXV, 2, June 1977.

appears that the structure of the publicly maintained system of education, as it was developed in the inter-war period and indeed up to the
early 1960s, was based on even more shaky foundations than has yet
been realised. All the more reason, then, to break free of this system
by the development of comprehensive education and the abolition of
streaming, as has been the trend over the last ten or fifteen years.

Burt remained active well into his eighties (he died in 1971 aged 88).
Towards the end of his life he entered energetically into polemics
against modern educational developments, being by far the most
prestigious and authoritative of the contributors to the notorious
series of Black Papers on education and similar publications.[1] Burt
used this opportunity to reiterate his "authoritative" pronouncements
as to the hereditary determination of intelligence (*Black Paper 2*), and
as to "The organisation of schools" (*Black Paper 3*) where again he
argued for streaming and early selection, just as he did in the 1920s and
1930s. Indeed the whole Black Paper phenomenon relied very heavily
indeed on the contribution of the three psychometrists, Burt, Eysenck
and Lynn—all of whom take roughly the same line.

The most damaging charge against Burt is that he invented data to
suit his hereditarian thesis. Professor Jack Tizard (Professor of Child
Development in the University of London) has stated that the discre-
diting of his work has cast doubt on his whole line of enquiry. It would
have the same effect on that branch of science (psychometry) as the
finding that the Piltdown skull was a forgery had on palaeontology.
"But Burt not only discovered the bones, he gave the vital dimensions
and estimated the intelligence quotient" (*The Times*, 25 October 1976).
Professor and Mrs. Anne Clarke, the former at present Professor of
Psychology at Hull University, who themselves worked closely with
Burt at one time, make a similar point, but quite legitimately take the
criticism further. Their own investigations "revealed gross inaccuracies
and internal contradictions" in Burt's work; "since no one who knew
Burt could possibly accuse him of incompetence, there remains only
the possibility of dishonesty". He was obsessed, they add, "with the
importance of heredity as a major determinant of human differences—
and this meant that he was 'responsible for misleading many of those
engaged in the scientific study of man' " (*Sunday Times*, 24 October
1976).

Put in another way, what Professor and Mrs. Clarke are saying is
that ideological convictions as to the power of heredity were held by

[1] See pages 241 ff for comments on one of these.

Burt with such striking power as to blind him to the elementary requirements of scientific procedures both in the collection and in the presentation of evidence. In this sense the revelations as to Burt's procedures and practice bring into the clear light of day the full extent to which ideology has penetrated into this field of science—even of its dominance by strongly held presuppositions of enormous social and political significance. The liberal belief that science is unaffected by, or neutral in relation to, ideology has received a very severe blow indeed.

This aspect of the issue is brought more and more to the front when the fascist press in this country is examined. "Nationalists believe that intelligence is mainly genetically determined, and so the differences in intelligence and other mental abilities between the races are inborn and hereditary," writes Steve Brady in *Britain First* (January 1977), adding, "Therefore, we believe that the world intellectual leadership shown by the White Race [*sic*] is due to our unique genetic heritage, whose dilution by mixing with alien stock would be an irreversible catastrophe for all mankind." We have heard all this before, of course, from the mouths of Hitler, Goebbels, Rosenberg, Streicher and many others, and seen the practical application of this doctrine in the death camps of Nazi Germany. The support, and indeed heavy reliance by such journals on the teaching of Burt, Jensen, Eysenck and others is natural and only to be expected. Burt, Brady goes on to explain, is important to Nationalists "because, in 50 years of work, he found a great deal of evidence in support of the idea that intelligence is mainly inherited, rather than environmentally determined". The critique of Burt's procedures has been carried through by "mavericks and cranks" against "the reputation of an eminent and well-respected scientist".[1]

This is one example from many that could be given of the use made of hereditarian theories based on intelligence testing data in the "nationalist" press. As might be expected particular emphasis is put on Arthur Jensen's conclusions, in his original *Harvard Educational Review* paper, that the IQ's of blacks in the United States average some 15 points lower than whites. "The intellectual inferiority of the Negro", it is stated in bold black type under the heading "The Negro Brain" (in *Spearhead*) "is then a genetically inherited mental trait, just as skin pigmentation is a similarly inherited physical trait". This is backed up by drawings of the skulls of the orang-utan, Negro, and European,

---

[1] "Media smear IQ pioneer", by Steve Brady, *Britain First*, January 1977. This is the paper of the National Party.

with the statement that "the low forehead of the Negro restricts the cranial capacity for the frontal region of the brain";[1] and elsewhere by graphs and histograms presenting in as striking a form as possible Jensen's conclusions on comparative intelligence levels of blacks and whites.[2]

The Nationalist press, of course, appeals partly to a working-class readership and therefore nowhere publicises Burt's firm conclusions as to average intelligence differentials among social classes in Britain, which, according to Burt, "prove" that the working class have low inherited intellectual capacity (see pages 78ff. below where this matter is discussed). It was this, in fact, that was Burt's main thesis, consistently reiterated since he was himself chiefly concerned with educational and eugenic issues in this country; he expressed doubts (unlike Eysenck) about Jensen's racialist conclusions. This is not referred to in the Nationalist press, but the use made of Burt's prestige as a scientist and his support for the hereditarian hypothesis in his Black Paper articles is immediately linked to Jensen's work and to racialism.[3]

These two theses, that concerning race and that concerning social class, are necessarily linked together in intelligence testing and have been from the very inception of the mental testing movement. Francis Galton, its founding father, maintained the real objective existence both of racial differences and of social class differences in mental ability.[4] These both formed the original ideological basis of the eugenics movement from the turn of the century and before. It is, perhaps, significant that both "theories" were developed and strongly propagated by Galton who originally elaborated them in the heyday of British Imperialism when the movement was born, and when "scientific" techniques began to be developed to support or "prove" the truth of these original assumptions—or ideological positions (as in fact they were).

It is clear, then, that the whole question of human capacities, of the interpretation of these by the mental testing movement and of alternative interpretations offered by Marxists and others, is still of crucial importance today. The papers in this volume are mainly concerned with the educational implications of these theories, since it was here that they found their immediate application in this country. In the last

[1] *Spearhead*, April 1976. This is the paper of the National Front.
[2] *Britain First*, May 1977.
[3] *Spearhead*, November 1969.
[4] See Francis Galton, *Hereditary Genius*, Fontana Library, 1962, pp. 414–415 and *passim*. The first edition of this book was published in 1869.

few years, however, the racial implications of mental testing theories have gained in importance—for obvious reasons. The critique offered in this volume is equally relevant in this sphere as in education.

BRIAN SIMON
November 1977

INTRODUCTION

Why should a publisher think it worth while to reprint, in 1971, a small book *Intelligence Testing and the Comprehensive School*, first published in 1953? The reorganisation of secondary education on comprehensive lines is now well under way, the 11 plus examination has been largely superseded, and it might well be thought superfluous to revive arguments in favour of a change in this direction. But, on the other hand, even older arguments are revived in an attempt to slow down, and effectively to limit, this new development. Moreover, attempts to reanimate the ideology of "intelligence" testing in the United States, as a barrier to the declared policy of desegregating schools, indicate that there are powerful social and political forces in favour of reinstating the doctrine that intelligence is innate and impervious to educational influences, to the detriment of social and educational advance. This is one of the matters examined in this volume which includes, in addition to the book mentioned, several articles discussing the same general question—as this has been broached or restated at various times over the last twenty years. Most of these articles were written not so much for specialists as for the general reader.

It is always easier to defend the *status quo* in education than to make a viable case for change which, in the nature of things, involves embarking on a relatively untried road. When it also entails, as it must in the case of extending a full secondary education to all, encroachment on what has been a minority privilege then there are bound to be claims that established values are being fatally undermined. From here it is a small step to the assertion that political aims are shaping policy when only educational considerations should operate. Thus educational change is discredited by those who would like to keep things as they are—as if this were not itself an essentially political stance, particularly at a moment when technological progress is about to take men to other planets and there is every reason to suppose that social progress could, and must, keep pace. It may, then, be because the book here reprinted controverts this conservative view, because it set out to look at the *educational* reasons for eliminating early selection—and for discarding the system of testing which bolstered a divided school system —that it is thought worth rereading today. In any case, it certainly has to do with the contemporary history of education, that is the state of the educational system eighteen years ago and the controversies that accompanied growing recognition of the need for change.

Teachers are subject to many influences in their daily work which it is not easy to disentangle. We like to think, no doubt, that we are always guided by the latest findings of objective, or scientific research, and indeed one of the reasons for accepting "intelligence" testing wholeheartedly was the belief that it represented the very latest and best method of plumbing the child mind. Armed, then, with this method it was the teacher's task to shape his work within the school accordingly, as the school system itself was shaped by a selective process based on classification by Intelligence Quotient (or I.Q.). The result was the establishment of a closed system, subject to the ideas which directed the process of mental measurement itself.

But where did these ideas come from? For a considerable time no one asked this question. The assumption was that they, too, must be above reproach, or beyond social influences, conceived in the rarified atmosphere of purely scientific enquiry by some process of immaculate conception. This was not, however, the case, nor could it be. The scientist, taking up themes broached by his predecessors, brings to his work—just as does the teacher or anyone else—attitudes of mind, pre-dilections, which favour the choice of one subject or method of enquiry rather than another. But over and above this, in the case of mental testing the nature of the existing system of education, current policies of maintaining or adapting that system, were inevitably a decisive influence in determining the direction of development. It could not be otherwise, since the tests used within the educational system were framed precisely to the end of making that system, as it then was, work smoothly. In other words, since the requirement was to select a given proportion of children from each age group to go to the academic grammar school, the tests sought to discover ability to profit from "a grammar school education" as normally conducted. That they were called "intelligence" tests necessarily upheld two interdependent assumptions: that "intelligence" is to be equated with facility in following academic studies of a particular kind, and that academic studies of a particular kind are essential to minister properly to the intelligent. There could hardly have been a better recipe for maintaining the *status quo* in educational organisation and method—and at a time when the rumblings of an approaching technological revolution were getting ever nearer and louder.

How this closed system evolved, operated and was broken down is one of the matters discussed at different points in this volume. Here it need only be said that, after a period of apparently impregnable stability, the disintegration of the stratified school system was comparatively rapid, allowing the less opportunity for a revolution of ideas. Consequently old attitudes still persist, to retard the kind of developments in educational practice which are as essential to technological and social advance as they are to the realisation of individual potentialities. Moreover, to recall former controversies is to raise various questions that are still actual—for instance, to what extent should teachers depend on the advice proffered by experts, in say psychology or sociology, or how far are they bound to weigh up and modify advice from various quarters in the light of professional experience in the practice of education?

Here it is relevant to describe—since my own views have been criticised as politically motivated in the manner already referred to—how my own study of "intelligence" testing arose directly from experience as a teacher.

When demobilised from the army at the close of the war I became a teacher in Manchester—a form master, and general subjects teacher, to a "B" stream in an urban secondary modern school, serving a working-class area where a large proportion of fathers were employed in engineering. The children were lively, intellectually curious and with many potentialities, though as things then were most left at 14 a school which had not effectively outgrown elementary status and could offer little, or no, encouragement to stay longer.

From here I moved to a boys' grammar school in an adjoining area, to act for several years as form master to first forms of 11-year-olds. It was a joy to teach these boys when they first entered the school, so infectious was their vitality and enthusiasm. One had only to ask a question for hands to shoot up all round, almost every child straining at the leash to provide an answer. Here, again, were potentialities, heightened perhaps by the stimulus of being among the selected few to get to this school. But there did not seem to me to be any fundamental difference between these and the first group of boys I had taught.

Then I was drawn a little further into the machinery. Approximately ninety boys entered the school each year from some thirty junior schools, since this was the only maintained boys' grammar school in the local authority area. On entry, according to the approved methods, they were allocated to three streams—A, B and C—according to their placing in the 11 plus examination which comprised tests in "intelligence", English and arithmetic (the last two closely resembling the first). It happened that I was form master to each of these graded classes in turn in successive years. It was impossible to detect any substantial difference between these carefully differentiated groups, in terms of liveliness and curiosity, or aptitude to learn. But they, and I, had yet to learn what could be done to muffle this, to substitute for a general optimism and confidence a growing lack of trust and sense of failure.

At the close of their first year in the new school these twelve-year-olds were set an examination covering the main subjects studied. The aim was not so much to see where strengths and weaknesses lay, with a view to remedying these in the coming year, but to use the list of results to reshuffle the pupils so that those capable of getting the best marks in examinations were put together under the rubric "A". Accordingly some were moved up from the B, and even the C, stream while others were moved down to make a place for them. Up to this time I had shared the common illusion that tests were reliable indicators of potentiality—the kind of potentiality which it is difficult for a mere teacher to discern—but I was beginning to have doubts. Accordingly I decided to test the system of streaming by comparing the order in which the boys were placed by examination results at the close of the first year with the order in which they had been placed by the 11 plus selection examination. There was a negative correlation.

What does this mean? Looked at one way, it means that if the ninety boys who entered the school at 11 had been placed in streams on the opposite principle from that used—if the top 30 in the selection examination had been labelled "C" and the bottom 30 labelled "A"—this would have been a more accurate classification than the one actually adopted if their achievement at the end of the first year is taken as a criterion. More generally, it implied that all this administering of tests, with the aim of achieving the finest degree of accuracy in differentiating children, had a good deal more to do with ideas in the heads of teachers than potentialities in children; or, since this is less than fair to teachers, that the whole operation was essentially a product of the known narrowing of the path to higher education at the end of the grammar school. Since only a given, small, proportion could then enter universities or colleges, it became the task of the school to select, re-select, groom, forward, that small contingent duly labelled "A" to give at least these boys (from an unfavoured area) a good chance of success in a competitive race in which Eton, Winchester and the rest were also entered. Actually about half a dozen got to university each year, and when a boy once won an open scholarship at university the whole school was given a holiday.

In due course it became evident that the same principle—if such it can be called—governed the whole school system, internally and externally. Clearly the process I was witnessing went on in all primary schools straining towards the 11 plus, as observation confirmed. Then, the education authority operated what was known as a "late developers" examination at the age of 13, whereby boys at the top of the given secondary modern school classes had a second chance to get into the single grammar school. Only a few were successful, some three or four each year, and the boys who entered were usually graded into the third year "B" class of the grammar school. Almost without exception, I noticed, these boys did extremely well and accordingly graduated into the "A" class. The question obviously arose, were these really "late developers" or was this merely a euphemism for rectifying mistakes in the selection examination? A related question was why were so few boys successful in the 13 plus examination? If the few who came did so exceptionally well wasn't it reasonable to suppose—remembering those bright lads in the "B" stream of the modern school I had first taught— that there were plenty more who would have done quite well enough? I came to the conclusion that, perhaps inadvertently, the norms of the 13 plus tests must be kept artificially high (as could be arranged when tests were standardised for this particular purpose) to avoid an embarrassingly large number of children passing which in turn would have stretched the system at the seams and raised questions about the validity of 11 plus selection.

Doubts were enhanced by a third, depressing, factor. The lively boys I had known, and enjoyed teaching, in the first year "C" stream had by the third and fourth year in grammar school become passive noncooperators. Once among the selected few in the borough they were now "the dregs" of this school and saw no reason to respect an institution that so degraded them. Any teacher who had to take 3C or 4C in the late afternoon—or, for that matter, at almost any time—was assured of the full sympathy of his colleagues in the staffroom, if usually expressed in a ribald manner. It was by now taken for granted that these boys were unteachable, as in fact, given the ethos of the school, they were. In one such class a boy, with an IQ of over 140, retained much charm if caught off guard but his talents were usually turned to directing the policy of teacher baiting. And, on reflection, one could not blame him or the others. Who, then, or what, should rightly be blamed? Today we know a good deal more about this process of alienation, both in relation to grammar and secondary modern schools, from the fascinating and comprehensive investigation in which Lacey and Hargreaves have been engaged.[1] In the late 1940s, when nearly every school large enough for the purpose was streamed as a matter of course, one was only at the stage of beginning to ask whether these schools were not *creating* their own problems.

Nor did the question relate only to the "C" stream with its offhand, anti-school, attitudes. There was almost as great a difference between the "A" stream of the fourth year and the eager 11-year-olds I had once taught, insofar as classes had become docile, passive, difficult to stimulate to anything but note taking of a kind related directly to preparation for examinations. I remember on one occasion setting out deliberately to break this syndrome, to get a lively reaction that would make for active learning, but the upsetting of the academic equilibrium released a spate of negatively aggressive behaviour rather than attaining any positive result. In the circumstances it was impossible to take comfort from the fact that at least so far as the "A" stream was concerned the school was doing a good job. Manifestly, while failing the boys as boys, it was processing the type of first year undergraduate of which universities bitterly complained; though themselves largely responsible for the product by virtue of their selection procedures to which the school conformed. In short, not only the "C" boys had been sacrificed to the system but also its favoured object, or justification—those labelled "A".

All this was nearly a quarter of a century ago. Only a handful of comprehensive schools had recently come into being of which little was known. For the most part these were in sparsely populated rural areas—such as Anglesey and the Lake District—where it was impractical to introduce a sophisticated paraphernalia of single-sex selective schools. There was, therefore, no alternative school experience on which to draw. It was also well before the explosion of higher education which in due course made hay of official calculations about the limited number capable of reaching the sixth form, which in turn was used to rule out the more general provision of comprehensive schools and keep the system closed. On the other hand it was not long after

---

[1] Colin Lacey, *Hightown Grammar. The school as a social system* (1970). The school here analysed bears a striking resemblance to the one in which I taught, though in Lacey's study streaming was only begun at the end of the first year. D. Hargreaves, *Social Relations in a Secondary School* (1967) refers to a modern school.

the war during which unexpected potentialities had been discovered when urgently needed, where no one expected to find them; when people had risen to the occasion (as it was often said) or risen well above themselves which, in the circumstances, was an even more illuminating idea. By comparison the school system appeared to be (as indeed it was) run on the assumption that no child could ever rise above himself, that his level of achievement was fatally determined by an IQ—"his" IQ as it was generally thought to be. Was this not the very negation of an educational approach? That question inevitably arose after seeing the effect of schools on children, and it led on to another.

Every teacher sets examinations, designed to test work that has been done and the degree to which children have mastered it. There are various ways of drawing up questions, ranging them in order of difficulty, allotting marks, ensuring a particular spread or concentration of marks and so on. How, then, were these all-important tests of "intelligence" constructed and marked? To arrive at an answer to that question involved reading volumes about the theory and practice of mental testing—from those of the founding father, Francis Galton, through the works of Spearman, Burt, Ballard, Godfrey Thomson, Terman, down to present day practitioners—and, also, required study of the chief technical aspects. In the process a picture began to emerge, from what initially seemed a vast confusion, or at best an admixture of dogged persistence at the technical level and highflown metaphysical speculation about the nature of the human mind and its faculties.

This branch of research had been initiated by psychologists, in the first place in terms of devising a scale to differentiate individual children for clinical purposes. But social demand had quickly led to something very different, adaptation of this technique to the purpose of mass testing and classification. As results accumulated these were subjected to intensive analysis. For this purpose statistical methods were used so that vital points of interpretation were decided in terms of selecting a particular statistical technique from among those convenient to the purpose. All this had an effect in modifying the construction of tests. But as the machinery of testing advanced by this process, and was increasingly called into use, inconclusive arguments about the nature and derivation of the mental attributes being measured were buried or overborne. An analogy might be a caterpillar tractor successfully traversing a bottomless swamp; so long as it gets across there is no need to think in terms of constructing a solid causeway, attention concentrates on maintenance and refuelling of the machine. And this, it seemed, was what the current generation of mental testers was chiefly engaged in. Pressed to provide a means of classifying large numbers of young children, who must be fitted into existing schools, they provided tests by the score to meet the demand, never pausing to ask unresolved questions which did not, anyway, obtrude. In the outcome an approach was introduced into the educational system which, however suitable it may have been for clinical purposes, had inherently anti-educational implications.

Try to make a precise classification of the children in a classroom, in a situation when first one, then another, makes his mark in varying ways and it is the teacher's aim to stimulate as many as possible to activity so that learning is maximised and differences minimised—the two aims are contradictory.

The teacher's concern is to promote learning, to take the children from point A to point B (if one can formalise to this extent), and it is to achieving this movement that his efforts are bent. By contrast the psychometrist, attempting to classify ability precisely across the spectrum, is like a collector of butterflies hovering with a pin, anxious to range each in an appropriate order and to this end necessarily ruling out the essential mode of activity of the organism. Allow a general subservience to this approach and education falls by the wayside, children cease to be developing young human beings and are classified under the petrified pattern of the A, B, C drawers of specimens. In sum, to the extent that the diagnosis of "intelligence" had come to dominate school practice, education had been virtually displaced as the prime task—this, in favour of a continual process of docketing and classifying without regard to children's general welfare or feelings which must obviously condition their intellectual achievements. So schools became dehumanised—and there was no indication of any possible improvement, rather things were likely to get worse.

Yet, by this time, in the early 1950s, evidence was beginning to come to hand (particularly from the United States) showing that the individual child's IQ does not normally remain constant. This indicated that, contrary to repeated claims, psychometrists were not accurately measuring a predetermined and unchangeable quality of mind. Clearly this important fact should be made known and the whole matter brought out into the open. Above all the need was to reinstate education in the centre of the picture, as the creative task of teacher and

school, and to do this required detailed questioning of the whole—
as it now seemed monstrous and alien—edifice of testing superimposed
on the school system. It was to this end that the book reprinted here
was written, in such a way that parents—whose objections to the arbitrary operation of 11 plus were beginning to become vocal—could gain
confidence in challenging the "experts" who so confidently and
arrogantly labelled their children, in effect for life.

A year later, in 1954, a book dealing with more technical aspects
came from a psychologist working within the field—*The Appraisal of
Intelligence* by Alice Heim. This book, which is extremely critical both
of the methodology and the theoretical assumptions underlying testing,
was reprinted in 1970 with an introduction suggesting that it is more
relevant now than when it first appeared. Here is an indication that
whatever adjustments psychometrists may have made in their theory
and practice (and important modifications were made as is indicated
later in this volume) they have not abandoned their basic positions.

On the other hand, the thoroughness with which schools have
changed, particularly primary schools when freed from the tyranny
of the 11 plus, may be gauged by considering the first and last chapters
of my book, written eighteen years ago, in relation to present developments. Several of the points made—for instance, that streaming increases
differences between groups of children—have been confirmed by research findings.[1] On the other hand it was difficult to foresee the extraordinarily inspiriting effect elimination of 11 plus selection would have
on junior school children and teachers, documented in the Plowden
Report (1967), which justly refers to a "revolution" in primary schools
with facilities to make the most of new opportunities. By comparison
the perspective for the unstreamed junior school outlined towards
the close of my book now seems somewhat limited. It is a matter in
which I am happy to be proved wrong, or a lesson, if you like, in the
extent to which thinking can remain conditioned by prevailing practice
even when there is every effort to transcend it.

There are, I have found, two main routes of escape from this con-
finement. One of these is historical, the other comparative. Historical
study brings to light the process of formation of the school system as a
whole, both in terms of its structure and in terms of ideas about
education crystallised in forms of organisation and methods of teaching
within the school. Moreover, to study different periods in history is to

---

[1] P. E. Vernon (ed.), *Secondary School Selection* (1957), pp. 42–43; J. W. B. Douglas,
The Home and the School, (1964) p. 118.

become aware of radically different attitudes to education succeeding each other—but not in the way usually suggested in textbooks, that is, through a steady process of enlightenment in theory and practice. On the contrary, at some moments—notably during revolutionary periods—there may be a sudden realisation of the potentialities of education closely related to the current experience of changing long-established institutions or planning the redirection of the social process as a whole. Alternatively, when a society is stagnant, such ideas are submerged or forgotten, and the task of schools is emphasised not in terms of preparing pupils to make new discoveries about society and themselves but in terms of shaping units to occupy a given slot in a social order; and just as that order appears unchanging so also do human powers. Again, at certain times the salient characteristic is a conflict of educational ideas, reflecting different and opposing interests within the social order. Such, for instance, was the case in the nineteenth century when it was the aim of government to establish a limited system of elementary and moral instruction for the working class of an increasingly industrialised society, but members of this class themselves voiced far wider aspirations for access to knowledge and the development of human powers.

There is a parallel between this phase and the conflict of ideas accompanying the establishment of secondary education for all, one necessarily extending again to the political field since education is of central importance to the social order. Today the points at issue are much more complex than they used to be since they are now often discussed in terms of specialist psychological and sociological findings. Thus in this century restrictive educational policies have been supported by the argument that the working class have been proved to lack intelligence, a point argued by psychometrists with a wealth of technical detail. Whereas in the Victorian age politicians established a basic differentiation by arguing, quite openly, that the governing class must have a markedly superior kind of education in order that the working class should respect them as beings of a different and superior order.[1]

To approach present complexities historically is, then, a material aid to disentangling the influences or ideas at work, even if now operating beneath the surface. There is an attempt to examine the phenomenon of selection and streaming within the school historically, up to the early 1960s, in one of the articles printed here.

[1] The argument used, for instance, by Robert Lowe. Brian Simon, *Studies in the History of Education*, 1780–1870 (1960), pp. 355–56.

Another way of getting outside the prevailing system of education, as it were, is by the comparative method, adopted recently by official bodies such as the Crowther and Robbins Committees. When it has long been asserted that the majority of children are incapable of significant educational achievement, that to restrict the provision of a full secondary education to 20 per cent or less of any age group is to take sensible account of the limited distribution of "intelligence" in any and every population, then it is startling to discover that other countries proceed on altogether different assumptions with impunity. Here the example of the U.S.S.R. has been particularly illuminating to English educationists and it was certainly one which assisted criticism of the selective system here and the ideas derived from "intelligence" testing which underpinned it.

In the U.S.S.R. the primary educational task during this century has been the eradication of illiteracy, and the establishment of a system of schools to raise the educational standard of whole populations, some of which had no written language. Approached by way of the doctrine of "intelligence" the problem would have appeared insoluble, or the way would have been open for an attitude similar to that in some quarters in America today where it has been suggested that a whole race—one cruelly oppressed for centuries—may be inherently defective intellectually; black means stupid by comparison with white. This represents an extension of the view long canvassed by psychometrists in this country—as a result of applying particular types of test and analysing results in a particular way—i.e. that by comparison with the English middle class, the English working class is inherently lacking in intellectual powers, or mentally unequipped to profit from anything much more than elementary instruction. In fact, in the 1930s mental measurement was quite extensively used in the U.S.S.R., particularly in the cities. Confident in the efficacy of their instruments of measurement, psychometrists began to dictate to teachers in the schools— much as they were doing in this country in the late 1940s and 1950s. Use of tests inevitably led to discrimination against working-class children and this controverted the policy of creating a unified school system directed to raising standards all round, as an essential aspect of the change from a backward and imperialist to an industrialised and socialist economy. Accordingly testing was eliminated from the schools as early as 1936 and psychologists consciously turned their attention to investigating the learning process and ways of facilitating it.

Consequently—as I discovered on visits to the Academy of Educational Sciences in Moscow in 1955 and subsequent years—the approach adopted in psychological research is diametrically opposed to that of mental measurement. For, while the latter is only concerned with an end result at a particular moment when the child is tested—and throws no light whatsoever on the process leading up to this position, which is the main matter of interest to teachers—Soviet research was integrally concerned with investigating and furthering the process of learning. And this not so much in terms of formulating an all-embracing "learning theory" but of working towards one, not least in directly educational terms—for instance, in terms of studying the psychology of learning, or teaching, elementary skills such as reading and writing up to complex subjects such as mathematics and physics. Again, all this is relatively familiar today, with similar developments in the United States and on a lesser scale here, but it was strikingly new then and correspondingly important to the task of freeing schools from the doctrine of limitation of abilities in order to redirect attention to education. For instance, Soviet psychologists argued that it is impossible to assess "child development" without taking full account of education which is manifestly a key factor in that development—from which one came to see that the psychometrists, unable to eliminate educational influences, were in effect indirectly assessing their incidence even while asserting that their tests measured inborn powers exempt from "environmental" influence.

The general nature of this work is reviewed in two papers in this volume, one given at a meeting of the British Psychological Society in 1962. It is discussed in more detail in the introductions to two volumes of papers translated from the Russian, to remedy the then almost complete ignorance here of these research findings.[1] Mention should also be made of the translation of an original and elegant study of identical twins by A. R. Luria, which has been influential out of proportion to size in drawing attention to the role of language in mental development.[2] There could hardly be a more telling contrast of two different methods of approach than the latter study, concerned to penetrate the nature of the learning process, and those reporting reiterated tests of identical twins by psychometrists concerned only to establish how far IQ level ought to be attributed to heredity, how far to "environment".

---

[1] *Psychology in the Soviet Union*, ed. B. Simon (1957), *Educational Psychology in the U.S.S.R.*, ed. B. and J. Simon (1963).

[2] A. R. Luria and F. Ia. Yudovich, *Speech and the Development of Mental Processes in the Child*, ed. J. Simon (1959).

Perhaps the most important lesson learned from Soviet psychologists, in relation to the problem of "intelligence" testing, is that its very point of departure—which determines the whole direction and nature of investigations and the interpretation of findings—is very much open to question; that is, the concept that human mental powers depend on the interaction of heredity and environment. This assumption, dating back to the biological origins of psychometry at the close of the nineteenth century, necessarily delimits findings for it can only be postulated either that heredity is the chief factor at work (which in the present state of knowledge is speculation, however thick the cloud of statistics) or that "environment" (the vaguest of general categories confusing together influences of a qualitatively different order, natural and social) is the major influence. The only other way out of an arid controversy is to suggest, as has recently been common form, that more allowance ought to be made for continued interaction between these two "factors". The point to be made here is that the initial assumption rules out an understanding of the specific role of education in the social environment and activity of human beings. Only by eliminating preconceived ideas about the nature of human development, which equate this with animal development, and by taking integral account of the social context can there be an objective approach to study of the specific qualities of human learning and the role of education in the formation of social man—a point that arises in several articles here.

This draws attention to the fact that the rise of sociology, and the accumulation of sociological research, has had a considerable effect in undermining the positions established by "intelligence" testing. With an increasing demand for ability as the extent of the technological revolution began to be recognised, there was a growing realisation that the highly selective system of secondary education led to a great wastage of ability, by comparison with the educational practice of other countries, including competitors in the industrial field. There is an interesting parallel here to the late nineteenth century when there was also a turn to comparative studies in order to underline the need for educational advance. Official reports on educational policy also began to draw on sociological evidence. The first to do so was *Early Leaving* (1955) followed by the Crowther Report *15–18* (1958), which by underlining the social barriers hampering working-class children relegated arguments about relative intelligence to the background and paved the way for the Robbins Report (1963). This produced a massive body of evidence which, in turn, tended to relegate arguments about the "pool of ability", a term suggesting a reservoir that could easily be drawn dry. The Robbins Report substituted the concept of the widow's cruse, a bottomless source, and recommended that higher education be greatly expanded and made available to all who qualified.

With the implementation of this policy, resulting in an expansion of higher education which was earlier discounted as impossible on theoretical as well as practical grounds, the old pressures on the second-ary system have been mitigated. Indeed the way has been cleared for the development of comprehensive secondary schooling, also dismissed on theoretical grounds as undesirable a decade before—and indeed virtually forbidden to education authorities by successive Labour and Conservative ministers of education in the critical period of reconstruc-tion after the war.[1] But already in the 1950s the 11 plus, the pivotal point of the selective system, was beginning to break down as evidence accumulated of error or injustice and the anti-educational effect of selection at an early age. In the circumstances psychometrists were forced to revise some of their more categoric statements, the essential theoretical support of the selective system, and this public recantation had an effect in hastening the process. It was made in the report of a special working party set up by the British Psychological Society (1957) framed in part to meet public criticisms of the whole practice of mass testing and of the circular arguments used to support the IQ as an accurate measure of innate ability. This report indicated an intention to retire to slightly less entrenched positions; that is, no longer able to assert that "intelligence" tests measure an inborn power imper-vious to improvement by education, if only because it has been shown that many children improved their IQs, it allowed that "environmental" influences have an effect, particularly in early childhood. But to go only so far meant that selection, or streaming, within the junior school was now deprecated and, in effect, no further effort made to defend the 11-plus—which, by now, enlightened education officers were virtually refusing to operate and which in time became the common butt of an increasingly informed body of educational correspondents in the daily press. From a theoretical point of view, however, the psycho-metrists by abandoning heredity for environment merely switched from the roundabout to the swing without giving any evidence of a

[1] The implementation of this policy was discussed in B. Simon, *The Common Secondary School* (1955).

intention to leave the fairground. One of the papers in this volume is a response to the British Psychological Society report, written in 1958.

A major question that has been brought to the fore by the present rapid scientific advance is the relation between different branches of science, not least because it is at the meeting-point of established disciplines that new and vital fields of study arise. And keeping in touch is important for other reasons. "Intelligence" testing could not have dominated the school system for so long as it did—nor the ideas deriving from it have retained their hold as they still do in some quarters—had findings in adjacent fields been brought to bear to question large assumptions arrived at in a facile way. This is indicated by the sharp criticism, in 1970, of Arthur Jensen's attempt to reinstate the whole ideology of "intelligence" testing in the United States, criticism from geneticists, social psychologists and others, outlined in an article in later pages of this book. To return to the earlier analogy, what Jensen has done is to lower probes into the swamp of statistical calculation and speculation supporting the machinery of "intelligence" testing and suggest that solid rock is to be found in terms of scientific findings—a procedure necessarily involving highly technical arguments about statistical methods and their application which only a few other psychometrists have at their fingertips. But it is only necessary to compare the assertion that variance in "intelligence"—one of the most complex of human attributes however defined—is 80 per cent determined by "heredity", with the statements of scientists engaged in new branches of biological research, to see how irrevocably psychometry is rooted in the biology of the day before yesterday and forced to return to yesterday's discarded findings.

"Controversy concerning the relative influence of heredity and environment in determining intelligence", writes a contributor to the latest edition of the American *Encyclopaedia of Educational Research*, "has subsided greatly since the early days of intelligence testing. The belief that intelligence is completely dependent on genetic influences without appreciable change by environmental factors is now seldom held."[1] But, while this is the point to which the B.P.S. working party retreated in 1957, the minority view could be strongly urged anew in 1970, owing to the essential limitations of psychometry and the strong pressures of social forces in America unwilling to allow equal citizenship to blacks. By contrast, a scientist at work in the new field of ethology, reviewing the old antithesis, writes:

[1] *Encyclopaedia of Educational Research*, ed. R. L. Ebel, 4th ed. 1969, pp. 670–1.

"Ethologists claim that it is by no means proved, and is in fact highly unlikely, that manipulation of the environment (education in the widest sense) can mould man's behaviour beyond the boundaries of innately determined ranges, although the extent of these ranges is hardly known. At the moment it is neither scientific to claim actual knowledge of our innate behavioural equipment nor that we are infinitely mouldable . . . such questions have to be considered undecided until they are properly investigated."[1]

This assessment, made in an article describing recent research, not in the heat of controversy, indicates the difference between scientific caution and the approach of those psychometrists who are intent on establishing an interpretation arrived at by a statistical short cut from prepared positions. "Very little of the nineteenth-century picture of the world remains today", writes Harré in an introduction to the survey of key scientific developments from which the above quotation is taken. "A great revolution in concepts and ideas of nature has taken place." And one of the most characteristic attributes of twentieth-century science is "the extraordinary integration of the traditionally independent fields of physics, chemistry and biology". "The work of Bohr in physics joins with the ideas of Lewis in chemistry; the techniques of X-ray crystallography are the key to the deepest problems of molecular biology, and in the end of genetics; the notions of enzymes as organic catalysts, of hormones as messengers, of the chemical basis of electrical conduction in nerves, have led to the gradual unravelling of the mechanisms of life, and promise to provide an explanatory basis for the discoveries of the new science of ethology."[2]

All this has a bearing on human development, up to and including the operation of the human brain, and to take account of such advances is to reject the naïve biologism underpinning "intelligence" testing—and, it might be added, achieving a new circulation in some popularisations (or vulgarisations) of ethological findings. The leap ahead of the biological sciences, to subsume much of physics and chemistry, also brings to attention the relative backwardness of the social sciences. In this field, rather than reaching a stage of organised integration,

[1] N. Tinbergen, F.R.S., in *Scientific Thought 1900–1960*, ed. R. Harré, Oxford 1969, p. 260. Other articles in this survey on molecular biology, ecological genetics, cell biophysics, also underline the complexity of the matters coming up for investigation following on important new findings.

[2] *op. cit.* v–vi.

different branches of enquiry pursue separate and unco-ordinated paths, to the confusion of those engaged in education.

If, for instance, the educationist studies history he may learn from the textbooks that the structure of the educational system yesterday corresponded to the realities and outlook of a class society, but that today it is quite another matter since legislation recognises the right of all to education and schools can easily have an enlightened approach to children as children. If he then turns to sociological findings, it may well be to learn that the class conditioning of children, both outside and inside schools, is one of the most important factors with which the teacher must contend, not only in terms of relative deprivation or privilege but in more complex ways. In some instances he may also be given to understand that there is nothing much he can do about the matter since "society" is the overriding influence; he, too, has been formed by his social origins and environment, as he was formed so he is and the same goes for the children before him who cannot transcend their social conditioning either. If the teacher looks to psychology, to seek a way out, he may come up with the advice that all a child is destined to be is included somewhere inside him and it is the primary task of education to find ways of bringing what is inside out, a view which co-ordinates comparatively closely with that of mental testing while leaving sociological findings altogether aside. It is difficult to reconcile such contradictory advice, offered without any common framework of reference, and this is nowadays the overriding problem of the educationist.

In one of the papers reprinted here on Karl Marx's thought in relation to education, given to initiate a course on sociological thinkers, I have outlined the Marxist approach as relevant to this question of a common framework. Marx brought historical, economic, philosophical and sociological thinking into relation in attempting to arrive at an understanding of the mechanics of capitalist society, or, more widely, the laws governing social development. This bringing together of different disciplines is again on the agenda today with sociology attempting to become more historical, history to take account of sociological findings, the development of social psychology and so on. But to seek a common framework is not merely a matter of synthesising disparate disciplines in an arbitrary way, nor of expecting to find a final answer to the question how the world works which can be applied dogmatically in any and every situation. Rather it is a question of finding a viable mode of operation and that is what, it seems to me, the Marxist approach provides. In the case in point here, for instance, it aids recognition of the essential interdependence of branches of scientific enquiry which at present maintain a separate existence—which, indeed, became established separately because they deal with intrinsically different matters and each of which has accordingly developed a particular methodology, or terminology, which in turn underlines differences. Nevertheless all these branches of enquiry have a common origin and end, in that they are conducted by human beings living in societies of a particular kind and applied within those societies. When specialisation outruns the application of knowledge, or scientific findings are not adequately applied to humanist ends, then there is uneven development and the interdependence of knowledge is shrouded. But it is fatal to lose sight of it, and, paradoxically, as fatal to blur essential distinctions.

I once tried to explain this as follows, when discussing the different branches of knowledge, or disciplines, on which education draws directly and indirectly:

"Disciplines, as they come into being and develop, do not merely lay claim to territory and fence it around. Each may cultivate a particular field in a particular way, but there remains an essential interdependence, and as all continue to develop these interrelations become more complex. For instance, to take a single strand, one might argue that the study of living beings begins with the life sciences, reaching through physiology and neurology to investigation of the human brain. Findings in this field provide a starting-point for the scientific study of psychology which, however, develops its own approach and methods proper to a new level of investigation. The findings of psychology provide a necessary foundation for educational enquiry, which also develops methods appropriate to another province, and is dependent as well on other disciplines such as sociology. It is the *progression*, I think, that we need to understand, particularly the nature and degree of interdependence, for some of the worst mistakes have followed from transferring techniques and concepts uncritically from one province to another. One may instance the application to human society of biological concepts, or the case I have discussed, the way in which psychometry was applied in the educational field. Techniques, it may be noted, are particularly insidious because they appear to be merely tools, whereas in fact the tool may comprise a specific theoretical approach."[1]

[1] *Education: the new perspective* (Leicester, 1967).

This summarises one of the lessons learned from the study of "intelligence" testing and its effect on educational thinking as well as practice. That these depressing, and oppressive, ideas and the divided system of education they upheld, are now being actively overcome means that there is a new perspective for education. It remains to make good use of new opportunities and that is material for another book. But this one has a brief epilogue on the implications, for schools, of the present outcome of past struggles to make way for educational advance. The point is put in this way to emphasise that it is not so much the stage reached that is important but the direction in which we now move. To decide rightly about that direction, whether in terms of educational theory and the extent to which it depends on other disciplines, or in terms of educational practice and how schools can best be organised on new lines, needs much hard thought on the part of teachers and educationists. But it is by no means only they who should think about and decide the matter. There was never more need than today to bridge the gap between specialists and consumers of their advice or services, as well as divisions between specialists themselves, and nowhere is the need greater than in education which is the heart of the social order.

If this book contributes to bridging that gap, and ensuring that never again can the education service be so isolated from the community under the umbrella of anti-educational ideas as in the heyday of "intelligence" testing, then it will have served its purpose.

PART I

INTELLIGENCE TESTING
AND THE COMPREHENSIVE SCHOOL

PREFACE

Every now and then there appears a book which makes a big, even a decisive, impact on developments in the particular field with which it deals. I venture to suggest that this will prove to be such a book.

It tackles the most topical and one of the most fundamental problems of British education. Have we achieved "secondary education for all", the reform that was the keystone of the Education Act, 1944? If not, why not? What are the fundamental misconceptions and practices that stand in our way? .

Mr. Simon puts his finger on the spot. He shows how the practice of intelligence testing is used to justify the curtailment of opportunity from the junior school onwards; he shows also how theories based on intelligence testing uphold a form of school organisation, and forms of teaching, which make secondary education for all impossible.

Mr. Simon has had a varied educational experience—in central, secondary modern, all-age, and grammar schools, followed by a university education department—which brought the problem of intelligence testing home to him and caused him to study the subject. He here explains, in a brief space and with admirable lucidity, how tests are constructed and given and how the results are interpreted and used. His criticisms will greatly strengthen and clarify the present, mainly instinctive, rebellion of parents, teachers and administrators against methods of selection at 10 plus.

The ground cleared of many misconceptions, Mr. Simon points the way forward—the Comprehensive School. Though he can necessarily only deal with the subject in brief outline, he makes a clear exposition of the case for this, the only method of providing a real secondary education for all.

G. C. T. GILES.

ACKNOWLEDGEMENTS

I have to thank many practising teachers in all types of school, including the new London comprehensive schools, for the benefit of frequent discussions on the issues raised in this book, more particularly in Chapters I and V.

My thanks are also due to Mr. J. C. Daniels, who has given me valuable assistance with the sections on intelligence testing.

I gratefully acknowledge the permission of the University of London Press to reproduce some figures from *A Guide to Mental Testing*, by R. B. Cattell, and of Cassell and Company and Sir Cyril Burt to reproduce some figures from *Intelligence and Fertility*, by Sir Cyril Burt.

B. SIMON.

1952

THE DIVIDED SYSTEM OF EDUCATION

The School and the Parent

A child's school life between the ages of seven and eleven is often a closed book to his parents. A few children will talk volubly about the happenings of the day when they come home to tea; but most tend to regard school as a world to be kept secret from their parents, a sphere of activity where they lead an independent life. This is a natural reaction and one that most parents respect.

Even when a child does talk about the teachers or about lessons, no clear picture of the school's organisation and aims can be built up. Young children have no other course than to take what happens at school for granted; they can hardly question or criticise. They are naturally unlikely to see what is significant and important in school organisation and activity and to hand on a clear picture to their parents.

The parents who, according to the law, deliver their child to school at the age of five are, then, sending him out into a relatively unknown world. Though at many nursery and infant schools a fairly close contact between teachers and parents is maintained, with the child's transfer to the junior school at seven this contact is usually broken. Most parents have neither the time nor the knowledge, nor possibly the means, of finding out much about how the school is run. An occasional visit on an open day and perhaps a single interview with the head teacher may be all the contact that they achieve.

Only where there is an active parents' association will they have any real opportunity of hearing talks on the work of the school and meeting the teachers. In general, however, they will assume that the teachers are skilled practitioners, that they know their job, and that it is not the parents' business to interfere.

Most parents, however, have fairly definite opinions about their own child. They know the things he is good at and have a fair idea where his weaknesses lie. What do they expect from the junior school? Probably not more than that it will give their child the opportunity to learn, to develop those activities to which he seems particularly suited, to bring him on where he is backward, and, in general, to give him a systematic, useful education, especially in the basic subjects, so preparing him for further education. They will also expect their child to have as fair a chance of these things as any other child attending a State school.

Perhaps the mother may pass by her child's school during the day. During lesson time all will appear quiet and orderly to the outsider. She may catch a glimpse through the ground-floor window of a class of children busily writing, or of the teacher at the blackboard, the children with heads raised, listening; she may see a physical education lesson in the school yard, or hear a class singing in the assembly hall. The children are learning new skills, new activities. Or if she passes during the break, she will see the children surging across the playground, shouting, singing, playing games, running about at a breakneck speed, but by some sixth sense never colliding. The air is full of the noise children make when released for a few minutes from the necessary constraint and discipline of the classroom.

Seen in this way, the school seems outwardly to have a single purpose. It appears to be a place where all children are taught to master the basic skills and activities necessary to social life, where they learn to make friends, to realise their own personality, and to prepare for their later independence and maturity.

Such, at least, is the apparent purpose of the junior school.

One School or Three

But penetrate within the school, examine its structure and organisation in detail, and the outward appearance of unity is at once shattered.

It is perfectly true that the school day usually starts with an assembly of all the children, when the head teacher sometimes talks about matters of interest to the school as a whole. It is also true that the children come together at play-time, sometimes for games, and to a lesser extent for activities run by the teachers out of school hours.

But for the main business of the school—that is, for teaching—there exists not one school, but two, three, and sometimes even four different "schools". These "schools within a school" can best be likened to conveyor belts, moving at different speeds, and moving also progressively further apart. It is a fact, little appreciated by many parents, that only those children who have obtained a place on the fastest of these belts have any real chance of being deposited in a grammar school at the age of eleven. The decisive step influencing the future career of any child is made, not at ten or eleven, but at seven or often even at six, when the child is still in the infant school.

Almost every junior school in the country of the requisite size is organised in this way. Schools are described as two-stream schools or three-stream schools, indicating the number of parallel classes for the different years, and implying, not only movement at a different pace, but also the existence of banks separating one stream from the other.[1]

Streams are normally called "A", "B" and "C", "A" being the quick stream and "C" the slow. The "B" stream is betwixt and between. Big schools with an intake of more than 120 children each year will also have a "D" and even an "E" stream. This system permits of a "streamlined" education, although such a conception will seem to some to contain a contradiction.

As a matter of fact, teachers, who are practically forced to organise schools in this way, often seek to hide the fact that the schools are "streamed" from the pupils. This they do in the interests of the children, who are, of course, very sensitive to the judgments of adults, and who like to receive encouragement in their efforts to master knowledge and skills. To label a class "C" makes it fairly clear to the children what their teachers think of them. As a result, these children are not unnaturally liable to get dispirited, and to lose confidence in their own abilities.

In many schools, therefore, the streams are not labelled "A", "B" and "C", but "X", "Y" and "Z", or even "P", "Q" and "R". Sometimes they are called after the initials of their teachers. Occasionally, even Greek letters are used, perhaps on the theory that children of eight or nine are not likely to understand this language. There is no end to the ingenuity of teachers in evolving methods of concealing this system of organisation from the children. But in spite of all these precautions, the children normally manage to penetrate these defences. It is very difficult to conceal the truth from children, especially in a matter that so intimately concerns them.

Once a child is placed in the "A", "B" or "C" category at the age of six or seven, he is almost certain to remain in it as he grows older. The reasons for this will be discussed later. The result, however, is clear. It is that the average junior school of 480 children usually consists not of one but of three schools, with a divided internal structure as outlined below.

[1] Some schools in country districts, and a few in the towns, are not large enough to allow for this form of organisation.

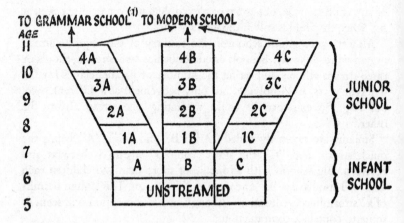

Streaming, Its Cause and Effect

This form of organisation is forced on the schools by the selection examination, popularly known as the "scholarship", which is usually taken at the age of ten. Success or failure in this examination determines the kind of secondary school to which the child will go at eleven.

It is well known that this examination is highly competitive, much more so today than before the 1944 Education Act, in spite of the increase in the number of grammar school places. Very many parents feel, rightly or wrongly, that their children should go to the grammar school; but, in fact, on an average in the country as a whole, there is room for only one child in five in these schools. Nevertheless, most parents expect the junior schools to prepare their children so that they will be able to jump the hurdle of the examination successfully.

At the same time, junior school headmasters and teachers like to get a good proportion of their children through the examination. Teachers are very anxious to do the best they can for the children under their care, and many feel that to make a special effort to get more children a place in a grammar school is well worth while. A child who goes to such a school has the opportunity to gain qualifications necessary for all the better jobs, and the grammar school also opens up the road to the university and the professions. Naturally, a junior school teacher will take a pride in sending on as many of his pupils as possible to a school which can offer these opportunities.

---

[1] The proportion of the "A" class who win places in grammar schools varies, of course, from school to school and year to year.

But it has been shown by experience that the *simplest* way of getting the largest number of boys and girls through this examination is to stream; to test all the children as early as possible, pick out those who appear to be the most advanced, put them together in one class and press on, as quickly as possible, especially with those subjects in which the children will eventually be examined. The "A" stream is therefore formed, as soon as the children come into the school at seven, though in many cases they have already been partially sorted out in the infant school, and come up, as it were, already hand-picked. The "B" and "C" streams similarly take shape.

As soon as a school is streamed, a certain rigidity is bound to set in. In the "A" stream are to be found all the children who can read well, write well and do sums well. In the "C" stream are all the children who cannot read or write, or who are only beginning to make out the words with difficulty and who are not good with figures. It is therefore not surprising that, by the end of the year, the "A" stream will have made comparatively greater progress than the "C" stream, where many of the children may not even have reached the point from which the children in the "A" stream began.

Towards the end of the year, the head teacher, wishing to be fair and to give each child the opportunity that he seems to merit, may decide to give a test to the whole year, in order to help him decide whether some children should be moved from the "B" to the "A" stream, or vice versa.

To give such a test fairly, he must set the same questions to all the children. But in arithmetic, for instance, the "A" stream will normally have got considerably further ahead than the "B" stream, and will certainly be a long way ahead of the "C" stream. Inevitably, the results of his test will show "A" children at the top, "B" in the middle and "C" at the bottom.

On the next page is the result of such a test in English and arithmetic done recently by children aged ten at a two-stream junior school (the marks on the different papers are combined):[1]

These results may lead the headmaster to suppose that his original sorting out of children has been amply confirmed. If there are one or two "B" children with higher marks than one or two of those in the "A" class, as there are in the example given below, he will probably transfer them. But in the main there will be no change. The tests used

[1] Classes are unusually small in this school, as it is situated in an area where the child population is declining.

Position	Mark	Stream	Position	Mark	Stream	Position	Mark	Stream	Position	Mark	Stream
1	129	A	17	111	A	32	97	A	47	90	B
2	125	A	17	111	A	32	97	B	47	90	B
3	124	A	19	110	A	34	96	A	47	90	B
4	120	A	19	110	A	34	96	A	50	89	B
4	120	A	21	108	A	36	95	B	51	88	B
6	119	A	21	108	A	36	95	A	52	87	B
7	118	A	23	107	A	36	95	A	52	87	B
7	118	A	23	107	A	39	94	B	54	86	B
9	117	A	25	106	A	39	94	B	55	84	B
9	117	A	25	106	A	41	93	B	56	82	B
11	116	A	27	104	A	41	93	B	56	82	B
12	115	A	28	103	A	43	92	B	58	81	B
13	114	A	29	102	A	44	91	A[1]	59	80	B
14	113	A	30	100	B	44	91	B	59	80	B
15	112	A	31	98	B	44	91	B	61	76	B
15	112	A							62	75	B

seem to reflect the "abilities" of the children and to justify the whole process of streaming.

But, of course, it often happens that the "B" and "C" streams have not even covered the syllabus on which the test is set, and so may never have been given the chance of mastering the techniques required to answer some of the questions. Even if they have covered the syllabus, they will probably not have done so as intensively, and they will have had less practice, since the teacher had to start at an earlier point and could not go so quickly as the teacher of the "A" stream. Results, such as those given above are, therefore, by no means surprising. They do not so much warrant conclusions about the abilities of the children as simply reflect the inevitable results of streaming. They indicate also how it is that the divisions between streams tend to widen as the child moves up the school, so that transfer between streams becomes progressively more difficult. From this follows the tremendous importance to the individual child of his original placement in a particular stream when he first enters the junior school. If he is allocated to the "C's" at the age of six or seven, it is practically certain that he will still be in a "C" stream at the age of ten or eleven, when the examination is taken.

The decision taken at this early age, based, as it normally is, on the

[1] This child was in the "B" stream throughout the school, until the final year, when he was transferred to the "A" stream. He was not, however, able to catch up with the others

child's ability in reading, writing and arithmetic, often determines his future. What, then, are the most important influences affecting the child's abilities in these subjects at the age of six or seven?

There are, of course, many reasons why some children are much better than others at reading, writing and arithmetic, when they first enter the junior school.

If a child comes from a home where the parents often tell him stories, where they read to him and take trouble to buy him suitable books, where they encourage him to paint, to draw, to write, and generally to express himself, then it is almost certain that by the age of six he will be talking fluently, reading well, and be generally interested in new activities. Such a child will almost automatically find himself in the "A" stream.

The parents of another child may rarely read anything but the newspaper. They may lack the facility for telling the kind of stories that appeal to children and so arouse the imagination. Possibly the father may be too tired after a hard day's work and travelling to give his child much attention; or the constant battle to make ends meet, perhaps with a large family and a small house, leaves the mother with little time for extras. The child of these parents is left a good deal on his own. He may develop all kinds of abilities, learning to fend for himself and developing initiative and independence beyond his years. But he may not learn to express himself clearly, and his reading and writing will progress slowly; he will more than probably find himself with the "C's".

The infant school cannot equalise these differences, and indeed, when it also is streamed, it does not set out to. Many children leave infant schools still unable to read or write.

And because some children enter the junior school at seven with less equipment of a certain kind than others, often for reasons which have nothing to do with character, interest or intellect, their paths will diverge from the start and will never meet. The former are labelled backward, the latter bright, and the labels will stick. The junior school teachers are necessarily affected by the class with which they are confronted, and affect it in turn. The "A's" are more rewarding, more interested in new activities; the "C's" have first to be provided with the necessary background before even reading has any meaning. And so the distance between the streams becomes more marked as the children go through the junior school. Moreover, even though it is usual to keep the "C" class smaller than the others, it is often too large to allow for much individual attention, which backward children particularly require to initiate them in reading and writing. As a result, semi-literacy or even illiteracy may not be overcome at one end of each age group in the junior schools, while at the other the children are being rigorously drilled in the basic subjects of the selection examination.

The normal junior school, therefore, is almost inevitably organised, not so much with the aim of providing the best possible education for all the children, as with that of obtaining the greatest number of "scholarships" or passes in the selection examination at ten. The tragedy is that many people, including some teachers, regard these two aims as synonymous. In fact, they are mutually exclusive.

Even the "A" stream, the few favoured children, do not get "the best possible education". The selection examination is ahead and profoundly affects the curriculum. "Some headmasters", stated Mr. R. Morley, an experienced teacher, in the House of Commons recently, "have moulded the whole of their curriculum around the grammar school entrance examination. From the time the child comes into the primary school at the age of seven, his attention is directed towards (this) examination. The whole of the primary school curriculum is distorted and warped . . . and |this warping . . . is a very evil thing."[1]

The headmasters concerned could well argue that they are only doing efficiently what the system requires of them. But that this distortion of junior school education is widespread is commonly admitted. In some schools it goes so far that Mr. Clegg, the Chief Education Officer for the West Riding, has felt impelled to write: "If the Committee were to decide that henceforth they would select for grammar schools solely on the children's ability to do long division, this form of calculation would be the main and most serious occupation of certain junior schools for the whole of their four-year course, to the detriment of many other activities which ought to be occupying those years."[2]

Even for children in the "A" classes, therefore, what should be education tends to become a narrow training in a few subjects. To achieve the necessary conditions for this concentration on the few, the rest of the school is separated into divisions which, it might be argued, tend to create the very backwardness which the school, in theory, exists to overcome. Actually, the "B" class often becomes a pale reflection

---

[1] *Hansard*, February 17th, 1953, 311–12.
[2] A. B. Clegg, "Some Problems of Administration in West Riding Grammar Schools", University of Leeds Institute of Education: *Researches and Studies*, January, 1953, VII, 9.

of the "A" class, following the same narrow curriculum several steps in the rear; there is still a faint hope of a successful examination result here, at least in some schools. The "C" class, however, deprived of the stimulation of those who find the subjects easier and more interesting, and conscious of their position in the school, find the struggle for literacy a hard and often unrewarding task, in spite of the help of the most devoted teachers.

Summarising the effects of this system from the children's point of view, it may be said first, that it practically determines their future at the age of six or seven; second, that it leads to a mechanical and distorted form of education; and third, that it isolates the children from each other, and so breaks up the unity of the school.

From the teachers' point of view, streaming is usually justified on the grounds that it is easier to teach a class with a roughly similar level of attainment, especially where there are forty-five or fifty children in a class. Most people would admit that there is some truth in this contention, though if it is "easier" to teach an "A" class, it is probably more difficult to teach the "C's". There are many points which could be made here, both for and against, but at the moment this discussion is not relevant. We are not concerned with what is the "easiest" way of teaching, but with the effect that present methods have on children. If this is bad, then, however difficult it may be, new methods should be evolved; if this means changing the structure of the educational system, the necessary changes should be made.

Some pioneers among junior school heads who find the system, with its attendant evils, abhorrent to their educational purposes, have abolished streaming in their schools. This is not an easy thing to do. It may meet with opposition within the school, since some of the teachers, especially those who regard themselves as "A" stream teachers, may oppose the change; it may involve standing out against external pressure; above all, it requires a re-thinking of the whole question of the content and methods of education to meet the new conditions of teaching and the new purposes. But where success is achieved, as it has been, such a school presents a challenge to the educational world, embodying a more humanist conception of education, and showing that there is an alternative which can be put into practice now, given the necessary conviction, energy and skill.

Nevertheless, these pioneer schools are fighting a difficult battle, and it would be illusory to suppose that their example can be widely followed while selection at ten continues to operate.

The Great Divide

In his last year at the junior school, the crucial moment comes, the child sits the selection examination.

Everyone knows the heart-burnings caused by this examination in innumerable homes throughout the country. This is the moment that has been prepared for, for weeks and months and years. It marks the parting of the ways, and in this sense it determines the child's future.

What is not so generally recognised is that for some 60 per cent of the children the die was already cast four or five years before, when they were first placed in lower streams. Many of these children, however, now go through the farce of taking the examination. In this way, the illusion that they have an equal chance is fostered.

For one or two days the children write busily on printed sheets of paper, usually filling in one word answers to questions in English arithmetic and "intelligence";[1] some, like Sir Winston Churchill at the Harrow entrance examination, may only succeed in making a large blob of ink, but they are unlikely to be selected as he was.

Teachers then spend hours (at very low pay) marking each question mechanically with the aid of a key, and totting up the marks. The papers are then sent to a central office, where marks are added to other marks, and age allowances and other modifications mathematically calculated. A list of the children in their final order is eventually made out. The dividing line between "pass" and "fail" is now drawn at a certain point, according to the number of grammar school places available in the area. Finally the parent receives a printed letter informing him that his child has, or has not gained a grammar school place, as the case may be.

Such, in brief, is the procedure of selection. Of course, it varies in detail from city to city, and county to county, since each education authority has the power to choose its own method. In some cases, the child's school record, or the teacher's estimate of his "ability", is taken partially into account; in others, much careful attention is devoted to the so-called border-line cases, those who just pass or who just fail. But refinements in selection are rarely concerned with more than the minority on the border-line.

The actual point at which the dividing line is drawn varies considerably from area to area, and even within an area. In the West Riding in 1952, for instance, there were in one district grammar school places

---

[1] Recently some local authorities have included compositions and comprehension tests in addition to the so-called "objective" tests in English, arithmetic and "intelligence".

for 40 per cent of the children; in another for only 15 per cent. A child in the first district could get to a grammar school with a mark of 59 per cent, while in the second the lowest score which secured a place was 70 per cent in the same examination. About 1,700 children in this county who had marks over 59 per cent failed to win a place in a grammar school.[1]

In spite of this wide inequality of provision, the dividing line between "pass" and "fail" is incredibly precise: "Under the present system", writes the Chief Education Officer for the West Riding, "admission may be determined by a fraction of 1 per cent."[2] Suppose there are 500 grammar school places to be competed for by 2,500 children. The 500th child gets an average mark on, say, five papers, of 60·2 per cent. The 501st gets 60·3 per cent. The cut-off point will then be 60·25 per cent. The former goes to a grammar school, the latter to a modern school. And, of course, just above and just below them will be grouped many other children who share their fate.[3]

In this way, the examination acts as a great sorting machine, separating the children into two or sometimes three groups. The children have arrived at the point of "all change". Friends in the same form, brothers and sisters from the same family, may be sent off to different types of schools, some to wear the caps and blazers of the grammar school, others to the modern school. From now on each of these groups will receive a different type of education, and their opportunity to make the most of their lives will vary accordingly.

The Secondary School

It is after eleven, therefore, that the conveyor belts separate, and now the gulf is so wide that it is extraordinarily difficult to jump from one to the other. In some areas, it is true, there is an opportunity to transfer from one type of secondary school to another at the age of twelve or thirteen. But, like the border-line selection, this concession affects only a handful of children. The vast majority, well over 95 per cent, stay in the type of school for which they have been selected.

At the grammar school the child will get an academic education, for

[1] A. B. Clegg, 7, 8.   [2] A. B. Clegg, 9.
[3] Mr. Ben S. Morris, Secretary of the National Foundation for Educational Research, drawing attention to this question, cited the case of 140 "border-line" children competing for eighty places. The total marks obtainable in the examination was 500. All 140 children obtained over 400. They were separated by only twenty-two points (*Manchester Guardian*, October 16th, 1952).

the grammar school is geared to the university and the professions; like the junior school, it prides itself chiefly on that small proportion of its pupils (sometimes about 10 per cent though often less), who are selected for higher education, and, like the junior school, it tends to subordinate all education to this end.

But the way to the university is narrow, and the majority of grammar school children have no hope of reaching this goal. Many become bored and unco-operative at the age of thirteen or fourteen, and cease to derive much advantage from their education. Although full of life and potentiality, they fill the grammar school "C" and "D" streams (for these schools also are streamed), and many fall out of the course early. These are the "early leavers", or "misfits", about whom educationists hold conferences. They and their parents are condemned on all hands. But the parents, though anxious for their children to have a good schooling, did not themselves choose the grammar school curriculum. In many districts there is in any case no alternative, for secondary technical schools are still very few and far between. It is not, after all, the parents who are responsible for the inability of these schools to provide the majority of their pupils after fourteen or fifteen with a suitable curriculum and methods of teaching. The main influences determining the grammar school curriculum are the university entrance requirements, which inevitably dominate these schools, just as the selection examination dominates the junior school; and grammar school teachers, like those in the junior schools, are naturally anxious to assist as many children as possible towards a higher education. If the grammar school ceased to place its main emphasis on winning university places, if it changed its structure, organisation and curriculum to meet the needs of the high proportion of its children who at present have no chance of achieving higher education, it would immediately lose caste. Rather than risk this, it is easier to rationalise the children's failure as being the result of their own lack of ability, and to claim that many of the children who have found their way into these schools should not be there at all.

While the secondary schools are so organised that the grammar school almost monopolises the road to higher education, neither this nor any other type of secondary school can provide a general, all-round education. The very existence of the grammar school inevitably de-limits the scope of the secondary modern school, which is cut off from the universities, the professions, and higher education generally. In those districts where there are secondary technical schools, the modern schools are also not required to prepare children for another wide range of activities. The position of these schools in the structure of the educational system ensures that they can have no clear aim beyond providing a four-year course of teaching for those on the way to work at the age of fifteen. Since, in many occupations, the workers are not supposed to contribute any intellectual power or scientific knowledge to the processes of production, this aim does not call for any particular kind of education. The result is that the secondary modern schools are supposed to concentrate on "projects" and "practical activities" of all kinds, and that a scientific and systematic education is considered out of the question. Fortunately this advice is not always taken, but the success achieved in modern schools is achieved in spite of the conditions under which they have to operate, and is a testimony rather to the quality of the teachers and the children, than to the conditions in which they have to work.

Selection and the Education Act, 1944

At this point, parents may well ask: But why is it that this system still goes on? Didn't the Education Act open up secondary schools to all, and provide greater equality of opportunity? Why is it that selection at ten is more competitive now than before this reform?

In 1944, largely as a result of years of struggle by working-class organisations, progressive educationists and teachers, "secondary education for all" was by law established. But, in spite of certain important changes, such as the raising of the school leaving age from fourteen to fifteen, and the abolition of fees in maintained grammar schools, the new Education Act left things fundamentally as they were.

The old senior elementary schools were rechristened "secondary modern schools", so giving the appearance of equality with the "secondary grammar schools". But though some fine new modern schools have been built, in many districts secondary modern schools are such only in name. In reality they are the old senior departments of all-age schools, sharing a usually old and overcrowded building with the juniors. In a few places, "secondary technical schools" have taken the place of the old "junior technical" or "intermediate" schools. But most parents are well aware that their child is likely to gain a more tangible advantage from his secondary education if he goes to a grammar school.

The Education Act did not lay down this particular form of organisation for secondary education. It merely required that, after the junior school, all children should be provided with an education according to "age, ability, and aptitude".

Nevertheless, two main types of school still exist, just as they did before the war. One stems from the elementary tradition of the eighteenth-century charity-schools and the nineteenth-century church and board schools; the other from the traditional grammar schools augmented by county secondary schools after 1902. And because the latter are still the only schools leading to a definite qualification, the General Certificate of Education, and still have the monopoly of the road to higher education, the gulf between the two types of schools exists in spite of "secondary education for all"; indeed it has even widened, notwithstanding the efforts made by teachers to build up and broaden the education given in the secondary modern schools.

Competition for the grammar schools is now much sharper precisely because parents took the promise of the Education Act at its face value. And giving the old elementary school a new name is no more likely to take in parents than the labelling of streams with Greek letters deceives children.

The last ten or fifteen years have seen a tremendous increase in the desire of ordinary people that their children should have the opportunity for a real secondary education. During the war, the promise of a new deal in education was one of the things which made people feel that the sacrifices of war were worth while for their children's sake. It gave a deep social and human meaning to the struggle against fascism. The Education Act was, in fact, the only great Act affecting the social welfare of the people passed by the Coalition Government during the war. It evoked tremendous enthusiasm. It implied the promise of a new world.

This promise has not been fulfilled. In place of "secondary education for all", we have selection for a graded system of schools. Because of the new hopes aroused by the 1944 Act, methods of selection are more necessary and more important than ever before in the history of this country. And, in an attempt to allay doubts, to be "fair", the selection system has been made far more mechanical than it ever used to be, in spite of all the efforts made by examiners in certain areas to introduce some small degree of flexibility. For this reason selection for secondary education has today become far more competitive than it ever was in the past, and is now a public issue of the first importance.

Is there an Alternative?

Socialists, communists, and many educationists and teachers have for years fought to abolish this selective system in the schools; in particular, to do away once and for all with the need for this fatally important examination at the early age of ten, with its distorting effect on the child's education.[1]

There is a perfectly practical way of doing this. In fact one county, Anglesey, has already done it. The method is to provide a unified system of secondary education. This can be done by developing what is called the "comprehensive" secondary school. This type of school, as its name implies, is one which takes *all* the children, aged eleven and over, living in a particular area, in just the same way as the junior school now takes all the children. It is, therefore, a common school, which essentially treats all children alike as *children*, and abolishes the need for making fundamental distinctions between them at the age of eleven.

There is a long history of struggle for the common school in the working class movement, dating from the time when it first developed as an independent political force. It was in 1837 that the London Working Men's Association, precursors of the Chartists, first called, in the name of the working class, for a unified school system and the common school.

Before and after 1944, all the leading working-class organisations, including the Labour Party, demanded the common secondary school. But, except in a few areas, these have not yet been set up, in spite of the fact that a Labour Government was in power from 1945 to 1951.

The meaning, organisation and structure of the comprehensive school will be discussed again in more detail in the last chapter of this book. Reference is only made to it here to show that there is a perfectly practical alternative to the present divided system of secondary education, and that this alternative has strong popular and professional support behind it.

But in spite of this, we still have different types of secondary school, and for this reason we have selection and a "streamed" system of education, almost from the moment the children enter the State schools.

[1] The White Paper "Educational Reconstruction", issued by the Board of Education in 1943, said of selection: "There is nothing to be said in favour of a system which subjects children at the age of eleven to the strain of a competitive examination on which, not only their future schooling, but their future career may depend."

The Justification of Selection: *Intelligence Testing*

Fundamentally, the present selective and graded system of schools serves the needs of a class-divided society which is not able to utilise the abilities of all its citizens, and so dare not develop them to the full. It is the product of a social structure in which the leading positions in commerce, in industry, in the civil service, the army, the judiciary, and the professions generally are, on the whole, the monopoly of a small group.[1]

The secondary school system corresponds to this pyramidic structure and includes, of course, schools which have not yet been mentioned. At the top are the "public" schools, charging fees up to £350 a year, and below them a hierarchy, ranging from the direct grant grammar schools—such as Manchester Grammar School—through the ordinary grammar schools, the secondary technical schools, to the so-called selective central or intermediate schools which still continue in some areas; the modern school and the top forms of the old unreorganised all-age schools form the broad base, and educate the majority of working-class children.

The grammar schools are small and select because, owing to the static nature of our society, only a few people need to be recruited into the more influential positions. The underlying reason for the existence of the stratified education system is, therefore, to be found, not in the schools, nor in the children, but in the economic and class structure of society.

Naturally, every effort has to be made to make the present selective system appear both reasonable and fair. Official statements, of course, rarely mention the economic and social pressures on education. On the contrary, they attempt to justify the structure of secondary education on the grounds that it actually corresponds to the most fundamental needs of the children themselves.

It may perhaps seem a little ironic that a system which evinces such a lack of concern for the human needs of children, which decides their future by totting up marks gained at one examination, and which subjects many of them to an emotional and nervous strain of considerable intensity, should be justified specifically on humanist grounds. Nevertheless, this is the case.

The argument runs as follows: only a small proportion of children have the necessary intelligence to profit from a systematic secondary

[1] See M. Morris, *Your Children's Future* (1953).

education which covers the main areas of knowledge, and which opens the way to further education. The majority of children simply have not got the ability to follow such a course. For them, therefore, a benevolent State provides a different and far more suitable kind of education in the secondary modern schools. The only motive for providing two or more different kinds of schools is that there are, in practice, two or more different kinds of children, the existing types of schools being specifically designed to meet their needs.[1]

This arrangement, it is claimed, is justified by science as well as humanity, for there is today a reliable scientific instrument which helps administrators to decide whether any particular child is fit for a grammar or a modern school. This instrument is the Intelligence Test. Administer this test to any group of children at the age of ten, we are told, and the results will show clearly those who will be relatively intelligent in later life, and those who will be relatively unintelligent. It is, therefore, perfectly justifiable to separate the sheep from the goats at this early age.

The "intelligence" test is, of course, supposed to measure inborn intellectual powers, and only a certain proportion of children—about 15 per cent—are supposed to have the amount of intellect necessary to be able to profit from a grammar school course. In practice, as we have already seen, the proportion of children who actually qualify for grammar schools varies considerably from county to county, since some areas have grammar school places for only about 10 or 12 per cent, others for 30 per cent or even more. But contradictions of this kind are usually passed over in silence.[2]

During the last ten or fifteen years, the intelligence test has become one of the main ingredients of the selection examinations held by local education authorities throughout the country. Although the precise nature of the examination varies from place to place, according to the predilections of the authority concerned, this test is occasionally given double or even treble the weight accorded to other papers.[3] It must

[1] Or, as the Ministry of Education has put it with sublime simplicity: "Everyone knows that no two children are alike. Schools must be different too, or the Education Act of 1944 will not achieve success" (*The New Secondary Education*, Ministry of Education Pamphlet No. 9, 1947).

[2] "Most authorities stated, that the minimum standard of ability and attainment required for admission to grammar schools, was an arbitrary standard determined by the accommodation available." (*Transfer from Primary to Secondary Schools*, N.U.T., 1949, 81–2.) Accommodation available varies from about 8 per cent (Gateshead) to over 60 per cent (Merioneth) of the age group concerned.

[3] *Ibid.*, 93.

also be noted that the English and arithmetic papers most generally used are almost replicas of the intelligence test. The tests by which children are examined and streamed in the junior schools are also "objective" tests of the same kind. It is, therefore, no exaggeration to say that success or failure in the intelligence test means success or failure in the selection examination for the overwhelming majority of children.

Clearly the "intelligence" test merits the careful attention of parents, since it virtually constitutes the system of selection.

But it also deserves attention for a far more fundamental reason. In the last resort, it is the very keystone of the present educational system, for the theory that children can be divided into different groups, that they have fundamentally differing mental capacities which determine their whole future development, is derived from the theory and practice of intelligence testing.

The classic case for a selective system of schools and for the selection of an élite who have inherited "high ability", occurs in the Report of the Consultative Committee on Secondary Education (*Spens Report*, 1938); this sketched out, in general terms, the course of development for secondary education which has since been followed. It relied heavily on a certain conception of "intelligence":

> "*Intellectual development during childhood appears to progress as if it were governed by a single central factor, usually known as 'general intelligence', which may broadly be described as innate all-round intellectual ability. It appears to enter into everything which the child attempts to think, to say, or do, and seems on the whole to be the most important factor in determining his work in the classroom.* Our psychological witnesses assured us that it can be measured approximately by means of intelligence tests."

The Committee add: "We are informed that, with few exceptions, it is possible at a very early age to predict with some degree of accuracy the ultimate level of a chld's intellectual powers. . . ." From this evidence they conclude:

> "Different children from the age of eleven, if justice is to be done to their varying capacities, require types of education varying in certain important respects."[1]

[1] *Report of Consultative Committee on Secondary Education*, H.M.S.O., 123–5. The italics occur in the original text.

The Spens Committee accordingly proposed that there should be three distinct types of secondary school: grammar, technical and modern, the three types which have now come into being.

If this theory is correct, then it is clear that the case for a common secondary education is seriously weakened; it would be ridiculous to suggest that a similar education should be given to children whose intellectual capacity has been determined at, or even before birth, in such a way as to set clear and definable limits to their educational attainment. In this case, it would be more efficient, and possibly even more humane, to provide several different kinds of education, adapted to different levels of inborn intelligence.

If, on the other hand, this theory is false, then the main theoretical justification for the existing divisions within the field of secondary education falls to the ground. The common secondary school appears as the evident alternative.

Intelligence tests are, therefore, of crucial importance. Not only do they provide the practical means of selection, and so smooth the functioning of the present system, but also the theories which have evolved as a result of testing justify a divided educational structure, and indeed lead logically to more exact and precise streaming than that already described.

It is impossible to advocate the unified junior school and a common secondary education with any real hope of success until we are clear about this question of inherited "intelligence".

2

WHAT IS AN INTELLIGENCE TEST?

Before we go on to discuss the theory and practice of intelligence testing in detail, it will be as well briefly to indicate the main features of the tests themselves.

An "intelligence test" is supposed to measure a child's inborn "intelligence", or "mental ability". His capacity to profit from education supposedly depends on the amount of "intelligence" he possesses.

Tests are of two main types: individual and group tests. Individual tests are administered to one child at a time. The best known is the original Binet–Simon test, first drawn up in France in 1905 for the purpose of diagnosing mentally defective children. This test has since been revised to adapt it to conditions in this country and America, and is still the test most widely used in psychological clinics. It is not, however, used for selection for secondary education, since to administer it to one child takes a trained psychologist about forty minutes; to test a whole age group of children in this way would clearly be impracticable.

There are other forms of individual tests, known as performance or manual tests, which are used for particular purposes. But, like the Binet–Simon test, they take some time to administer, and so are not used for selection. For this reason, individual tests are not discussed in detail in this book.

The group test, on the other hand, can be administered to a large number of children simultaneously. It also has other practical advantages. For example, it does not need the services of a trained psychologist; any teacher, after a little instruction and advice, is competent to take charge of the testing process.

Group tests were, in fact, specifically designed for testing large numbers of people in the shortest possible time. They were first developed and applied in the U.S.A. in 1917 and 1918 for the purpose of sorting out recruits to the U.S. Army. The experience gained was later turned to producing tests designed to sort out large numbers of children in the schools.

Although group tests vary slightly according to the theories of the constructor, they have essential features in common. Each child is provided with a printed test paper, usually containing about 100 individual questions. In answering these, the child normally has to choose the correct answer from among several alternatives which are presented to him. Typical instructions are as follows: "In answering the questions there will be *nothing to write*. You will have to pick out the correct answer and *underline* it only." Or again: "You will not have to write anything at all, but only underline certain words and put crosses in certain squares."

These instructions are important, since they are an essential aspect of what is called the "standardised test situation". The aim is to ensure that "all children who are subjected to the test shall do it under as nearly as possible identical circumstances".[1] The underlying assumption here is that, if exactly the same instructions are given to all children, they will all react in an exactly similar manner, and their performance may be safely and accurately compared.

With every test, therefore, a detailed set of instructions is supplied, which the teacher should follow exactly. These tell him how to distribute the tests and precisely what he should say to the children. A forced brightness is often demanded. In one test, for instance, the supervisor says: "You will like this. Look at what the book says on the front cover. Write your names where it tells you to do so. Have you all done this? Pencils up when you have finished. Now read what it says. You will like this book", and so on. No child may start until the word is given.

Nearly all group tests have a time limit. They are, therefore, partially speed tests, purposely designed so that very few children finish completely in the time given. The instructions impress this on the children: "Work through (the questions) *as carefully and quickly as you can* . . . Each test has to be finished in a certain time, so do not waste time on examples that you cannot do." The object here is to ensure that the tests differentiate effectively between the children. Given the kind of question asked, the most practicable way of ensuring this is to ask so many questions that even the fastest worker cannot complete the papers with any regard for accuracy.

Many tests are divided into a number of sub-tests, each occupying a page in the booklet. When this is done, a time limit is set for each page of about twenty questions. The standardised instructions may read as follows: "See that each pupil is working on the right page. After

[1] P. E. Vernon, *The Measurement of Abilities* (1940), 171.

the exact number of minutes specified below (from three to ten minutes), say to the pupils: 'Pencils up. That was well done. Now look at the next page. Are you ready? Do what it tells you to do there. Ready! Begin!' "

This formula has to be repeated five times in a test lasting thirty minutes. Timing is done with a stop-watch.

Most intelligence tests include a "battery" of sub-tests, each sub-test consisting of questions similar in type, but varying from easy to difficult. The increasing difficulty of the questions is a principle as essential to the tests as the time limit, since it also ensures that the final marks will differ considerably. There are, however, "omnibus" tests, in which different types of questions are mixed up together, though the general order of difficulty is preserved. These have no "batteries" of sub-tests, and simply an over-all time limit.

The questions asked may vary considerably in detail, but are all similar in type. Most of the common forms used are listed below; most of the examples given are taken from actual tests for children of about eleven:

(1). *Opposites*

(*a*) (*The testee underlines the correct word from those in brackets: sometimes he is asked to pick the most nearly opposite.*)

1. Hot is the opposite of (wet, comfortable, cool, wintry, cold).
2. Gift is the opposite of (theft, expense, parcel, unkindness, enemy).
3. Famous is the opposite of (poor, failure, ancient, unhappy, unknown, shy).
4. Inquisitive is the opposite of (uninterested, forgetful, eager, knowledge, anxious, queer).

(*b*) (*The testee underlines two words which mean the same, or nearly the same, and a third word which means the opposite of the other two.*)

1. Below, begin, grow, common, collect, end.
2. Attempt, audacity, timidity, lucidity, brazen, boldness.

(2) *Analogies*. (*The testee underlines the correct word from those in brackets.*)

1. Wear is to clothes as eat is to (hat, table, food, plate, fork).
2. Flavour is to mouth as colour is to (ear, brush, paint, nose, eye).
3. Fire is to heat as lamp is to (flame, candle, see, light, soot, dark).
4. A is to Z as birth is to (marriage, cradle, mother, death, birthday, B).

(3). *Synonyms.* (*The testee underlines the correct word from those in brackets.*)

   1. Big means the same as (fat, tall, brave, large, heavy).

   2. Kill means the same as (murder, shoot, destroy, slay, bury).

(4). *Classification.*

(*a*) (*Five words are given: the testee picks out the one word most unlike the others in meaning*).

   1. Red, green, blue, wet, yellow.

   2. And, but, if, now, although.

(*b*) (*The testee underlines the word in brackets which is like the three in capital letters, but different from all the others.*)

   1. BREAD, FRUIT, MEAT (baker, eat, butcher, pudding, recipe, delicious).

   2. ENLARGE, STRETCH, EXTEND (compress, elastic, intend, strengthen, increase, twist).

(5) *Mixed Sentences.* (*The testee works out the phrase, and decides whether it is true or false. Alternatively, he underlines* "*unknown*".)

   1. A roses odour pleasant have. True. False. Unknown.

(6) *Reasoning.* (*In the first example the testee underlines the best answer.*)

   1. Peter is taller than James. Edward is not as tall as Peter. Who is the tallest?

     (1) Peter.

     (2) Edward.

     (3) James.

     (4) Cannot say.

   2. Five girls whom we shall call F, G, H, I, J, sit side by side on a seat.

     F has H next to her on her left, and J next to her on her right.

     G sits with I and J on either side of her.

     Who sits one from the right?

   3. If an inch is longer than a foot, write the first letter of the name of the longer unit, but if not, write the last letter of the name of the day of the week that today is.

(7) *Alphabet Questions.* (*The alphabet is printed, and the questions based on it.*)

1. What letter comes midway between G and O?
2. Suppose the first and second letters of the alphabet were interchanged, and also the third and fourth, and fifth and sixth, and so on. Which letter would then come seventeenth?
3. One day of the week begins with the third letter after T in the alphabet. Write the second letter of this day.

Some tests consist only of verbal questions of this character. Others include problems involving numbers. The testee may be asked, for instance, to complete a number series (e.g. 1, 3, 6, 10, ... what comes next?). Other number questions are put in the form of letter codes and puzzles. Finally, some sub-tests may be non-verbal, that is, the questions may be concerned with the relations between shapes instead of the relations between the meanings of words or sentences. Some psychologists hold that to ask only verbal questions is to handicap children whose vocabulary is limited, and they have therefore sought to construct tests which will reveal the child's supposed innate intelligence without requiring a knowledge of words. Non-verbal questions of this kind are sometimes included in intelligence tests used for selec-

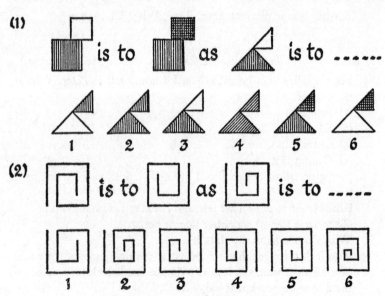

tion, though the weight of opinion seems to favour the verbal test for this purpose, in spite of the fact that verbal knowledge clearly depends largely on schooling and opportunity.[1] Some examples are given on page 56. The testee is asked: "Which shape will you choose to finish the sentence?"

When the children have completed the test, it is marked, again in a standardised way. Tests are so constructed that all the answers can only be either right or wrong. The process of marking is, therefore, quite "objective": each marker is provided with a key, and simply tots up the correct answers. In the U.S.A. this process is often further simplified by the use of a special kind of carbon paper which records *only* the correct answers, and so allows for final marking by an electrical machine.[2]

When tests are used for a selection examination, the score got on the intelligence test is given whatever weight the particular authority favours, and then added to the marks gained in the other tests (usually English and Arithmetic). An age allowance is then made, based on a complex statistical procedure. The object here is to prevent younger children being penalised, and older children gaining an advantage from their age differences. In this way each child's individual mark is computed, and the final order of merit of the children, from which the selection is to be made, is compiled.

This is all that is needed if the test is used for selection. If it is to be used to establish the child's intelligence quotient (I.Q.), which theoretically provides a measure of his intelligence, the test has to be "standardised". This is a complex process which is discussed in the next chapter; at this stage it is enough to say that the average score for each age group of children is calculated. For instance, the scores of children aged eleven years six months may average out at 120. Then any child, whatever his chronological age, who scores 120, is said to have a "mental age" of eleven years six months. From this, the I.Q., which

[1] Professor Vernon writes: "But since one of the most important, if not the most important use of intelligence tests is that of predicting scholastic aptitude, and school work is itself predominantly verbal, verbal tests are certainly the most useful" (Vernon, 182–3). The Moray House Intelligence Tests, very widely used by local authorities for selection, are almost entirely verbal tests. As for the non-verbal tests, psychologists now agree that the child's general verbal and educational background considerably affects his score, for a summary of some evidence on this point, see: J. D. Nisbet, *Family Environment*, 1953.

[2] In this way no subjective factors enter into the marking of tests, that is to say, the marker never has to use his own judgment as to whether one answer is better than another. This is held to be one of the strong points of tests.

actually expresses the ratio between mental and chronological age, is worked out by the following formula:

$$\text{Intelligence quotient} = \frac{\text{Mental age} \times 100}{\text{Chronological age}}$$

If, for instance, one child aged ten years six months, and another aged fourteen years, both score 120 on the standardised test, then each has a mental age of eleven and a half, and their intelligence quotients work out as follows:

$$(a) \ \text{I.Q.} \ = \ \frac{11\frac{1}{2} \times 100}{10\frac{1}{2}} \ = \ 109 \cdot 5$$

$$(b) \ \text{I.Q.} \ = \ \frac{11\frac{1}{2} \times 100}{14} \ = \ 82 \cdot 1$$

On the surface, intelligence tests appear very simple. Actually they involve a number of difficult logical, statistical and philosophical problems, both in their construction and in the interpretation of their results. Some of these will be discussed in the next two chapters.

3

THE PRACTICE OF INTELLIGENCE TESTING

Why These Particular Questions?

The crucial problem posed by the preceding discussion of intelligence tests is this: Why is it held that questions of the particular type outlined —synonyms, antonyms, number series, etc.—test intelligence?

The short answer to this question—and it needs to be made quite clear at the start of this discussion—is that no one thinks that these questions test intelligence in the sense in which the term is normally used in daily life.

This may seem surprising, in view of the supposition that this is precisely the intention of tests. But the public may be forgiven for the misunderstanding. The real state of affairs is not often explained, mainly because educational psychologists are not clear about this issue themselves.

Probably most people use the word "intelligence" (or the adjective and adverb "intelligent", "intelligently") to describe how a particular individual has behaved in a particular situation. We may say, for instance, that a rock-climber made an intelligent use of the holds in mastering a difficult climb, or, to put it in another way, that he displayed intelligence in the choice of holds; we may say that Dennis Compton played a googly in an intelligent way, or that a bricklayer overcame a difficult problem in an intelligent manner. We may say also that a boy who is doing well at school is intelligent.

Without probing further into the precise meaning which may be assigned to this word, we can at least recognise that these judgments all have one feature in common, they describe the way an individual behaves in situations that occur in the course of living. In practice, it is by the careful observation of human *behaviour* of this kind that judgments are made about individuals.

The normal use of the word "intelligence" implies, therefore, a functional intelligence, *one that is revealed in the course of action.* It is, of course, common knowledge, that a man may be very intelligent in one particular field, and yet quite unintelligent in another. For instance, if Dennis Compton and our rock-climber were transposed, it would probably be impossible to make the same judgment of their actions as was made in the case of the activities with which they are familiar.

Similarly, a university professor may display unbounded intelligence in his analysis of the structure of the atomic nucleus, in literary criticism, or in some other field of study, and yet make ridiculous statements about, for instance, sex, religion, the population problem or communism. Further, as far as his family or human relations generally are concerned, he may behave in a distinctly stupid way.

It is not with this kind of intelligence that tests and test questions are concerned. It is easy to see that the practice of mental testing, as already described, inevitably excludes the exercise of what might be called functional intelligence. This remains true in spite of the psychologists' claim that they do attempt to measure, to some extent, some "aspect" or "component" of what might be called "daily life" intelligence.[1]

In the first place, the group intelligence test isolates the individual from all social relations and from any "real life" situation. Under the control of an automaton teacher, divested of his usual characteristics, the child is presented with a set of symbols to manipulate, items of a "restricted and artificial type".[2] The test situation clearly differs, in a most important respect, from most situations with which the individual is faced in the process of living.

Secondly, the questions asked exclude, or attempt to exclude any emotional response; this is done in an effort to isolate the pure "intelligence" which the psychologist seeks to measure. In a life situation, the individual's feelings, his emotional responses, play an essential part in his total response. They are equally involved even in the most standardised test situation. But every effort is made to eliminate individual human responses. Questions which might arouse an emotional feeling are regarded as "invalid" (giving a "wrong" estimation of the individual's intelligence), precisely *because* the individual has an emotional response to them. For this reason the intelligence test is deliberately constructed so that questions are remote from "real life" situations.

[1] Thus Vernon talks of "the intelligence which we recognise in daily life . . . which we wish to measure" (Vernon, p. 194). Burt claims that the meaning of "intelligence", "which corresponds to the usage of most psychologists" is the "innate component" of " 'intelligence' as manifested in daily life", *and* " 'intelligence' as measured by some one test (without adjustment for irrelevant factors)". (Burt, *Intelligence and Fertility*, 1946, 41.)

[2] Vernon, 194.

What, then, is the intelligence that is measured by tests?

Most psychologists argue that it is a quality of mind, a kind of essence, *inherited by the child at birth*, in much the same way as he inherits blue eyes or black hair. Sir Cyril Burt, for instance, suggests that all children are born with a varying amount of "innate general cognitive ability", and this is what the tests measure with a greater or lesser degree of accuracy.[1] Some psychologists go further and give a more precise definition. Thus, Professor Knight has defined the intelligence measured by tests as "the power to discover relevant relations and the power to educe relevant correlates".[2]

This last definition is based on the theories of Charles Spearman, a psychologist who attempted to bring order into the practice of mental testing in the 1920s. Spearman recognised that tests could hardly be called scientific when no two psychologists could agree either on *what* they were measuring or *how* to measure it. He collected some twenty definitions of intelligence, all mutually exclusive, and showed that no concrete evidence had been adduced to support the claim that the tests really did measure any of the hypothetical qualities defined.[3]

He then himself entered the field, but with certain definite ideas about the nature of "mind" or "thought", and with a strong belief in the efficacy of certain forms of statistical calculation. In brief, he made up a number of tests, administered them, and, after making certain calculations with the results, claimed that these supported the suggestion that all human minds have a central "power" (he called this "general mental energy" or "g") which can be accurately measured by certain kinds of tests. He avoided the use of the word "intelligence" owing to the varying meanings that had been assigned it.

These conclusions were immediately subjected to criticism by other psychologists. Some did not believe that the kinds of tests used by Spearman were acceptable; others took exception to his statistical calculations, and showed that by applying slightly different rules, quite different results could be obtained. Since this time, many more tests

---

[1] Cognition: "Action or faculty of knowing, perceiving, conceiving, as opposed to emotion or volition" (*Concise Oxford Dictionary*).

[2] R. Knight, *Intelligence and Intelligence Tests* (4th Edition, 1948), 29.

[3] For instance, intelligence is "the power of good responses from the point of view of truth"; "the ability to act effectively under given conditions"; "the capacity to acquire capacity" for "success, either past or present"; the power of "abstract thinking"; "the capacity to profit from experience" (C. Spearman, *The Nature of Intelligence and the Principles of Cognition*, 1927, 12–15).

have been administered and many more calculations made, but it is true to say that the nature of "intelligence" is as obscure as ever it was; whatever it is that tests measure, this thing cannot be defined in a way that both commands general agreement and is in any degree precise.

Some psychologists skirt the problem posed by the lack of definition in this way: We agree that intelligence cannot be defined, but we have good reason to believe that it exists. It is for all practical purposes, sufficient to say that *intelligence is that which is measured by intelligence tests*. This latest definition deliberately deprives the word of any meaning external to the test itself. It enables us, however, to re-phrase the question posed at the start of this chapter, which should now read: "Why is it held that questions of this particular type test the intelligence that is measured by intelligence tests?" The question has, of course, become quite meaningless. This helps us to come to an initial conclusion: whatever psychologists may argue in theory, in *practice* intelligence is definable only in terms of the actual questions in tests. In other words, tests are not objective. The subjective element, the personal judgment of the psychologist, is decisive, because he chooses the actual questions which he *thinks* test what he *thinks* is intelligence. No amount of objective marking, or standardisation of the test situation, can redress the balance.

Professor Vernon puts it in this way: "All the test items or sub-tests are selected in the first place on the basis of subjective opinion; they must appear to the tester to involve the exercise of intellect."[1] Now a test constructor may hold one of several contemporary theories as to what it is that he is testing. He may hold that "relational thinking" is important, and so set out to test this, or he may hold that other thought processes are relevant, and attempt to test these as well. In either case, he can only reach this essence that he wishes to measure through the medium of words, figures or shapes; he must decide what type of question to ask, and in what form these questions are to be put. It is clear, therefore, that the items of any intelligence test, and the intelligence test as a whole, embody not some objective criterion of intelligence but only the constructor's ideas about it.

There are a number of checks which a constructor can make in order to decide whether his questions are good ones for his purpose; these will be referred to later, but here the important point to emphasise is the arbitrary, subjective nature of the actual questions themselves.

[1] Vernon, 176.

An analysis of the kind of questions, which test constructors have chosen as "involving the exercise of intellect" is instructive, in that it shows that tests must involve a great deal of acquired knowledge. A verbal intelligence test for children of about eleven, chosen at random, shows that in order to have the necessary data to answer some of the questions at all, the testee must know the following things (only a few examples are given): the meaning of such words as "spurious", "antique", "external", irregular", "inexpensive", "affectionate", "moist": that a sovereign is made of gold, while a florin is made of silver; that pearls, emeralds, sapphires, diamonds and rubies are precious stones, while gold is not; the relative functions of telephone and telegraph; the use of thermometers; the reasons for saving money; the purpose of charitable societies; what a cubic block is; what a code is; what a clerk's job is; that ledger-clerks work in banks; what an individual's "mechanical bent" is; what a person's "inclinations"are; that a shorthand-typist is expected to be able to spell well; what "the adjustment of an individual to his vocation" means; and finally, that a parlourmaid is not expected to do the sewing in a house!

Such knowledge may seem obvious to the adult and even to the fortunate child of eleven, but it is by no means so obvious to the average child brought up in an overcrowded house in the centre of an industrial city. One might say that the information required for success depends directly on social status. Many working-class children will never have heard the subject matter of some of these questions discussed, and yet the questions cannot be answered unless the *meaning* of each of the words is fully grasped.

The test quoted was compiled in 1925. Of recent years, much effort has been devoted to eliminating questions which discriminate so evidently on class lines. But this has inevitably led to the formulation of ever more tortuous questions, without removing the fundamental objection. It is impossible to make questions progressively more difficult without bringing in unusual words or peculiar sentence construction, as some of the examples given in the last chapter clearly show. As a result, children who have not had the opportunity to read widely, or to acquire verbal facility, must always be at a grave disadvantage. Indeed, it is no exaggeration to say that the difference between social classes is most easily to be discerned in differences of expression, vocabulary, and sentence construction. The most common grammatical "errors", in the formal sense, are precisely those forms of speech which are generally current in local dialect. In short, it would be difficult to find a more effective method of differentiating children, according to social environment, than the standard verbal intelligence test.[1]

The fact that these tests discriminate against the working class has been admitted by educational psychologists. In an entirely praiseworthy attempt to overcome this difficulty and to produce a really "fair" test, some have tried to evolve "culture-free" tests—that is, tests which involve acquirements more equally available to children from all social classes. Non-verbal tests, which consist only of shapes and figures, and possibly pictures, are of this character. But these are also open to objection, because mastery of shapes and figures varies with the character of the child's education and his home environment. It follows that a test of this kind is also bound, primarily, to test educational attainment.[2]

It has already been noted that the tests used for selection are primarily verbal and number tests, and success in these evidently depends, to a large extent, on how effectively a child has been taught, either by his teachers, his parents, or others; in other words, on the general opportunities he has had for learning. These opportunities, of course, vary considerably with variation in economic status. One has only to compare the education of a child in a private preparatory school, with classes of ten to fifteen, with that of the average child in a city school, with classes of forty-five to fifty, to recognise how wide are the differences in educational opportunity between middle- and working-class children.

It is not, therefore, surprising that experimental work with tests has shown first, that a very close relation exists between tests results and educational attainment, and, second, that there is a similarly close relation between test results and social class. We have seen that test questions inevitably favour the middle-class child, and that it is the questions, and only the questions, which determine and define the kind of "intelligence" that is being measured. It may be concluded, on these grounds alone, that the "intelligence" measured by tests is anything but a pure intellectual power; it evidently comprehends what can only be described as a class element.

[1] A recent test of this type, widely used for selection at ten, included among only eight contiguous questions, the following words, the precise meaning of each of which had to be fully grasped before the questions could be answered correctly: expose, confess, position, uncertain, insult, offence, frail, sturdy, fragment, inquisitive, anxious, eager.

[2] Comparing non-verbal to verbal tests from the point of view of "fairness", Vernon concludes that the former ". . . of course, are open to analogous defects" (Vernon, 182).

The Distribution of Intelligence

Another set of arguments about the validity of intelligence tests may now be examined. When tests are given to large numbers of children, and all the scores are plotted out on a graph, a certain recognisable pattern emerges. This curve is supposed to indicate how intelligence (as defined by tests) is distributed among the population as a whole.

Here some interesting points arise. Though parents are accustomed to think about intelligence tests in terms of an individual child's results —George has an I.Q. of 100 and Betty an I.Q. of 120—and to assume that this represents some absolute measurement of the child's intellectual powers, it is really quite unjustifiable to give an *individual* label of this kind at all. A test result only tells us what the child's status is *in relation to* all the other children who have done the same test. The most that can be said is that George is *less* "intelligent" than Betty, and *more* "intelligent" than another child with a lower I.Q. This illustrates that tests are unsuitable instruments for diagnosing *individual* human qualities; their primary function is to classify, sort and arrange people, according to certain criteria.

Discussing the limitations of the statistical methods fundamental to the practice of intelligence testing, Professor Vernon points out that their "fundamentally abstract nature . . . needs to be stressed. They are adapted primarily for mass-investigations of measurements obtained from large numbers of persons, and such investigations are apt to lose touch with the concrete individual case".[1]

From the very outset of mental testing, psychologists have been primarily concerned with the question of the *distribution* of intelligence among a whole population. When only very few tests had been constructed and administered, attempts were made to calculate, from such results as were available, the probable distribution of "intelligence" among thousands and millions of people. This was not the result of mere scientific curiosity; it was quite essential to the further development of tests that there should be such a general picture. Without it, no classification of children or adults was possible, nor for that matter, could anyone claim that their test was a "valid" measure unless the results showed a distribution of "intelligence" approximating to that produced by other tests purporting to measure the same thing.

But this is also a matter of public interest, because, if it can be shown that, for instance, 20 per cent of the population have a relatively high

[1] Vernon, 3.

intelligence, and 80 per cent a relatively low intelligence, then various conclusions follow in the sphere of practical public policy, especially as regards education and schooling.

The conclusion arrived at was that the distribution of "intelligence" follows a normal curve. What is meant by a normal curve? This is a technical term implying that the majority of measurements obtained in an investigation cluster about the average mark; only a few extreme measures are recorded, and the number of measurements at given intervals above the average is the same as the number below.

It is easier to understand if represented in a diagram. Let us take, for example, the probable heights of ninety-nine Englishmen chosen at random. If these were plotted on a graph, we would tend to obtain the following figure:

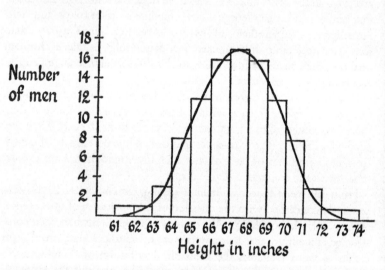

In the figure above, each rectangle represents the number of people whose height falls between certain limits. In this hypothetical group of ninety-nine people, one is between 61 and 62 inches tall, one between 62 and 63 inches, three between 63 and 64 inches, and so on up to the largest group of seventeen people whose height lies between 67 and 68 inches. Those taller than this are distributed in an exactly similar manner to those below this height. Once these figures have been plotted out, a curve can be constructed, as above; this is the normal curve.[1]

[1] The example is based on that given by P. B. Ballard, in *Mental Tests* (1937 Edition), 115–18.

Now it is clear that, since "intelligence" cannot even be defined, there can be no way of knowing how it is distributed, whether in this way or any other. But unless the general distribution of "intelligence" can be calculated in some way, adequate tests, purporting always to measure the same thing, cannot be constructed. Faced with this contradiction, mental testers have made what can only be an assumption: that "intelligence" is normally distributed. In the nature of the case, there can be no scientific proof that this is so.[1]

As a result, arguments about test construction and test results tend to revolve within an enclosed circle. "Well-constructed tests always tend to yield a normal frequency distribution; hence we are entitled to regard departures from normality as indicative of bad construction or bad scoring", writes one authority.[2] A little later in the same book the same proposition is advanced in a somewhat different way. A test, it is said, should be "of such a length, and contain questions of sufficient ease and difficulty, to differentiate among both the poorest and the best pupils, and to yield an approximately normal distribution".[3]

In other words, the psychologist constructs his test in such a way that it will tend to give a normal distribution of scores, and no other. Any test which gives a different distribution is "badly constructed"; it is accordingly jettisoned as a "bad" test of "intelligence". The fact that accepted tests always give an approximately normal distribution of scores is then advanced as proof that "intelligence" exists and has been adequately measured by the tests concerned.

Even an approximation to the normal curve is considered adequate to sustain the approved position. For example, the large scale testing of Scottish children in 1939 brought results which did not exactly follow the normal curve. But these discrepancies have been described as relatively slight, so that *for many practical purposes* we may continue to regard the distribution of intelligence, *when measured by an adequate test as normal.*"[4] But for all practical purposes an adequate test is, by

[1] It has sometimes been argued that early experiments with tests proved that "intelligence" is normally distributed without the aid of any statistical procedures. But in these experiments the test used was the Binet test—one not now accepted by psychometrists as a scientific test of "intelligence"; further, though the particular version of the Binet test used was constructed without the statistical aids now generally employed, the acceptance or rejection of questions was based on a principle which made an approximately normal distribution a foregone conclusion. See L. M. Terman, *The Measurement of Intelligence* (1919).

[2] Vernon, 27.

[3] *Ibid.* 39.

[4] *Ibid.*, 21. (My italics.—B.S.)

definition, a test which is so constructed that it will tend to give a roughly normal distribution of scores. To conclude from a large-scale application of such a test that *intelligence* is normally distributed, is merely to reiterate the assumption with which the psychologist embarked on the investigation. The distribution proves no more than that the test was efficiently constructed within the arbitrary limits set. It certainly does not even begin to prove that "intelligence" is always to be found in certain fixed proportions in every population.

On the contrary, any mathematician could easily demonstrate that, by careful choice and arrangement of questions, it is difficult to avoid obtaining a normal distribution of scores. If, for instance, a test of ninety questions is constructed so that, on average, 10 per cent of children get the first ten questions wrong and 90 per cent get them right, 20 per cent get the next ten questions wrong and 80 per cent get them right, and so on up to the last ten questions which 90 per cent of children omit or get wrong and 10 per cent complete correctly, then the scores are bound to fall into a pattern roughly corresponding to the normal curve. This is mathematically determined. And, of course, this is precisely how test constructors arrange the questions when they choose items of "varying difficulty" and put them in an "order of difficulty", controlled also by time. If the test contained eighty questions which 90 per cent of children get right and only 10 per cent get wrong, and ten questions which 10 per cent get right and 90 per cent get wrong, the scores would not, of course, be normally distributed. There is nothing to show that the latter would be a worse test of "intelligence" than the former; but the former test is, of course, preferred because the normal curve provides a basis for all kinds of theoretical arguments and is, besides, far the most convenient from a statistical point of view.

There is, however, no reason why test scores should not be distributed in a whole variety of other ways. It would be perfectly possible to construct intelligence tests which gave all manner of different distributions.

Why then, is it so easily assumed that "intelligence" *must* be normally distributed? The bias in favour of normal distribution is partly to be explained by the fact that certain physical characteristics, such as height, are normally distributed. A further argument is derived from certain human performances. Measurements of the number of times children can tap with one finger in a minute, or the number of words they can write in the same time, are often normally distributed. If all these various human attributes are distributed in this way, why not also "intelligence"?

This kind of argument by analogy has no scientific validity. It might just as well be argued that some physical characteristics—such as weight and hair colour—are not normally distributed. Performance tests are not so much tests of mind, as of muscular co-ordination and control. To argue about the fundamental nature of mind by analogy from such physical characteristics is an exceedingly dangerous proceeding, since the brain and the higher nervous system represent a qualitatively different organisation of matter, about whose structure and functioning extremely little is as yet known.

The assumption that "intelligence", itself an indefinable quality, is normally distributed is, then, nothing but a shot in the dark. Nevertheless, the broadest possible assertions are based on the curve of normal distribution. If it is assumed that this curve illustrates the distribution of a key human power, "intelligence" (and not merely the distribution of test scores as a result of applying "well-constructed" tests) then it can be asserted that there must always be a few people with high intelligence, suited to posts of responsibility and "leadership"; the vast majority are merely average, and are not likely to achieve much in their lives—they are doomed to be the followers of the few intelligent leaders. Many people genuinely believe that this is the case, that there is some natural law which operates to ensure that human beings have varying powers in just these proportions. No better justification could be found for the necessity of providing different "types" of schools for different "levels" of "intelligence".

Many people appear to think that intelligence is "obviously" distributed in this way. In any school, they say, you will find at the top of the "A" stream a few highly intelligent children; at the bottom of the "C" stream a few very unintelligent children, while the majority lie between these extremes. Objective (new-type) examinations, they say, give the same result.

But this argument shifts the discussion from intelligence to educational attainment. It is perfectly true that, in our society, at present, with the schools organised in the way that has been described in the first chapter, the children's educational attainment will tend to be distributed in this order. This arises from our whole selective system and the process of streaming, which ensures a wide spread between the attainment of the best and the worst, and which operates to widen this spread as the children grow older.

To argue from this situation that intelligence, if it exists, is also distributed in this manner, is quite unwarrantable. If our schools were organised, not on the present competitive, individualist basis, but instead in such a way as to provide the conditions for bringing all the children on at a relatively equal rate, as is done, for instance, in the U.S.S.R., Poland and elsewhere, then an entirely different distribution of educational attainment would be achieved. In the U.S.S.R., for instance, the examinations each year are so designed that nearly all the children of a particular class are expected to pass them. They mark the achievement of a certain definite educational stage for all children, and the teacher and class as a whole specifically set out to see that all its members are capable of passing the examination. The very small proportion, probably about 7 per cent, who do not achieve the required standard, usually cover the course again. The result is a more equal level of educational attainment than is achieved much here.[1]

This does not mean that all children are held down to a dead level; some, for example, may have ranged much wider than others in the usual studies. It does mean that, so far as important basic knowledge and skills are concerned, all children are helped to reach a definite standard.

In this country, however, the concept that nearly all the children should attain a given educational level is considered as being either undesirable or impossible of achievement. The schools are organised to provide for a differentiation between children, and the new types of "objective" examinations, often used in junior schools as well as in the selection test, *specifically set out to ensure that these differences are underlined, by deliberately excluding questions that all the children can answer.* "In new-type examinations", says Professor Vernon, speaking of one-word tests in English, arithmetic, intelligence, and so forth, "several sections of the work may be omitted altogether if they are likely to be known so well that more than 95 per cent of the students would answer questions on them correctly. *It is a pure waste of time to include items which everyone can do.*"[2]

New-type examinations of this kind reflect the objectives of a highly

---

[1] Annual examinations in the Soviet seven-year school (seven to fourteen) start when the child is eleven. These are partly oral and partly written. Failure in more than two subjects involves repeating the year's work. (See G. C. T. Giles, "Why Soviet Teachers oppose Intelligence Tests", *Anglo-Soviet Journal*, XIV, 1, 13).

[2] Vernon, 260. (My italics.—B.S.)

selective educational system, and are specifically designed to facilitate its working. Their function is therefore the opposite of that of examinations in socialist countries, which mark the completion of a stage of work by all children. The first type of examination deliberately excludes questions which all the children can do, while in the second type all the children are expected to be able to do all the questions which are set on the year's work. These opposing concepts of the role of examinations reflect opposed views on the function of teaching and education.

The present distribution of educational attainment in the schools of this country is a product, not of the nature of the "child mind", but of the social and economic factors which determine both the structure and organisation of the educational system, and the wider opportunities of children to learn and develop. To derive from the situation, as it exists today in our country, evidence for the existence of a basic law— that "intelligence" is always normally distributed—is just as questionable as are all the other arguments in favour of the normal distribution of "intelligence".

The Construction of Intelligence Tests: (a) Arranging the Questions

The main way of ensuring that the scores of intelligence tests are normally distributed, is to include questions carefully graded in an "order of difficulty". But other techniques have also to be employed. It is important to examine them carefully, since if we understand how a test is constructed—with the aim of making it a kind of mental foot-rule—we will be in a better position to assess its value.

We may begin by describing a simple method, which, though no longer used in the pure form described, has provided the starting point for the more sophisticated procedures of today.

The psychologist starts with, say, 200 questions, varying from easy to difficult, all of which he thinks will test intelligence as he conceives it. He sets these questions to a group of children who have already been approximately graded by their teachers in what the latter think is the correct order of intelligence; the teachers will have relied partly on their own judgment, partly on the results of examinations and other relevant information in making up their list. The psychologist's aim is to pick, from his 200 original questions, the 100 which discriminate best between the children according to the grading provided by the teacher, and which produce an approximately normal distribution. In other words, he intends to keep only those questions (usually about 100) which seem to give the "right" assessment of the children.

For instance, to take an extreme example, he may find, on analysing the children's answers to one particular question, that nearly all the children graded highly by the teacher have got it wrong, while nearly all those graded low for intelligence have got it right. This question he will inevitably throw out as a bad test of intelligence.

It is highly improbable that such a clear-cut situation would arise. More usually, correct answers will be given by some children graded as intelligent and some graded as unintelligent. The task is then to choose those questions which have the "right" *proportion* of correct answers from each section, so that, in the test as a whole, the children graded by the teachers as intelligent come out at the top, and those graded as unintelligent at the bottom.

The final test evolved will, therefore, consist of the hundred questions which discriminate best among the children according to the judgment of the teacher and the psychologist. It must also give approximately a normal distribution of the test scores. Questions which seem to upset this normal distribution are, of course, jettisoned.

Any test, therefore, consists of questions graded in difficulty, from those which all the children can get right, to those which very few get right. The cut-off at the top is also ensured by making the test into a speed test, i.e. allowing only so many minutes for each group of questions. Once more, this timing is so arranged that all children can answer some questions, but very few reach the end of the test; this gives scope to the child who works fast, enabling him to pile up additional marks near to the maximum level.

The Construction of Intelligence Tests: (b) Validating the Test

These procedures mark the initial stages of test construction. If the test is to make some claim to be scientific, various checks are required. The close relation between the test results and the teacher's estimates might, for instance, be due to fortuitous factors. In an attempt to ensure that this is not the case, the psychologist must go on to "validate" his test, i.e. to see whether it really is measuring whatever he set out to measure. To do this, he must check it against some other measure of intelligence, one, shall we say, which is generally accepted by other mental testers.

An analogous procedure would be the following: if I want a bit of string which measures exactly one yard, I could cut off a length which I *think* approximates to a yard, using some household article as a rough guide. This process could be said to be equivalent to the construction of a test as described above. But in order to ensure that my bit of string is a valid measure, I must test it against a ruler, and if necessary add to it or subtract from it, so that it does measure exactly one yard.

If I suspected that my particular ruler at home was inaccurate, and wanted to be very precise, I could go to the extreme length of testing my string against the agreed measure of one yard, a length of bronze kept at a constant temperature of 62° Fahrenheit at the Board of Trade.

This procedure is relatively straightforward. But to attempt to check a test which is designed to measure so elusive and indefinable a quality as intelligence, is quite another matter. There just is not, nor could there be, any objective criterion, against which the test can be assessed.[1]

Such criteria as have been used, therefore, are admittedly subjective, that is, they reflect the opinions of certain people as to what constitutes intelligence. If these criteria are influenced, for instance, by social considerations of any kind, then, of course, these immediately become of crucial importance, since the criterion of intelligence once established, is embodied and perpetuated in intelligence tests.

There are two methods which have been commonly used to validate tests. The first is closely akin to that of test construction. Once a test has been constructed in the way described, it is given to a different, and probably a larger, sample of children; these again have been arranged in an order of intelligence by the teachers. If the new results of the test with this larger group also correspond reasonably closely to the teachers' judgment, the test is regarded as a valid test of intelligence, and, as such, it may find its way into general circulation.

Now, teachers' ratings of children's intelligence are often profoundly influenced by what are, as far as intelligence testing is concerned, entirely extraneous considerations. For instance, if the child is industrious at school, attentive, co-operative and willing, a teacher may be inclined to rate him high for intelligence; on the other hand, children who dislike school, get into trouble, and do not work well, possibly for emotional or other reasons, are likely to get a low rating. Similarly, teachers may sometimes, quite unconsciously, be biased in favour

[1] "The validation of intelligence tests . . . is particularly difficult, since we possess no objective criterion of intelligence, etc., with which to compare them." Vernon, 175.

of a child who is well dressed and has no accent. Finally, a teacher's rating is bound to depend to a considerable extent on the child's educational attainment, which, as has already been argued, may itself partly depend on all sorts of social factors independent of the intellectual make-up of the child.

For all these reasons, teachers' estimates of intelligence are liable to be strongly influenced by social considerations, and on the whole to favour the middle-class child. For this reason they have been described by psychologists themselves as "highly fallible".[1] To validate a test in this way is bound to lead to the embodiment in the test of a criterion of intelligence which discriminates against the working-class child.

Teachers' estimates, though so clearly unscientific guides, were used until quite recently to validate tests. Even psychometrists must, therefore, admit that much unfairness has resulted for thousands of children in selection, based on these tests. Even more important, the tests evolved in this way, have established criteria of intelligence which have been perpetuated by the continued use of the tests.

The second method of validating a new test is to check it against an old one. This is quite simply done. The two tests are given to the same group of children; if both put the children in roughly the same order, the new test is considered valid. This may seem to be satisfactory until one asks, how was the other test used itself validated—what claims has it got to represent a standard or criterion of intelligence? There can only be two answers to this, the other test was itself either validated against a third, earlier test, or it was validated against the estimates of teachers.

This second method is, therefore, a replica of the first at one remove. The test that is used itself embodies all those social considerations already mentioned. The only difference is that it is less trouble to validate a test in this way. The method is, if anything, even less exact, precisely because it is less direct.

There is one intelligence test which has often been used for the validation of new tests, but was not itself fully validated against teachers' estimates, although these were used. This is the original Binet–Simon oral test, administered to one child at a time.

First evolved nearly half a century ago, for the purpose of diagnosing mental defect, the Binet test differs from modern group intelligence tests in many important respects. It includes, for instance, a group of differ-

[1] Vernon, 175.

ent questions for each age level, as well as a whole variety of questions which differ qualitatively from the ingredients of the normal verbal intelligence test. For instance, the child is asked to give change for money, to name coins, to do simple monetary addition, to repeat a number series, to name the months of the year, to define certain objects, to make rhymes, to interpret pictures, and so on.[1] The test, therefore, does not set out to measure the child's supposed capacity for relational thinking ("g"). It aims rather, by including different kinds of questions based largely on the child's everyday life experiences, to enable the psychologist to make a rapid assessment of a child's status in relation to the average performance of children on the test. The Binet test, therefore, though for long the only one in the field, is now critic-ised by leading educational psychologists as "a distressingly unscientific instrument" which measures "an unanalysed hotch-potch of abilities". For these and other reasons, says Professor Vernon, the validity of the Binet scales "is open to doubt"—that is to say, the test cannot claim to embody an objective criterion of intelligence. Consequently, although several group intelligence tests have been validated against the Binet–Simon test, this is no longer regarded as satisfactory by modern psychometrists themselves.[2]

Psychologists are well aware of the inconsistencies in test construction and the bias that enters into tests through the methods of validation described. They have, therefore, sought to discover some method which would not be open to these charges. They claim now to have found it, "We can now", says Professor Knight, "employ an exact mathematical criterion to assess the extent to which any particular type of problem measures intelligence."[3]

The mathematical criterion is that of factor analysis. Put simply,

[1] Some of the tests of information were dropped from the New Stanford Revision of 1937.

[2] Vernon, 173, 193, 195. In spite of the sharp criticism of the Binet test by nearly all leading psychometrists, it is still regarded by practising psychologists, especially clinicians, as, in practice, the most satisfactory mental measuring instrument. This is surely a reflec-tion of the basic theoretical confusion in this field of work. One psychologist, however, blames the clinicians. "The retention of the Binet tests in a good deal of clinical work to-day, is alike a great tribute to the early genius of Binet and to the conservatism, rather than the scientific conscience of the present generation of clinical psychologists." R. B. Cattell, *A Guide to Mental Testing* (2nd Edition, 1948), 13.

Compare Vernon, who, although characterising the test as "distressingly unscientific", adds that from this test the psychologist "obtains a much more complete and practically useful view than he could from a more scientific measure of cognitive intellectual ability". Vernon, 194.

[3] Knight, 44.

the procedure is as follows: the constructor first makes up his questions, some of which he will later jettison. He sets them to a group of children. He then compares the result for each item (the proportions of right and wrong answers) with those for all other items; alternatively, he compares groups of items with each other. These comparisons are made statistically, that is to say, the constructor looks for a certain statistical pattern in the results. All items which fail to conform to this criterion are jettisoned. When the required pattern is achieved, it is claimed on mathematical grounds that the test items are consistent with each other, and so are measuring one and the same "thing"— and since the questions are those which the constructor assumes test intelligence, it is said that the test measures intelligence.

Although this method does not rely on teachers' estimates of the children's intelligence in the construction of the test, it clearly lays a far greater emphasis on the original choice of the questions themselves by the constructor, and it is precisely here that the subjective factor enters most obviously into the construction of the test. We may note that the kinds of questions asked are still much the same as those used in tests twenty or thirty years ago, before this method was developed. The significance of this new departure is that absolutely no attempt is now made to measure the test against any external criterion of intelligence; this is actually regarded as the main strength of this method of validation.[1]

What emerges from this discussion of test construction and validation is that the criterion of intelligence embodied in the tests is one determined by social considerations. In the case of tests constructed and validated against teachers' estimates, as many were until quite recently, this was entirely self-evident, and admitted by psychologists themselves. Both the character of the questions and the external criteria of intelligence employed were clearly subjective. In the case of tests constructed and validated by the method of internal consistency however, exactly the same limitations apply, only in a more subtle or veiled manner; they are now part and parcel of the mathematical tech-

---

[1] It is worth adding that the acceptance of this form of mathematical validation itself depends fundamentally on the acceptance of Spearman's theories. Possibly this is the reason why these theories, once vigorously attacked by other psychometrists, are now more generally accepted. Internal validation appears to be scientific, by contrast with the other methods, which are obviously subjective. Thus Cattell, who gives the impression that there is an interpretation of intelligence agreed to by all, says: "So long as controversy existed as to what was meant by intelligence, no test could be truly validated, and the design of tests perforce remained a matter of personal taste." Cattell, 5.

niques used. The only difference between the two methods is that the second places much more reliance on the questions, themselves chosen subjectively, and refers to no other outside judgment of intelligence at all. In this sense, the method of validating by internal consistency is even more questionable than the older method, however biased the outside judgments may have been. In sum, the attempt to attain greater objectivity has resulted only in a more subjective approach, in a greater reliance on the constructor's own judgment.

The Construction of Intelligence Tests: (c) Standardising the Test

There is yet another step in the process of preparing a test, that of standardisation. Though many tests used in the selection examination are not standardised, any test which is to be put on the market and used to calculate a child's mental age and I.Q. must go through this further process.

It has already been noted that a mental test result only indicates the standing of a child in relation to the other children who have taken the same test. If this status is to be interpreted in terms of an individual intellectual "label", what are called "test norms" must be established for each test.

In order to get "norms", the test must be set to a very large number of children of different ages, but approximating to the age-group for which the test is specifically designed. The large sample chosen (it should consist of several thousands of children) ought, in theory, to represent a complete cross section of the population from the brilliant to the imbecile, and from the highest social class to the lowest. When all the results are available, average scores for all the children, for each month of each age between, say, eight and thirteen, must be worked out. Once these averages are settled, the score of any child of a particular age may be checked against them. If his score falls exactly at the average, a child is awarded an I.Q. of one hundred; if his score is the same as the average score of children older or younger, his Intelligence Quotient will be proportionately above or below one hundred.[1] The

---

[1] The process sounds simple, but is, in fact, so complicated and so expensive that it is almost, if not quite, impossible to achieve in such a way that norms have any real validity, even according to the criteria of psychologists. Thus Vernon mentions the "almost insuperable difficulties" involved "in collecting standardisation groups which will be truly representative of all children of a certain age". He adds: "The origin and adequacy of many of the published test norms are so dubious that we would advise testers in schools to treat them all with caution, and when possible, to do without them." Vernon, 81-2. See his discussion of this subject, 79-87.

actual spread of I.Q.s obtained from any particular test, incidentally, depends entirely on the constructor's own decision. Some tests give much higher or lower I.Q.s than others, and, for this and other reasons, the I.Q.s got by children on different tests cannot be compared, a fact that comes as a surprise to many who have been led to believe that an individual child's I.Q. represents something quite definite.

Standardisation is important in this respect. It fixes as the "norm" the standard of achievement recorded by children who are subject to the widest inequality of opportunity. Once concretised in this way, these standards will become self-perpetuating, and wherever the test is applied, it will discriminate between children on what can only be described as class lines. It is evident that the proficiency of the children in the standardisation group to answer the questions in the test must itself vary with educational opportunity, home background, stimulus to achievement, and so on. It will do so the more clearly since, if the standardisation group has been carefully selected, it will include fixed proportions of children from different social and economic classes. Since, in a class society, *on average*, the higher the social status, the greater the likelihood that test questions of the kind described can be successfully answered; a test standardised in this way is bound to set standards of "intelligence" which are largely class differences disguised. It is an inescapable fact that the middle class child will always *tend* to do better than the working-class child, as a necessary result of the way in which the tests are constructed, validated and standardised.[1]

Intelligence and Social Class

That, on average, the working class turns out to have less "intelligence", as measured by tests, than other classes, is a foregone conclusion. Nevertheless much energy has been devoted to proving this point with the aid of surveys of the relative "intelligence" of different social and economic classes or occupational groups, undertaken with intelligence tests.

Two tables given by leading psychologists are reproduced on pages 79 and 80.

The most important single conclusion that emerges from this discussion of the construction of tests, is that the "intelligence" measured by tests is a class-conditioned attribute. A class element enters into the

---

[1] The fact that individual children from very poor homes sometimes do well on tests in no way invalidates this statement.

TABLE I*

Intelligence of Parents and Children Classified according to Occupations

		Average intelligence quotient	
Class	Occupational category	Children	Adults
I.	Higher Professional: Administrative	120·3	153·2
II.	Lower Professional: Technical Executive	114·6	132·4
III.	Highly Skilled: Clerical	109·7	117·1
IV.	Skilled	104·5	108·6
V.	Semi-skilled	98·2	97·5
VI.	Unskilled	92·0	86·8
VII.	Casual	89·1	81·6
VIII.	Institutional	67·2	57·3

* Table I is taken from Burt, 14. In explanation, Burt says: "The data for children refers to pupils attending London schools only. The data for adults was largely obtained during investigations carried out for the National Institute of Industrial Psychology."

practice of intelligence testing, at almost every stage; first, and most important, in the choice and character of the questions; second, in the method of putting the test questions together, and validating the test as a whole; finally, in the process of standardisation. All these processes militate against success on the part of the more culturally deprived section of the population. It follows that an investigation of the class distribution of intelligence is bound to give precisely the result it does, and indeed these results are the best possible confirmation of our thesis.

Some American psychometrists[1] have recognised that intelligence tests "prove" something that is patently false, namely, that working-class children are more stupid than middle- and upper-class children. When they tested children in novel "real-life" situations, for example, constructing a "soap-box" automobile from old pram wheels and grocers' throw-outs, working-class children showed resourcefulness of a kind seldom displayed by those more fortunate children used to receive their toys as presents. An individual intelligence test consisting of items of this character could easily be constructed, which would turn the tables printed above on their heads—it would embody a criterion of intelligence which favoured the working-class child just as the present verbal tests discriminate against him. But such a test would give such

[1] A psychometrist is a psychologist specifically concerned with mental measurement (e.g. intelligence testing).

TABLE II*

Number tested	Occupational category	Average intelligence quotient
30	Secondary School and University Teachers	151
25	Physicians and Surgeons	146·5
20	Civil Engineers	142
15	General Business Managers	137
250	Nurses	122
33	Carpenters	98
33	Machine Operators	96
12	Welders	87
19	Factory Packers and Sorters	78

* Table II is extracted from a larger table given in Cattell, 32. Terman analysed the social status of the higher I.Q. group of 1,000 unselected children: "Intelligence of 110 to 120 I.Q. is approximately five times as common among children of superior social status as among children of inferior social status. . . . The group is made up largely of children of the fairly successful mercantile or professional classes." Of I.Q.s between 120 and 140 he writes: "In a series of 476 unselected children, there was not a single one reaching 120 whose social class was described as 'below average'. Of the children of superior social status, about ten per cent reached 120 or better. The 120–140 group is made up almost entirely of children whose parents belong to the professional or very successful business classes. The child of a skilled labourer belongs here occasionally; the child of a common labourer very rarely indeed." In other investigations, however, he found even brighter children "from very inferior homes". Terman, *Measurement of Intelligence* (1919), 95–6.

different results from existing tests that it would undoubtedly be rejected on the grounds that it did not test "intelligence". This is another indication that a class criterion of intelligence has by now become inseparable from the whole practice of testing.

The American investigators conclude that the first criterion for determining whether an item should or should not be included in a test, must be that it does *not* discriminate between children from different social and economic backgrounds. "In each mental system area, the test maker must select problems common to the culture *and practice* of all socio-economic groups in the population to be tested."[1] Hence the search for so-called "common culture", or even "culture-free", tests, which really would give everybody a fair chance. But in a class society there is not a common culture, while the search for a culture-free test is obviously a chase after a will-o'-the-wisp; the questions must be formulated in words or symbols of some kind, and the testee's familiarity with these will depend on his life experience,

[1] Davis and Havighurst, "The Measurement of Mental Systems", *The Scientific Monthly*, Vol. XXVI, No. 4. (My italics.—B.S.)

and so will differ from person to person and, in general, from group to group. The suggestion that human intelligence might be measurable by the development of a new kind of test which actually eliminates all words and symbols is an absurdity. One of the most important single differences between human beings and the animals is that the former can communicate through speech and its derivatives, reading and writing. To attempt to eliminate all words and symbols because, in a class society, many children lack the opportunity to master the basic skills, is to reveal the limitations of this society and to illustrate the dead end reached by mental testing.

Intelligence tests can never be "objective", can never reach the supposed elusive and independent inner essence of mind which psychologists attempt to measure. Instead they are bound sharply to discriminate against the working class. And since these tests are used, in practice, to select children for secondary education, this discrimination is particularly evident in this field.

Nor is this simply a conclusion from the foregoing analysis. Recently a detailed investigation was made by two sociologists interested in the effect of the 1944 Education Act on the social composition of the children at certain grammar and modern schools.[1] Basing their analysis on a careful assessment of the social background of the pupils, these investigators found that "The difference in social composition between the two types of school is striking. The secondary modern schools cater very largely for the sons of manual workers, especially the semi-skilled and unskilled". This class was also "markedly underrepresented" in the grammar schools investigated; in none of these did they constitute as much as a quarter of the pupils, and in one only 6·9 per cent. Conversely, very few middle-class children were found in secondary modern schools. The investigators conclude: ". . . despite the changes introduced into secondary education by the Education Act of 1944, it remains the case that a boy has a greater chance of entering a grammar school if he comes from a middle-class rather than a working-class home". In explaining how this situation has come about, they rightly point "to the crucial role played by intelligence tests in the present selection procedure".

[1] A. H. Halsey and L. Gardner, "Selection for Secondary Education", *British Journal of Sociology*, Vol. IV, No. 1, March, 1953. This study is part of research being undertaken under the aegis of the Department of Sociological and Demographic Research of the London School of Economics. The sample investigated consisted of some 700 boys aged thirteen to fourteen years in four grammar and five secondary modern schools in Greater London.

4

INTELLIGENCE TESTING AND
SELECTION FOR SECONDARY EDUCATION

The Changing Intelligence Quotient

Selection for different kinds of secondary schools at the age of ten can only be justified on the grounds that the child mind has a single central factor ("innate all-round intellectual ability"), which determines the ultimate level of his intellectual powers, and which can be reliably measured at an early age.

Leaving aside, for the moment, the many theoretical problems involved in this hypothesis, and ignoring also the evident bias of intelligence tests already described, we may inquire, on the purely practical plane, whether the scores obtained by children on tests are *reliable* measures.

Intelligence tests can only claim to be reliable measures of an innate quality if children, tested a number of different times over a period of years, consistently obtain an approximately similar Intelligence Quotient.

In the 1920s and 1930s, it was widely held that a child's I.Q. remained constant as he grew older. This view was not, however, based on long-term studies of individual children, since, at that time, no such investigations had been carried through. It was based primarily on the results of testing groups of children two or three times at fairly short intervals, results which showed that, *on average*, the I.Q. remained roughly constant.

For instance, Terman, discussing this question in 1921, wrote: "speaking roughly, 50 per cent of the I.Q.s found at a later test may be expected to fall within the range between six points up and four points down. . . . It is evident, therefore, that the I.Q. is sufficiently constant to make it a practical and serviceable basis for mental classification."[1]

The last part of Terman's statement was repeated, while the qualification in the first sentence was conveniently forgotten. All that Terman in fact claimed was that "roughly speaking" half the children tested a

[1] Terman, *The Intelligence of School Children* (1921).

second time showed a variation of up to about five points. The other half showed an even greater variation, nor does he indicate how large were the individual changes. Clearly this is not convincing evidence for claiming that the individual child's I.Q. remains constant; nevertheless it was consistently suggested that this was so.

The theory of the constant I.Q. has, however, recently had to be abandoned as a result of long-term researches undertaken primarily in the U.S.A. These have shown beyond any doubt that children's scores vary from year to year, some steadily increasing, others decreasing, yet others oscillating up and down although usually showing a long-term trend. For a child's I.Q. to remain the same year after year is entirely exceptional. Further, it has been demonstrated that the longer the time interval between the first and the last test, the greater, in general, is the discrepancy between the scores.[1]

In view of this it can hardly be claimed that the tests are a reliable measuring rod of that supposedly innate and unalterable quality, "intelligence". Children's scores on a particular test at the age of ten have significance for that moment in time only. If the same test were given to the same group either a year later or earlier, the scores would almost all be different, some considerably so, and the actual order in which the children were placed would also be very different. Practically this means that the group of children selected for the grammar schools by a certain test at ten would be different from the group selected at nine or at eleven or twelve, even if a proportion of the children were in each group.

In addition, all kinds of influences may affect the child, and so his score, under the conditions of the actual selection examination; influences which the psychologist would regard as strictly irrelevant. For instance, the child's attitude to the test and his own emotional reaction at the time will, to some extent, determine his success. If he is sick or tired, or suffering from any degree of nervous strain, he may not do himself justice.[2] He may be unfamiliar with examinations,

[1] See *Transfer from Primary to Secondary Schools*, N.U.T. (1949), Appendix iii, by Dr. C. M. Fleming.

[2] The degree of strain imposed on children by this examination is not commonly realised. One teacher who noticed symptoms of anxiety and worry in her class a year before the examination, did a careful investigation and came to the conclusion that the examination was "a positive danger to the mental and physical well-being of many children in my class". Several showed signs of nervous instability, many complained of disturbed nights, especially on the eve of the examinations. "I had a smashing night's sleep—I took four aspirins." Their dreams are significant. "I had passed it, and got a bicycle but it was in pieces"; "I had a nightmare and went into Mummy"; "I dreamt of fainting half-

become overawed, and muff his papers. There are half a hundred possible reasons of this kind why a child may do less well than he normally would, or again why some children might do better than usual. It has even been shown that the way the test is supervised, whether strictly or slackly, has a profound effect on the children's scores.[1]

Clearly children cannot be compared to machines giving always a constant output. On the contrary, the way they behave at a particular moment may depend on all kinds of complex and subtle influences. For this reason alone, a group intelligence test score is slender evidence on which to base a final judgment of a child's ultimate intellectual development. Quite apart from this, the tests themselves are very unreliable as guides, partly owing to differences in methods of construction and validation. "Few experienced persons", writes Professor Vernon, "appear to put much trust in an individual's group test score, not only because of prejudice or conservatism, but also because different group tests are known to yield remarkably discrepant results. . . . A child who is given two or more may obtain I.Q.s differing by as much as thirty or even forty points."[2] One might add that practically no child will get exactly the same score if given the same test twice. And yet, as Mr. Clegg has pointed out, success or failure in the selection examination at ten is often determined by a decimal point on the examination as a whole, an examination dominated by one particular intelligence test, which, of course, puts children in a different order than would be the case if any other intelligence test were used.[3]

Psychologists themselves are, of course, aware of the limitations of group intelligence testing. Thus Vernon concludes that such tests "are not (very useful) for obtaining trustworthy information about indi-

---

way through"; "I went to sleep and woke up crying". The prizes offered by parents to this one class included: sixteen new bicycles, three watches, three puppies, a bedroom clock, a portable radio, a tennis racket, a "perm", a pair of roller skates, etc., "all", says the teacher "built up the tension, and sharpened the children's perception of their parents' fear". *Journal of the Institute of Education of Durham University*, Vol. 4, No. 23, May, 1953 (article on "The Scholarship").

[1] Vernon, 190, note 2.

[2] Vernon, 193.

[3] In view of this admitted fact, what can be made of the following claim on behalf of the Moray House Intelligence Tests, which are very widely used in selection examinations throughout the country (it is made in a pamphlet written to explain and publicise these tests to local authorities): "The discriminating power of Moray House Tests is such that it is worth taking these quotients [I.Q.s.—B.S.] to half points in order to avoid ties (though this does not, of course, mean that two repetitions of different Moray House tests will agree to half a point !)". The exclamation mark is the author's. Godfrey H. Thomson, *What are Moray House Tests?* (no date).

viduals", although they have their uses in the testing of groups, and for large-scale experiments.[1] Sir Cyril Burt, one of the two psychologists who gave oral evidence to the Spens Committee, has himself said: "No predictions are so confidently offered by the educational or vocational psychologist as those which are based on some such factor as 'g' or general intelligence. Yet again and again his forecasts are falsified."[2] This is the expert's view, yet in selection the results of these tests are treated as if they were trustworthy and normally given great weight; and, of course, as far as parents are concerned, it is the individual child and his future opportunities that matter.

Coaching for Intelligence Tests

The fact that an individual child's I.Q. varies from test to test, as well as from day to day and from year to year, is itself an indication that these tests are scarcely satisfactory instruments on which to base, not only the practice but also the whole theory of selection. But recently mental testing has suffered a much severer blow than any that have gone before. It has been clearly established that coaching in the "tricks of the trade" can have a profound effect on children's test results. Late in 1952, Professor Vernon announced that the *average* rise in I.Q. which was obtained from a limited amount of instruction in the technique of answering test questions was as much as fourteen points. One investigator actually raised the average I.Q. of a complete class by seventeen points after four hours' work, while with a similar class he obtained an increase of sixteen points after one hour only.[3]

Professor Vernon himself pointed out the significance of this discovery. The typical cut-off point for a pass into a grammar school is supposed to be at an I.Q. of 115. Normally 17 per cent of an average class of children may be expected to pass this borderline, and so win a

---

[1] Vernon, 193.

[2] Burt, *Factors of the Mind*, 1940, 229–30.

[3] Vernon, "Intelligence Testing", *Times Educ. Supp.*, January 2nd and February 1st, 1952. Professor Vernon later reduced the average rise to 11 points, indicating that there had been some confusion about the norms of the tests used. He reiterated, however, that "an appreciable proportion of the boys who took part in the experiments did show rises of 15 up to 20 or more I.Q. points" (*Times Educ. Supp.*, April 24th, 1953). In the original articles announcing his results he stated that these had been "substantiated by numerous experiments" other than those done under his aegis. In another article he stated, in answer to critics who asserted that the average gain was less than 14 points, that his figure was supported "by every other comparable research (carried out by six different investigators in three different countries) that has been done in this field". (*Times Educ. Supp.*, December 12th, 1952). See also letters in the same journal, December 26th, 1952.

place. But if this same class were coached and the average I.Q. rose fifteen points, exactly half the class would pass the borderline. In other words, 33 per cent of the class who, without coaching, would not have qualified for a grammar school, would do so after coaching.

Coaching for intelligence tests has, of course, been going on for a long time. Parents, not unnaturally, have bought practice test booklets and given their children instruction. In some junior schools the children spend many hours on different kinds of test questions. It has been known that this kind of coaching produced good results, but the implications for testing were so serious that this undoubted fact had been ignored. At a meeting of some two hundred Middlesex teachers in 1952, Professor Vernon, in his own words, "tried to play down the seriousness of coaching". He continues: "I was informed from the floor in no uncertain terms how widespread it was in the country."[1] Consequently, he embarked on the research outlined above. He found that his conclusions paralleled those of other researchers in the 1920s and 1930s; conclusions, incidentally, to which little or no attention was paid until it became impossible to avoid the issue.

It is natural that psychometrists should have tried to ignore the very considerable changes in test scores that result from coaching. Until recently, the *cornerstone* of psychometry has been that intelligence tests measure, at least approximately, the same inherited, unchangeable quality of mind—intelligence; and it is on this assumption, and this alone that their use in selection—and indeed selection itself—has been justified to the public. If a local authority can say to a protesting parent: we have scientific evidence that your child simply has not got enough intelligence to profit from a grammar school education, the parent has no alternative but to accept this dictum.

And yet it has been shown beyond any doubt that children can be taught to do intelligence tests, just as they can be taught to do English and arithmetic, chess and crosswords. If the reader will refer back to the examples given in Chapter II, he will recognise that there is nothing unteachable in the kind of questions or problems set. Teachers and parents, of course, have been aware of this, the number of practice tests on the market is sufficient indication of their wide and general use.[2]

---

[1] Vernon, *Times Educ. Supp.*, December 26th, 1952.

[2] The situation was well summed up by a correspondent to the *Times Educational Supplement*. (February 15th, 1952):

"That intelligence tests are susceptible to the effects of coaching has been suspected by practising psychologists for some time, has been known by teachers for years, and has never been doubted by parents."

Vernon's publication of his findings immediately raised a flood of controversy among psychometrists. Some asserted that the effect of coaching was not so great as Vernon claimed, but these he answered effectively. In any case, the argument as to whether the average gain from coaching is fourteen points or ten points or even less is irrelevant to the main issue. Dr. Alexander, psychologist and administrator, wrote an article in the official journal of the Association of Education Committees, claiming that any teachers "guilty of special preparation of children for such . . . tests are guilty of cruelty to children just as much as those who appear in court for physical cruelty to children". Adding that it was, indeed, "perhaps a more serious offence" than the latter, he concluded "for a teacher to be guilty of such an offence should be proper grounds for striking his name from the list of those qualified to teach".[1]

Clearly this question engenders much heat. But surely it is psychologists and administrators, whose claims have been proved false, who are at fault, rather than parents and teachers. No professional organisation of teachers has, to the writer's knowledge, ever committed itself as to the scientific and objective character of these instruments. In any case, Dr. Alexander's solution—that there should be no coaching—although supported by a few psychometrists, has naturally not been taken very seriously. As this step is clearly impracticable, many mental testers attempt to argue that the problem will be overcome if *all* children are equally coached for this test, and in order to facilitate this, they have produced booklets giving guidance on how to coach, including practice tests for use in the schools.[2]

But the peculiar and often absurd questions in tests were devised in this form precisely so that they should be "new" to all children and so fair tests of innate ability and not of acquired knowledge! Now that it is proposed that all children should be taught how to do these questions, it is clear that this position can no longer be maintained, and that

---

[1] *Education*, June 6th, 1952.

[2] W. S. James, Lecturer in Education at Bristol University, writes: "In the two counties where I serve as Chief Examiner, we have introduced coaching for intelligence tests into all primary schools [for limited periods—B.S.]. . . . With this end in view, a booklet will very shortly be produced, giving lessons and practice tests for use by pupils in authorities' schools during the few weeks before the examination" (*Manchester Guardian*, January, 1952). A review commending this booklet says: "Instructions are clearly printed in bold type, and in places are worded so as to create in the child's mind the idea that answering the questions is a pleasant pastime and not an ordeal" (*Schoolmaster*, March 28th, 1952).

tests will chiefly measure differences in opportunity. For there is, of course, no way of ensuring that all children are equally coached.

First, there is the difference in teachers: "It should be recognised ..." writes one psychometrist, "that universal coaching could very well introduce much greater unfairness. Children in schools with a high standard of teaching will gain more from their instruction in intelligence tests than others, and the chief virtue of the test, that it compensates for inequalities in teaching, will not only be lost but turned into an additional handicap for children from the less efficient schools."[1]

Second, there is the difference in the attitude of the children to this peculiar sort of "lesson". Some will be frankly bored, and who can blame them, especially since the "best" test questions are those with no meaningful content at all. And, if one can hazard a generalisation, it will be the children with most spirit in them who will pay least attention. Only the docile could easily submit.

Thirdly, how can one ensure that all children are coached for an equal length of time? This is obviously quite impossible. Some psychometrists argue that this does not matter, claiming that once children have learned the tricks in some three or four hours, it is difficult to produce any further improvement, however long they are coached. Hence Vernon's suggestion that coaching for all should take only three or four hours; "there seems to me", he says, "convincing evidence that any teacher or parent who spent longer on coaching would be wasting time and possibly even reducing the pupil's efficiency."[2]

The difficulty is that neither teachers nor parents are likely to be convinced by this argument, and for a very good reason. All the researches quoted have been based on *average* results; this, as we have seen, is the common practice of psychometrists. But the teacher is faced with a class of individuals, and of course the parent is interested normally in only *one* child. There is *no* evidence to show that the individual child, given intensive coaching over a long period, his co-operation being maintained by all kinds of incentives, will not increase his I.Q. score by well over the average; he may well continually increase it, if at a

[1] W. G. Emmett. Reader in Educational Research, Moray House, University of Edinburgh. *The Use of Intelligence Tests in the* 11+ *Transfer Examination.* Dr. Emmett supports Dr. Alexander: no one should be coached. Compare Vernon: "There seems to be little difference between different teachers as coaches", "Coaching for All Advised", *Times Educ. Supp.*, February 1st, 1952.

[2] Vernon, *ibid.*

decreasing rate, up to a very high point. And the methods of teaching "intelligence" will, with universal practice, certainly improve.

While psychometrists argue among themselves as to whether children should be officially coached or not, no way has or can be found out of the present impasse. If all are coached (a sufficiently futile process from the educational angle) the test results will measure differences in the amount and effectiveness of coaching. If coaching is officially frowned on, test results will still measure these differences, since, in practice, coaching will go on. In either case, a new element of unfairness is introduced into the selection examination. In sum, the revelations as to the effect of coaching have cast the very gravest doubts on the theory that "intelligence" exists and can be measured by tests.[1]

The Validity of Selection: (a) A Question without an Answer

The defects in the practice of intelligence testing, summarised in this chapter, have led to much heart searching among teachers, local authorities, psychologists, and indeed among all those concerned with the unhappy business of sorting children out at ten or eleven. Nobody is satisfied with the present methods or procedure, least of all the parents, as the pages of the popular and the local press abundantly testify. In particular, it is the intelligence test that is most sharply criticised. The I.Q. is under fire.

One county authority, Hertfordshire, announced early in 1953 its intention of cutting "the knot in which intelligence testers have entangled themselves" by dropping these tests from the selection examination, chiefly for the reasons given above. Other authorities are trying to work out methods of selection that put less emphasis on these scores. Articles in the educational press describing these methods reflect this unease. "Selection tests for secondary education are now under hot fire, and some of the shots are going home", writes a reviewer of a pamphlet on selection in Wiltshire.[2] "That there is widespread dis-

---

[1] Professor Vernon has suggested that coaching for intelligence tests, until recently regarded by everybody as educationally indefensible, may, in fact, be educationally desirable, since the "skilful use of intelligence test material" in school may "even perhaps" not only increase the children's scores, but also their ability to "use their brains", just as teaching in English or Mathematics may do. If it is once admitted that children can be taught to "use their brains", i.e. to act more intelligently, the whole case for selection on the basis of *inherited* intelligence is logically exploded; since the *only* rational justification for selection lies in the supposed innate and *unalterable* differences between children, so far as "intelligence", at least, is concerned (Vernon, *ibid.*).

[2] *Times Educ. Supp.*, November 7th, 1952.

satisfaction with the present system of selection for grammar schools needs no emphasis".[1] This, it may be noted, was written by a grammar school headmaster; there is no "system of selection" for modern schools. When Hertfordshire abolished intelligence tests, the *Schoolmaster*, organ of the National Union of Teachers, published a cartoon of a tank breaking through a wall described "I.Q. barrier", and headed the cartoon "Hertfordshire strikes again".[2]

But selection cannot be saved simply by abolishing the "intelligence" test, which has hitherto been the keystone of the whole system. What is the alternative? To hand over selection for grammar schools largely to the grammar school headmasters (as in Hertfordshire and Wiltshire), or to the primary school headmaster (as is apparently proposed in the West Riding), or, alternatively, to include different *kinds* of tests, (essay papers, comprehension tests and so on), as various other authorities are doing, does not solve the problem at all. Fundamentally the same kind of decision has to be made by somebody. Children must be sorted out at the early age of ten *according to predictions made about their future intellectual development*. The basic assumptions of intelligence testing must therefore underlie these "new" methods as well. The only difference will be that these methods, relying as they do to a greater extent on the personal judgment of one or two people, can make no claim to scientific validity at all. They represent an advance, therefore, only in this sense, that with the relegation of intelligence tests into the background, it becomes impossible for anybody to maintain that selection is a scientific procedure. The case against separating children into different groups at the age of ten becomes proportionately more overwhelming.

What is the answer of the psychometrists to these developments? It is a firm reiteration that intelligence tests are the best, the most "reliable", the most "valid" instruments for use in selection. Vernon, although expressing interest in the Hertfordshire experiment, described it as "a regrettable step."[3] Nevertheless, psychometrists themselves are unhappy about the situation. Some see little prospect of further refining or improving selection procedures: "we . . . [have] virtually reached the limit of valid selection under present conditions"[4]; and, referring to coaching, they complain that their work has been misunderstood:

[1] *Times Educ. Supp.*, October 3rd, 1952. F. C. Happold, Headmaster of Bishop Wordsworth School, Salisbury.
[2] *Schoolmaster*, January 16th, 1953.
[3] *Times Educ. Supp.*, January 16th, 1953.
[4] Vernon, *Times Educ. Supp.*, December 26th, 1952.

"... our present controversy would never have occurred had not educationists misused our instruments".[1] Mr. Ben Morris, Secretary of the National Foundation for Educational Research, points out that "objective tests are being used for purposes for which they were not originally intended". They were, he claims, intended for educational guidance not for selection, though they are still the best instruments for the latter purpose yet known. He concludes: "It is, however, up to the public to see that a system of secondary education is created in which effective educational guidance, as distinct from selection, becomes possible."[2] He is of course, perfectly right, but it must be noted that hitherto the public has been lulled into accepting the present selective system of education precisely on the grounds that these tests *were* valid instruments for selection.

By continuing to maintain that intelligence tests are the best instruments for selection, psychometrists are patently putting themselves in a false position. In the nature of the case, there can be no way of knowing what *is* the best method of selection, or, to put the same point in another way, the very nature of selection makes it quite impossible to assess its effectiveness. For that reason, the question "what is the best method of selection?" is of the same order as the old conundrum: "Have you stopped beating your wife?". It is impossible to answer definitely one way or another. If children have *not* got different quantities of the inherited quality "intelligence", which administrators can measure, if, in other words, there is no scientific means of differentiating between them at the age of ten, then there can be no "best" method of selection at all; the task is patently impossible.

When psychometrists claim that intelligence testing is the best method of selection, what they mean is that these tests appear to predict children's "success" at the grammar school (according to certain scholastic criteria) very slightly more effectively than other tests given to the same children at ten in the selection examination.

The claim is based on a comparison of the marks of certain children in intelligence and other tests at ten with their marks in grammar school examinations taken at fifteen or sixteen; each individual selection test, for instance English or arithmetic being compared with these marks independently. The procedure followed may be briefly outlined, for this is an important argument.

If a hundred children win places in a given grammar school, their

<hr />

[1] Vernon, *ibid.*
[2] *The Times*, August 29th, 1952.

I.Q.s can be listed in descending order from the highest of, say, 145 to the lowest of, perhaps, 112. Four or five years later their examination marks in a number of different subjects can be added up and their average mark worked out; the children can once again be listed in descending order from the highest to the lowest. These two orders may now be compared, and there is a method of expressing the *degree* of relation between the two sets of figures in one statistical term—a correlation coefficient. For instance, if the two sets of marks correspond exactly, with all the children listed in exactly the same order at fifteen as they were at ten, then the correlation coefficient is a positive unity: +1·0. If the two sets of marks are exactly opposite to each other, e.g. if the top boy at ten is bottom at fifteen and vice versa, all the others reversing their positions correspondingly, the correlation coefficient is a minus one: −1·0. The half-way position between these two extremes is expressed by a correlation coefficient of 0, implying, of course, that there is no relation at all between the two sets of marks. The intermediate figures between + 1·0 and − 1·0, therefore, describe different degrees of likeness between two sets of figures.

When challenged recently to show that intelligence tests were the best predictors of grammar school "success", Professor Vernon quoted as being typical of the "ordinary English grammar school" a correlation between I.Q. and School Certificate results of + 0·44,[1] a slightly higher correlation than was shown for other forms of assessment of children at ten.[2]

Vernon, in reporting this result, pointed out that "though the I.Q. is at least as good as the others, none of the correlations is high, and this explains why grammar school teachers find considerable discrepancies between entrance results and subsequent achievement".[3]

This is not in itself an impressive result when one considers all the

[1] *Times Educ. Supp.*, August 4th, 1950.
[2] These were: the special place (selection) examination, involving educational attainment tests, and the primary school teacher's assessments of the children. The correlations here were +0·42 and +0·43 respectively.
[3] Vernon, *ibid.* A correlation of +0·44 sounds reasonably high, but it actually describes a very slight degree of similarity between the two sets of marks. Suppose the test is to be used to select the best 20 per cent of the ten-year-olds for grammar school entrance, on the usual assumption that 20 per cent of the ten-year age group *only* have the intellectual capacity to profit from a grammar school education and so to pass the Certificate examination five years later. This correlation of +0·44 would mean that out of every twenty pupils sent to the grammar school, twelve would be failures according to the second test at fifteen. That is to say, in the grammar school there would be a 60 per cent failure rate in this second test.

claims that have been made for tests, and all the human problems involved in their use. But, even more important, though results of this kind may tell us something about the relative efficiency of different kinds of selection tests (if we accept the criterion of "success" chosen), they operate within the closed circle of the grammar school; they tell us absolutely *nothing* about what might be called the absolute efficiency of selection. In other words, no one knows, or could possibly know, how "successful" the 80 per cent of children who failed at ten or eleven would have been if they had won places at this type of school.

Obviously this is an unsatisfactory state of affairs. One way out of this difficulty is to sidestep it by simply assuming that the 80 per cent of children who fail to get into grammar schools, will vary in their attainment of "success" at fifteen or sixteen, to *exactly* the same degree as those who passed the selection test. It is not worth trying to puzzle out a "meaning" for this assumption in terms of any practical criterion of "success" it is possible to imagine. It is a purely statistical conception.[1] But a psychometrist prepared to make this leap in the dark finds it quite possible to compute what may be called the *total* "efficiency" of the intelligence test, and, far more important, to produce a more impressive figure. By simply making this statistical assumption he can raise the correlation coefficient from the meagre $+ 0·44$ to $+ 0·70$. One investigator has even claimed a correlation of $+ 0·84$ on this basis.[2]

It is worth pointing out that many leading psychometrists regard the basic assumption described above as unscientific and unjustifiable. But nevertheless the idea that there *is* a high correlation between test results and grammar school success tends to get about, and naturally the general public is in no position to argue. In practice there is *no* way of finding out how any child would have done at a grammar school if he is, for instance, in a secondary modern school; it is, in fact, impossible to

---

[1] This conception would only be valid if it could be shown that children's educational development is absolutely independent of the type of school to which they go; that is to say, that this development is determined wholly by factors internal to the child. But this is clearly a ridiculous proposition.

[2] If the correlation of $+0·84$ represented anything meaningful, it would lead to the conclusion that in an area where 20 per cent are selected for grammar school entrance, and this selection was made on the basis of I.Q. only (its purpose being to predict who is likely to be in the best 20 per cent of pupils after five years), 35 per cent of those sent to the grammar school would be failures at fifteen. McClelland, referring to a correlation of $+0·8$ in this connection, says: "These results show the uncertainty of any guidance given to a pupil solely on the basis of examinations and tests, no matter how complete or carefully conducted." Cf. McClelland, *Selection for Secondary Education* (1945), 124–5.

assess the efficiency of selection in any scientific way. Though intelligence tests may have a slightly higher correlation than other tests with later success at a grammar school, there may still be thousands and tens of thousands of children outside the grammar schools who would also have been equally "successful" had they passed at ten. And this, of course, is the only material point at issue.

The Validity of Selection: (b) Some Evidence from the Rejected

However, if we are really interested in finding out what children are capable of achieving, what the ordinary child is like, there are various ways in which it could be done, even within the limits of the present divided system of secondary education. But, as this matter is not at present apparently regarded as important, there are no researches to report; a few examples, mainly taken from the educational press, must suffice.

A recent article provides a good opening.[1] In this, a headmaster in an area with a high proportion of grammar school places, reports on his teaching of French to 1st form boys (aged eleven). He found in his class one boy (D) with an I.Q. of 105; another (A) had an I.Q. of 111, and had "just sneaked into a grammar school", since his total entrance examination marks (which included the results of other tests) were the lowest for the form; in another area, says the headmaster, "he would automatically have been transferred to a secondary modern school". What happened to these two boys? A became top of the class, "he was mopping it up and loving it". D came out fourth. And right at the bottom of the class of twenty-nine children was a boy with an I Q of 131, the third highest I Q in the class. Of three of his boys the headmaster concludes that they were "in this grammar school by the merest fluke, and I should not be surprised if one day they gain a modern language scholarship".

In another area the governors of individual grammar schools are allowed to award a small number of places in the school to boys who have been graded as below grammar school standard in the selection examination. The headmaster of one of these schools analysed the performance of forty-one such boys who, in other areas, would have been excluded from a grammar school. He found that "not only were the greater number of these boys well able to hold their own, but more

---

[1] "Grammar School Entrants", by a Headmaster, *Times Educ. Supp.*, October 24th, 1952.

than a third were above the grammar school average and several had reached an exceptional standard".

He also established that "the majority of (these) boys who have since done well had failed to obtain a grammar school grading because of a low intelligence mark". In this area, special attention is given to the examination, in an attempt to make selection as accurate as possible. But, concludes this headmaster, "those who base their opposition to the comprehensive school on the accuracy of the present system of selection would be well advised to seek firmer ground".[1]

Unfortunately, few schoolmasters make investigations of the kind reported in these articles, but if some children who scrape into the grammar school do so well, how many who fail at ten would have done so? Some indication may be gained from the experience of those authorities which allow a few children a second chance of qualifying for a grammar school at thirteen. All such entrants failed at ten, that is to say, the selection test predicted that they were incapable of profiting from a systematic education. Of children in this category the Chief Education Officer for the West Riding states: "in many schools . . . transfer cases have been outstandingly successful. Some have gained open and State scholarships. A considerable number have gained County Major Scholarships. . . . At least one gained a first-class honours degree at the University with the University medal for the best student of the year. Many have entered Training Colleges."[2]

The great majority of secondary modern school children do not get the chance of proving their powers in this way. The assumption is that they are incapable of such sustained intellectual achievement. The Ministry of Education seems to suggest that they are only capable

[1] "New Light on Secondary Selection", by a Grammar School Headmaster. *Schoolmaster*, June 12th and June 19th, 1953. Of the whole group of forty-one boys two "proved to be very weak and another five below average, eighteen seemed to be about average, eleven above average, and five outstanding".

[2] Clegg, 11. A very small proportion of secondary modern school chilren win a transfer at twelve or thirteen to a grammar school. It cannot be argued that these are all who are worthy of this "second chance". This question has been investigated by the National Foundation of Educational Research. Mr. Ben Morris, summarising their conclusions, has pointed out that it is difficult [impossible?—B.S.] "to find a valid basis of comparison between children who have for one or more years been immersed in totally different environments and pursuing divergent courses of study". He concludes: "The amount of transfer between secondary schools found to be necessary is, however, usually very low. This, unfortunately, proves nothing at all except that the pupils and the teachers in the schools have adapted to each other, or have come to accept each other. It proves little or nothing about the basic suitability or unsuitability of the children for the courses of study they follow." *Education*, October 31st, 1952, 602.

of learning through "practical activities", gardening, woodwork, dressmaking and the like. Only one child in 22,000 from secondary modern schools gets to a university—proof indeed!

It was impossible to challenge this assumption, except theoretically, until recently. The Bournemouth Education Committee has, however, given it the lie, and in no uncertain manner. They ran two experimental courses for the General Certificate of Education at two ordinary secondary modern schools. Forty-eight children took the examination (at "ordinary level") in 1952; some gained as many as nine passes, and the average was five. These results are at least as good as the average results in many grammar schools, and this in spite of the fact that standards have been raised well above the pass level of the old school certificate examination. "It has been noticeable that some pupils have been inspired by the thought of a 'second lease of life' when admitted to the G.C.E. classes", writes the Borough Education Officer; the two schools "have shown by their outstanding work what can be done by such pupils. Such a scheme demands hard work on the part of both staff and pupils, and they are both to be congratulated on the success which rewarded their efforts". He adds: "I believe . . . other secondary modern staff and pupils would welcome a similar challenge."[1]

The Bournemouth Education Committee's plan certainly, as they claim, "strikes at the root of the secondary allocation problem", and it is now proposed to institute G.C.E. courses in all the secondary modern schools in this town. But this, of course, does not solve what is politely called the "allocation" problem. To set up two different types of schools and then to give the same type of education in them is scarcely logical![2] Nevertheless, Bournemouth has certainly exposed in a dramatic way that the validity of selection at ten is a chimera.

Pupils in some other secondary modern schools in the country are beginning to be given the opportunity to take the General Certificate, and there is no reason to believe that they, and their teachers, will tackle it any less effectively than Bournemouth.[3] It is to developments like

[1] *Schoolmaster*, November 14th, 1952.

[2] The plan was tried out since Bournemouth do not wish to extend their grammar schools to meet the bulge in the birthrate which will begin to reach the secondary schools in 1956. Their existing grammar schools take about 24 per cent of an age group, well above the average for the country.

[3] A similar scheme operates in Southampton. In 1952, forty-one children, who had only begun to study for this course three years before (the normal length is five years), sat the examination, securing 127 passes in different subjects. Fourteen of these children then transferred to grammar school sixth forms (*Schoolmaster*, February 6th, 1953). In another authority in 1950–1, seven modern schools presented 176 candidates for the

this, as well as to the scholastic successes by "ordinary" pupils in the new comprehensive schools in Anglesey, Middlesex, London, the West Riding, the Isle of Man, and elsewhere, that attention should be directed if we really wish to assess the validity of intelligence testing and selection.

Finally, something could surely be learned from the very different proportions of children given the opportunity of a grammar school education in different parts of the country. This varies from about 8 per cent to over 60 per cent; the town of Nottingham, for instance, provides places for just over 11 per cent of an age group while Gloucester provides for about 39 per cent.[1] What proportion of the population is endowed with sufficient "innate general cognitive ability" to profit from a grammar school course, is it a half or a tenth? This is a question to which the supporters of a divided educational system, involving a selection examination in which the marks have to be worked out to decimal places, should surely return an accurate answer, if they wish their claims to be taken seriously.

But more important from our point of view, is it a fact that the grammar schools in Gloucester, for instance, have a far higher proportion of failures in later examinations than those of Nottingham or Gateshead? If the theories of mental testing are true this should, in general, be the case. But no research has been done to find out the facts. In the meantime it can be said that whatever the proportion of the population at grammar schools, these schools themselves are curiously similar. The children sit for the same examinations, and, although each school has its ups and downs, the actual proportion of failures and successes does not vary greatly. In other words, the success of a school seems to depend not so much on the "intelligence" level of the children as on the quality of the teaching, a quality, incidentally, which psychometry consistently ignores in its dictums on education.

What conclusion can be drawn from these examples? The most obvious is that there are many children outside the grammar schools who could profit from a grammar school education, whatever their recorded "intelligence" level and their achievement in the selection

General Certificate at Ordinary level and twelve at advanced. Of these, 129 (73 per cent) secured passes in at least one subject at ordinary level and ten (83 per cent) at Advanced, the latter being equivalent to the grammar school sixth form work. This authority expects more secondary modern children to take the examination as more courses are provided. *Times Educ. Supp.*, September 19th, 1952.

[1] F. C. Campbell, "Anomalies in Grammar School Placing". *Schoolmaster*, December 5th, 1952.

examination as a whole. How many there are cannot be known, but recent developments have shown that the number is far larger than has ever been admitted as possible, and this fact alone points to the overall inefficiency and injustice of the existing system of selection.

It is, however, possible to draw two opposite conclusions from this experience. Those who are dominated by the theories of mental testing and who subscribe to the doctrine of the normal distribution of intelligence, have now begun to argue that what is required is a whole hierarchy of different types of schools or courses specially designed to meet the requirements of children at each intelligence level. Some suggest that grammar schools should take not 15 per cent of the population, but only 5 per cent, or even 0·5 per cent—the really *brilliant* intellects; there should then be many other grades of school or courses right down to that which takes the really "unintelligent" child, innately incapable of any intellectual achievement.[1]

This, of course, reflects a pessimistic attitude to children and their "abilities". But what, in fact, is the kernel of this proposition? It is a suggestion that the whole structure of the school system should be made to conform to what is an unverifiable assumption about the distribution of an indefinable quality.

It is quite possible to reach an opposite conclusion. The evidence of this chapter has shown that where the restrictions surrounding the admittedly limited and academic grammar school type of education have been even slightly lifted, children and teachers outside these schools have proved their ability, and this in an examination whose standards have been considerably raised during the last three years. They have, therefore, given the lie to the selection examination. This suggests once more that it is quite impossible to achieve a "valid" form of selection, and that intelligence tests, which provide the justification for the present system of selection, are open to the most serious objections as predictors of future intellectual attainments.

This conclusion is becoming more generally accepted as the evidence accumulates. For instance, the Professor of Experimental Psychology at Cambridge University, reporting recently on a five-year investigation into the use of similar tests to select medical students, said: "I think it is clear beyond dispute that the predictive capacity of tests of

---

[1] Burt gives support to this view when he writes: "Obviously, in an ideal community, our aim should be to discover what ration of intelligence nature has given to each individual child at birth, then to provide him with the appropriate education, and finally to guide him into the career for which he seems to have been marked out." *The Listener*, November 16th, 1950.

this kind . . . is (with one possible exception) entirely negligible"; he is reported as adding that the view, once widely held, that tests of this kind reveal stable, relatively unalterable human properties, whether of intelligence or anything else, was almost certainly wrong.[1]

The Failure of Mental Testing

Mental testing has, then, been proved to be a failure in practice; and indeed to so great an extent that some education authorities have already dispensed with "intelligence" tests, and others are considering doing so. Why then has so much time been spent in analysing and criticising these tests if they are already on the way out? The answer has already been given. So long as there are different types of secondary school, offering very different kinds of education and opportunities to children, so long must *someone* make a judgment between children at the age of eleven. The fact that "intelligence" tests are being discarded does not mean that the ideas behind them have been dismissed. On the contrary, these ideas permeate education at all levels, and inspire both teachers' judgments of children and the other kinds of examination which serve as substitutes for tests. Most English and arithmetic papers set for the selection examination are very like "intelligence" tests, while teachers required to stream young children, to keep school records for use when the decision is made about the child's future, or to set their children out in an order of merit can only do so according to some criterion. The criterion they tend to use is that of "intelligence". It is, therefore, necessary to underline the fact that the rejection of "intelligence" tests in practice, implies also the rejection of the concept of "intelligence". This is clear if we recapitulate briefly the course of development of testing.

It was precisely because it was impossible for such judgments between children to be made fairly, without prejudice, and because the normal examination penalised the child from a poor home, that the "intelligence" test was first introduced in the schools. The idea was that, if the child's real innate powers could be measured, without reference to his acquired knowledge, then selection for scholarships would be truly fair. With the rapid development of the county secondary schools after the First World War, accompanied by the increase in "free places" to be competed for by examination, psychologists were faced

[1] Professor Sir Frederick Bartlett, in an address to a section of the First World Conference on Medical Education. *Times Educ. Supp.*, September 4th, 1953.

with the demand for an "objective" test of this kind. They, as much as anyone, were aware how fatal was the decision made at ten, and how unfairly it operated against the less fortunate child. "A simple method of testing the abilities of children has become in educational administration an urgent practical need", wrote Sir Cyril Burt in 1921, "No appeal is more often addressed to the psychologist than the demand for a mental footrule".[1]

In their attempt to construct this "footrule", psychologists set out with two hypotheses, without which their task would have been impossible, but for which there was as yet no scientific proof. They assumed (a) that children have certain fixed mental powers which can be measured with reasonable accuracy, and which remain much the same throughout life; (b) a necessary corollary of the first assumption, that these mental powers are inherited at birth.

Obviously there was no way of measuring these powers directly. The only thing that could be done, was to measure the *differences* between children, differences shown in the performance of certain basic mental tasks. The average performance of children in these tasks was worked out, and each child was then classified in an order in relation to this average. However, it was one thing to classify children in relation to each other, in answer to an insistent demand that children should be so "differentiated", it was quite another thing to claim that test results threw light on the individual child's inherited potentialities. It was in the effort to prove that they did, that is, to prove the initial assumptions of testing, that the various techniques, already described in Chapter III, were introduced. If it could be shown that test scores were always distributed in the same way, then it could be argued that tests were measuring the same "thing", i.e. "intelligence"; if it could be shown that scores remained constant, then it might be argued that "intelligence", as measured by tests, was an innate and unchanging power.

And so, gradually, a mass of data, and of theories derived from this data, were evolved; the aim was to establish that "intelligence" test results *prove* the existence of a mental power "intelligence", an inherited, unchanging characteristic. But the extent of the claims for "intelligence" tests soon began to vary with the extent of testing. When very few tests had been administered, the most extravagant claims were advanced with the greatest certitude. As testing became more general, and difficulties of various kinds emerged, the claims became pro-

[1] Burt, *Mental and Scholastic Tests* (1921), 1.

gressively less exaggerated and less assured. Finally, today, when almost every child in the country is tested at a certain stage, and when the weaknesses of tests have become so obvious that they can no longer be hidden, psychologists make hardly any claims at all. They now hasten to assure us that we must *not* suppose that tests reveal "entities of the mind" or "the fundamental elements of which human minds are compounded". On the contrary, "factors" extracted from test results, and "intelligence" is just such a factor, are "primarily . . . categories for classifying mental tests and examinations".[1]

Since absolutely no proof has been adduced that "intelligence" is a fixed quality of the individual human mind, it is obvious that there can be no proof that it is innate; the two propositions hang together. After half a century of research, and the widest practical use of mental testing, the original hypotheses on which the whole edifice has been raised remain unsubstantiated. It is now abundantly clear that testing is nothing more than a practically useful method of classification, a classification of children *in relation to* an arbitrary standard of "intelligence". That standard, as has already been argued, is necessarily one derived from our social practice. The brain worker or white-collar worker is socially more highly valued than the manual worker, no matter whether the former merely adds up lists of figures while the latter works a complicated machine demanding a considerable degree of technical knowledge and skill; B.B.C. speech is socially more acceptable than the dialect of the North Country. Social judgments of this kind are incorporated in tests, which discriminate between children primarily according to vocabulary and the capacity to manipulate the printed word in certain ways, and not according to their potential usefulness to society and humanity. As a result, many teachers in grammar schools now complain that it is the intellectual "spiv" who profits

---

[1] Some of the efforts to substantiate these hypotheses have not been referred to, for instance those arguments based on the results of testing twins. Psychometrists disagree in their interpretation of these results. Briefly, it is claimed that, on average, identical twins tend to have similar I.Q.s while progressively greater differences are shown, in ascending scale, when fraternal twins, brothers and sisters, and random pairs of children are tested. Some psychometrists argue that, if "intelligence" varies in this way with genetical make-up then the likelihood is that it is handed on genetically, i.e. that it is a unitary mental trait and innate. This is yet another argument by analogy, arrived at statistically. It is not generally accepted as conclusive because twins and siblings have also an environment more similar than other pairs. In addition, the genetical theories here taken for granted have been shown to be open to much the same objections as theories based on "intelligence" testing, so that it is rather a case of the blind leading the blind. So far as parents and teachers are concerned there must always be anxiety lest twins are separated at eleven, for group tests have been known to place even identical twins widely apart.

from the "intelligence" test, while the child of true worth is passed over.

In spite of the failure of mental testing, those interested in preserving the present system of secondary education still cling to the conception of "intelligence", refusing to recognise that the practical failure implies also a theoretical failure. But this, of course, is the case, and with this failure the whole selective system of education stands condemned. Obviously there can be no return to the equally arbitrary and unfair selection procedures which preceded testing. The conclusion must be that the fruitless and sterile search for a perfect selection technique should be abandoned, the divided or sub-divided system of education be ended, and that, in its place, we begin to make secondary education for all a reality, and provide the opportunity for the systematic and purposeful teaching of all children alike.

5

THE COMPREHENSIVE SCHOOL

Individual Differences and the Role of Teaching

The teacher who sets out to *educate* the children under his care, meets them as human beings. He first searches for ways of welding his class together into a group, knowing that learning is not a purely individual affair which takes place in a vacuum, but rather a *social activity*; and that the progress of each child will be conditioned largely by the progress of the group as a whole. He begins, then, by concentrating on the interests children have in common, rather than by underlining their individual differences. As the work of the class takes shape, however, individual children make varying contributions; some may draw well, others may be good readers, others may be quick with figures. The teacher's task is not, of course, to see that the children who are good at some particular activity shine to the detriment of their companions, but rather to see that each child contributes to and enlivens the work of the class as a whole, and that all encompass the necessary basic skills. There is no better means of ensuring this than the stimulus given by other children within a cohesive group.

The teacher who approaches his task in this way starts from a point of view diametrically opposed to that of mental testing. His attitude is essentially humanist. He recognises that learning is a process of human change, not merely the formal acquisition of knowledge. Above all, he starts out with the conviction that all the children under his care are *educable*.

This is not to say that he shuts his eyes to obvious differences in attainment. But it does mean that he refuses to be blinded by the assumption that degrees of attainment reflect degrees of "intelligence". He recognises that to ask: "Why is David better at reading than John", and to answer: "Because David is more intelligent", is little but a play with words; the answer is, strictly speaking, irrelevant; rather than explaining *why* David does better than John, and *how* John can be helped, this kind of answer simply suggests that John's parents are at fault and there is nothing the teacher can do about it.

To the important questions that the teacher asks about children's mental development, psychology has, as yet, produced little in the way of answer. Psychometrists have classified and attempted to measure hypothetical mental "abilities", but this very occupation has excluded adequate consideration of *how* children learn and change. They have suggested that these abilities are hereditary, but this again is no explanation of their nature. In this connection, all that can be said with a strict regard for scientific accuracy is that each child is born with a physiological make-up which *conditions* his development, which provides, as it were, *the point from which he starts*. There is no scientific evidence for the claim that the child's "mental capacity" is *determined* by this original endowment.

On the contrary, study of the brain and the higher nervous system suggests that precisely the opposite is the case. Pavlov, the great Russian physiologist and psychologist, was summarising a life-time of research when he wrote: "The *chief, strongest,* and *most permanent impression* we get from the study of higher nervous activity by our methods, is the extraordinary plasticity of this activity, and its immense potentialities; nothing is immobile or intractable, and everything may always be achieved, changed for the better, provided only that the proper conditions are created."[1]

These conclusions certainly lend no support to the theory of "fixed abilities". Rather they add conviction to the view that human beings are capable of change, of development, and that it is the job of the school and the teacher to provide the proper conditions for human development in this sense. Nor should these conditions differ for every child, or for groups of children. Under the influence of psychometry, we have tended so greatly to emphasise individual differences that we have been blinded to the simple fact that *all* children, except in the case of serious physical defect, develop according to a certain fundamental pattern. The conditions for human development for all children must, therefore, be broadly similar. It is not the school's function to discriminate between children, treating different groups or streams in a fundamentally different way. On the contrary, it must find the best way of helping all children to find the common path to maturity.

Nevertheless, at present children will enter the junior school with different levels of attainment in all activities, and especially in the important skills of reading, writing and arithmetic. It has already been suggested that these result primarily from the differing content of each child's activity, which is itself dependent on the varying opportunities of different social classes. In fact, the child's mastery of any field of

[1] I. P. Pavlov, *A Physiologist's Reply to Psychologists.*

activity does not and cannot arise "spontaneously", and, of course, teachers particularly recognise this. No child will be able to read well, or to play football or the piano, unless he has practice in these skills, unless he applies himself systematically to learn them, even if only in play. Only in this way will he develop the mental and physical co-ordination necessary to make a success of these activities. Here, it is clear, the level of achievement at any particular moment depends not so much on the child's inborn characteristics, as on the degree to which these have been modified in activity—in the process of practice. What is decisive is the opportunities for engaging in different activities, and the help the child is given to master these, to develop new abilities and to make new achievements. The teacher is specifically skilled at this extremely complex and important task. He sets about it in a systematic manner. To do precisely this is the essence of education.

The degree to which the teacher is successful in this aim will depend to a considerable extent on his attitude to his job; and this, in turn, is coloured by his attitude to children. If, led astray by the theories of mental testing, he believes that the level of a child's achievement is *predetermined* by the nature of his inborn "abilities", then all he can aim to do is to help children to make their inborn abilities actual. He does not conceive that a child can rise above his inheritance. From the start, therefore, he does not set out to educate in a creative way.

If, on the other hand, the teacher believes that the development of a child's abilities depends primarily on the careful control of his activity in school, that is on the nature and character of his own teaching, then his attitude will be entirely different. In this case, he holds that it is possible to *educate* the child in the fullest sense of the term, and he will exert his skill and his art precisely to assist him constantly to rise above himself, to make ever new achievements, and to overcome all obstacles in his path. He will recognise that the first condition for achieving this aim for *all* children in the school, whatever the initial individual differences between them, is the abolition of the streamed system of education.

The separation of children into different groups, labelled good, indifferent and bad, serves only to perpetuate these initial differences and even to create new ones. But these differences are, in an important sense, irrelevant to the school's purpose, which is to give a common, systematic character to children's activities in order to achieve certain specific educational aims. A school which sets itself other aims than this virtually abdicates its primary educative function.

The Common Junior School

The common junior school must be so organised that all children are given the opportunity to develop abilities. For this reason, children entering the school for the first time should be divided into different classes, not according to test results, but simply according to the rooms and teachers available, as is already done in schools which have abolished streaming.

At the outset, each class will include children of varying levels of attainment in different subjects; but this need not cause dismay. It is the task of the junior school to lay the foundations of learning; if in some cases these foundations have already been well and truly laid, so much the better, the task becomes—or should become—the easier. But education is not a race, to be won by the early starter or the fastest worker. It is much more than this. The common junior school will not, therefore, concentrate on picking "winners". Instead it will set out to provide the necessary opportunities for all-round development. The aim will be to raise the educational level of each class, by carefully planned stages, and to ensure that all children participate in the advance.

What problems would this radical change give rise to? First, it is difficult to plan a common education unless there is agreement on certain fundamentals; for instance, at what age children should be taught to read and write. At present there is no clear understanding on this point. Some infant schools embark seriously on reading not long after the age of five, others do not attempt to introduce it until six, and methods of teaching vary widely. The result is that the average junior school intake at seven includes both readers and non-readers, and this immediately poses a problem for the junior school. It is usually overcome by separating the two groups and placing them in different grades.

In the interests of the children, this question must be decided one way or the other. On the Continent, reading and writing is often not taught in a formal manner until the child enters the first grade at seven. If we followed this practice here, this function would devolve entirely on the junior school. But at present it is infant, rather than junior school teachers who are equipped for the task of teaching reading, and the child who cannot read at seven has already fallen fatally behind in the race.

A school which abolishes streaming must make universal reading its first major objective. Success can be achieved, as experience has proved, by giving the non-readers instruction in special small classes each day.

Progressive familiarity with books and practice in writing should, in any case, be the staple of the junior school course for all children. The experience of schools for backward children shows that there are very few who fail entirely to learn to read, given good teaching, plenty of individual attention and the necessary stimulus to achievement. If, early in their junior school career, all children can read, a common education becomes a perfectly practicable proposition.

Secondly, and this point has already arisen, greater attention must be given to the content of education and to methods of teaching the basic skills. The problem here is the evolution of new methods, adapted to the purposes of universal education, and this calls for scientific research and the exchange of experiences among teachers in unstreamed schools. There has been a considerable amount of detailed research into this matter, but a variety of different methods are still used. There are, for instance, not only different approaches to the teaching of reading, but also quite different ways of teaching arithmetic. Children learn to divide and subtract in one way in one school and in quite another in a neighbouring one. This naturally makes things difficult for both teachers and children at the secondary school. It also indicates how wide are the differences of opinion about the best methods of teaching the basic subjects. Certainly the most complex and difficult educational problems are here involved. But once more, though research must go on, some definite course should be decided upon and adhered to.

Third, and most important, the size of classes in the primary schools must be reduced to a maximum of thirty. Teachers have been putting forward this demand for years, since they, at least, are quite clear that, faced with classes of forty-five or fifty-five children, their task is virtually impossible. It is, indeed, a near miracle that illiteracy and backwardness are not more widespread today than they are. In the expensive preparatory schools, classes rarely exceed twenty for this age group. If these conditions are good for some children, they are good for all; they are indispensable if there is to be that modicum of individual attention which every teacher knows to be essential. At present many teachers cannot even hear all their children read once a day; there is just not time. But, though this reform is vitally necessary, it is not an absolutely essential condition for making some success in the abolition of streaming, as has been proved in practice by the example of schools which have carried this through.

What else does the child need from his junior school? First, a vivid and stimulating life, one that awakens his interests and makes demands on his energy and application. School should give the young child plenty of opportunity both for the exercise of individual initiative and for participation in the work of a group under the guidance of the teacher. In so doing it will be providing the conditions for the development of abilities. Secondly, the junior school must introduce the child to his cultural heritage, and to a wide range of activities outside the basic subjects. This is a stage in the child's development when interest is quickened, memorising comes easily, and children are particularly lively and receptive of new ideas. Yet at present many subjects—elementary history, geography, science, in particular—are elbowed out of the time table owing to the pressure of the selection examination.

Finally, the child needs to be taught. It may seem to the layman that this is an unnecessary point to make, but many educational theorists think otherwise, and one finds juxtaposed to the formal training of the "bright" children in the scholarship subjects an opposite method, "free activity", especially for the less "intelligent". The idea that children's learning depends entirely on innate "intelligence" has given credence to the view that, since no one can improve a child's abilities, the best thing to do is to leave him "free" to develop his own potentialities "spontaneously". The teacher, then, must abdicate his functions to the children, allowing them to follow their own interests at their own pace. This theory lies at the root of the "free activity" movement, which denies the value of the normal forms of class teaching, and relies on the child's own undirected activity as the basic form of education.

The adoption of "free activity" was a reaction from the atmosphere of the old elementary school. But, where carried to extreme lengths, it is the very negation of education. It is evident that the child cannot find out everything necessary for himself and choose his own educational path with judgment; he can only master the elements of knowledge if the school programme is systematically developed from one stage to the next. Children do not acquire social habits spontaneously, as every parent knows; they have to be taught. Moreover their insistent questions must be answered, some inclinations must be curbed, other interests must be fostered and new horizons opened. This is the process of education as carried on in every family. In school it becomes more systematic. The task is to give each child the tools and techniques that he will need and use throughout life, to introduce him to his social heritage. It is, then, the teacher's job to teach, to provide that careful guidance and control of the child's activity which alone will enable him to master new skills and social knowledge. This is, after all, the fundamental reason for the school's existence—the provision of skilled practitioners, trained to educate each new generation of children.

The aim of the unstreamed junior school must, therefore, be to bring each age group of children up to a minimum level of achievement; not in terms of rigidly set texts, as in the old elementary school "standards", but in terms of basic skills and techniques. What this minimum level should comprise both can and should be defined, so that every school can be clear about its basic scholastic objectives.,

Selection at ten makes this development impossible. The junior school can never be a common school, with a clear educational aim, for all children, until the threat of the selection examination is removed and the education and welfare of all children alike becomes the central objective. Once this is the case, the junior school will at last come into its own, as the foundation of an educational system designed to foster and develop abilities and to enable all children to make the most of their lives.

Are there Two Types of Mind?

Most people would agree, in general, with the foregoing analysis, even if they have reservations about particular points. But once secondary education comes into the picture real differences arise. Former practices and preconceived ideas of various kinds now begin to cloud judgment. Secondary education has, for long, begun at eleven. This age, it is often argued, marks a critical stage in the child's development. Those who uphold the theories of mental testing, using their own terminology, suggest that at about the age of eleven, individual differences become so great that a common education is impossible. While the "average" or "below-average" child, they contend, is incapable of abstraction and generalisation,[1] the highly intelligent, or "brilliant", child thinks naturally in abstractions. For the good of both, for the good of the country, these different "intelligence" levels must be separated. There must be two or more kinds of school.[2]

[1] "For normal or sub-normal children, natural endowment limits the number of things which they can do; for many of them the basic skills are as much as we can expect." Dr. Eric James, High Master, Manchester Grammar School. He adds, "with the brilliant person there is no such self-limitation", *Education and Leadership*, 1951, 54.

[2] As is argued, for instance, in the Ministry of Education Pamphlet No. 9 (*The New Secondary Education*, 1947), and in the Norwood Report (*Curriculum and Examinations in Secondary Schools*, 1943); though the conclusions of the latter are not directly based on the theories of mental testing.

But there is nothing sacrosanct about the age of ten or eleven. Children do not suddenly alter and become qualitatively different beings. On the contrary, the early age of ten became the age of transfer from the junior school mainly because of the leaving age of fourteen. In fact, it had already become established by the beginning of this century, though at that time it was not thought necessary to advance psychological theories to support the practice. Nor is it true that children can be divided, either at this age or any other, into two distinct groups; those who are and those who are not capable of abstract thought; those who learn through books and those who can only learn through "activities"; those who need the aid of concrete examples and those who can do without them.

These theories result, once more, from questionable psychological—and even philosophical—doctrines about the nature of language and thought and their relationship. In fact, every child who uses words is demonstrating that he is capable of generalisation and abstraction. Words like "table", "chair", "engine", refer to a whole group of similar objects, not only to a single concrete thing. With the development of speech, the child learns to represent to himself and to others general ideas as to the properties of the things to which he refers. He begins to perceive the essential similarities and differences between the qualities of things and of people: "this pillow is hard, that soft", "these sums are difficult, those are easy". This development is common to all children.

As he grows older, the child's knowledge of reality extends, and with it his ability to express this knowledge in the form of words. The degree of development naturally depends mainly on his education and his experience, but all children begin to perceive more and more complex relations between things and events; their thinking acquires greater depth, their ability to generalise and to understand abstract ideas becomes more marked. It is by systematic teaching, wide reading, and especially the mastery of language that children can be assisted in this development.

The child's capacity for abstraction and generalisation reaches a higher stage as he grows towards adolescence, if he is given opportunities for study and for exercising his mind. But, of course, this development does not take place in a vacuum. If no demands are made upon young people, at school or at work, if they have no guidance or serious education, then they are unlikely to become theoretical mathematicians or philosophers. It is only because children have always been selected at the age of eleven, and thereafter given very different kinds of treatment, that it is possible to argue that there are qualitatively different types of mind.

The idea that there are two quite different types of mind, one capable of coping with abstractions and the other earth-bound and unable to rise into the sphere of abstract thought, gives rise to the theory that there must be two different types of teaching at the secondary stage; in the grammar schools intelligent children can grasp ideas imparted to them verbally without difficulty; in the modern schools average children must be approached through the senses with plenty of concrete examples, and it is unlikely that they will be able to grasp a a systematic and reasoned argument.

This conception is strongly at variance with all that is known of the human understanding. All thought needs the aid of representation, sometimes of concrete objects, sometimes of symbols. This point itself can be made clearer by an illustration. No child or adult can easily grasp how an internal combustion engine works if nothing but a verbal explanation is forthcoming. In addition to theoretical instruction, it is necessary to see an engine operating, and, if possible, to examine a model cut down the centre which exposes the inner processes. It will help if diagrams are available of the more complex parts, and yet other aids could be used. But no one is likely really to master an internal combustion engine until he has taken one or more to pieces with his own hands and reassembled them himself.

Even the most "brilliant" must go through these mundane stages if they are to learn in any real sense of the word. Nor is it only in the scientific subjects that these considerations apply. In the study of history, geography, literature, the child has to form ideas about people and things outside himself, even those which belong to the past. Will he not form these ideas more correctly, the more concretely they are represented to him?

No one would seriously disagree with most of these propositions and there are, of course, grammar schools which teach science effectively and are quite prepared to use visual and other aids for other subjects as well. But in so doing, they undermine the theory that there is a gulf fixed between learning in the abstract, and learning through practice and concrete examples; that the former is proper to the "highly intelligent" and the latter to the "average" child. Yet it is this facile conception, which, translated into practice, vitiates much of the work of grammar and modern schools alike; the former, attempting to teach on purely formal lines, take the life out of knowledge, the latter, attempting to teach solely through practical activities, take the knowledge out of life. Such, at any rate, are supposed to be their respective spheres, though the underlying theory is belied by the practice of the best teachers in both types of school.

In reality, all human beings learn in a broadly similar way. While the human learning process differs qualitatively from that of the animals, there is no qualitative difference between different classes of men. All learn by relating theory and practice, thought and activity. There is no basis here for differentiating between children at ten.

Only if it could be shown to be essential that children aged eleven to fifteen learn different things, could it be maintained that they should be educated in different schools. But it is generally agreed that there ought not to be intensive specialisation at this stage, that during these years all children should be having a broad general education. In practice, in spite of important differences in approach and in the content of the subjects taught, the main elements of the curriculum up to fourteen or fifteen are similar in all schools.

Both modern and grammar schools include in their curriculum those subjects which cover the main areas of knowledge; language and literature, mathematics, science, history and geography, art, music and practical work of various kinds. In many modern schools a foreign language is included. The only subject in which the grammar schools have a monopoly is classics, and this for obvious reasons.

There is, therefore, general agreement that these subjects, should comprise the common core of education for all children. Once it recognised that there are no good grounds for separating children according to "innate ability", "intellect", "capacity", or "power of abstract thought", all that remains to be done is explicitly to recognise this position; to sweep away the selective system of secondary education, and to establish a common secondary education in a common school.

The Comprehensive School

A number of local education authorities, taking advantage of their powers under the 1944 Education Act, are beginning to establish common secondary schools, in spite of the many difficulties which are put in their way. There are, however, important differences of opinion about the organisation of the common school.

(1) There is first the opinion that, within the common secondary school, there should be three distinct streams, corresponding to the

grammar, technical and modern schools, in which different types of education should be given. A school organised in this way is usually called a "multilateral" school.

Although the multilateral school is, in outward form, a common school, its internal structure corresponds exactly to the existing divisions in secondary education. The children have to be selected for one of the three streams at or before entry, so that a school organised in this way, though mitigating some of the disadvantages of separate schools, does not overcome the major problem, that of selection at ten; at best, in those multilateral schools which provide a relatively common course for the first two years, it makes the transfer of children between different streams at thirteen easier. But the multilateral school, by definition, does not aim to give a common secondary education.

(2) The second point of view, today more general, is that the common secondary school should provide the same type of education for all children; a school organised in this way is usually called a comprehensive school. But there are differences of opinion about the organisation of the comprehensive school. Some educationists believe that special provision should be made so that individual children can "go at their own pace", or "be given every opportunity of working to the full extent of their capacity". In order to ensure this there should be a wide variety of optional subjects on which a considerable amount of time should be spent.

This form of organisation implies that the child is allocated to different classes for different subjects, and moves from class to class according to his individual achievement. He may, for instance, be grouped with advanced pupils in mathematics and with backward pupils in French, and he has, besides, the chance of taking or dropping other subjects.

The primary aim here is to achieve a flexible organisation. But the main emphasis within the school is placed not so much on common subjects and the achievement of a basic standard by all children, as on individual choice of subjects and individual mobility. The provision of many optional subjects, some of which may be chosen by some children and some by others, is an indication of the individualist nature of this conception.

In practice, though the aim is flexibility, time-tables organised on this principle cannot but become rigid, at least with present staffing ratios. Moreover, this method of organisation, based to some extent on the practice of the American high school, has certain evident disadvantages. Underlying it is the axiom that children, entering school at eleven, have differing innate "abilities" which they must be allowed to develop in their own way; hence the personal choice of subjects or courses and the allowance for children to work at different rates according to the horsepower of their internal "intelligence" engines, which must—so it is supposed—determine their rate of work.

Apart from its practical disadvantages, this form of organisation also breaks up the unity of the school. Carried to its logical conclusion it amounts to a denial of the role of the teacher and of any clear purpose for universal education. That purpose must be to teach children *how* to study effectively and how to work with others, in the course of an educational programme which effectively covers the main areas of knowledge. This should be the aim for all children; it cannot be achieved so long as the school is organised on individualist and competitive lines.

(3) But there is another way of organising the comprehensive school, one which accords fully with democratic objectives. That is to provide every child with the opportunity of following the same basic curriculum up to the age of fourteen or fifteen, and to lay the emphasis on this common core of teaching. At this age, after nine or ten years of schooling and the opportunities of learning, of reading widely, and of developing abilities, most children will be ready to take the decisive step of choosing their future career. Only at this age, then, should differentiation of subject matter for specifically vocational purposes begin, though the greater part of the curriculum should still remain common to all pupils. By this time all children should have reached a good standard of general education.

The experience of eastern European countries, and in particular of the U.S.S.R., shows that this is a practical objective. In the U.S.S.R. all children in the main urban centres will receive a common education up to the age of seventeen or eighteen by 1955; these conditions will be general throughout the country by 1960. It is the opinion of Mr. G. C. T. Giles, a grammar school headmaster who visited the U.S.S.R. with an educational delegation in 1952, that "the standard of the ten-year school corresponds very closely to the old matriculation standard in Britain". He goes on: "If this estimate is justified, it means that the majority of Soviet children now reach, by the age of seventeen, an academic standard approximately equal to that reached by our grammar school children a year younger. In ten years' time, practically all Soviet children will do so."[1]

The significance of this achievement is immense. It is a practical verification that all children *can* be educated, and up to a far higher standard than has hitherto been thought possible. The evidence quoted in Chapter IV points to the possibility of achieving the same result in this country, though this must—to a very considerable degree—depend also on greater equality of opportunity in the choice of careers.

The Soviet success is the result of stressing the formative role of teaching and education. In Russia, as in this country, mental testing began to dominate the schools in the 1920s. But the practice was abolished in 1936, and since then, responsibility for education has been fully restored to the teachers. They have been expected to arouse and maintain the interest of their pupils, to develop new abilities, and, in particular, to work out and apply new methods of teaching adapted to the purpose of universal education. There is no streaming in Soviet schools; each child covers the same basic educational course.[2]

This form of organisation can be adopted in this country also, though pressures on the comprehensive school will inevitably produce initial difficulties. But a start can and must be made, if we are to transform our educational system, in accordance with the 1944 Act, into a system genuinely providing "secondary education for all".

The main practical difficulty at first will be the pressure on the schools from the university. It is almost impossible for anyone to win a place at a university at present unless he is picked young, placed in a "fast" stream, and crammed in a narrow field of studies. This is the normal practice today in the grammar schools though it is condemned on all hands, in particular by most grammar school headmasters and university teachers. There will be obstacles to relieving over-specialisation in the secondary school, from which the children are the chief sufferers, until higher education itself is unified and much expanded, and until this country makes up its mind that it can afford to lengthen the normal university course from three to five years, as is now the practice in Eastern and Western Europe, America and the U.S.S.R.

The comprehensive school will face its most difficult problems in the

[1] G. C. T. Giles, "Why Soviet Teachers oppose Intelligence Tests", *Anglo-Soviet Journal*, Vol. XIV, No. 1, Spring, 1953.

[2] The Soviet decree abolishing the practice of intelligence testing in schools is published in full in *Soviet Psychiatry* (1950) by J. Wortis, also in *Moscow in the Making* (1937) by Sir Ernest Simon and others. The decree gives the main reasons for this step.

first few years, since its annual intake will initially consist of children who have suffered from streaming in the junior school. This will have created wide differences in educational attainment, and the school may be forced to take this into account. But once a common secondary education is established, the pressure to stream the local junior schools will be lifted. If these go ahead in the way outlined earlier in this chapter, then it is reasonable to expect that standards of achievement will be raised all round; after four years a group of children will enter secondary school who have never known what selection, testing, differentiation or streaming is, and whose attitude to education will be revolutionised accordingly.

Objections to the Comprehensive School

This, in brief, is the case for the comprehensive school. But in spite of its fundamentally humanist objectives, this conception is frequently held up to obloquy as doctrinaire. Those who advocate it are accused of attempting to fasten a dull uniformity on the schools, even of wishing to stamp out all individuality, and it is argued that they ignore all educational considerations.

It is unnecessary to argue the latter point; it has already been made clear that the case for the comprehensive school is based primarily on educational grounds. Nor do the other propositions stand up to serious analysis. Both the public and the grammar schools today give a common education to all their pupils, within the limits laid down by streaming, and this is recognised as the essential equipment of the educated person. The claim for diversity of education at the secondary stage is today an argument for the retention of privilege, couched in educational terminology, and grounded on the findings of "intelligence" testing. In practice, there is little diversity of education; there are only different measures of opportunity in different types of school. It is the "type" of school which marks the child for the rest of his life, and counts far more than his individual qualities in deciding his future achievement. On the other hand, it is evident that in our complex society, the higher the educational level the greater the individual's opportunity to express his personality.

There are some who oppose the comprehensive school on grounds of expediency. The grammar schools, they say, provide an education for clever working-class children equivalent to that provided for the children of the wealthy in the public schools; to "abolish" the grammar schools would, therefore, be a step backwards, it would reduce the opportunity of the working-class child.

No democrat can accept an argument which takes class privilege for granted, and assumes that the success of the few can only be attained at the expense of the many. So long as competition and selection remain, so long does the education of *all* children suffer; both that of the minority who are selected and of the majority who early drop out of the race. The only way of increasing opportunity for working-class children in general is by creating the conditions for educating *all* children at the secondary stage. These conditions do not exist today and cannot be created in the absence of a unified system of secondary schools.

Nevertheless, the problem of the "public" schools remains. These have no parallel in any other country in the world; they confer initial privileges on certain children regardless of intellect or worth, which it is impossible to justify. Pupils from these schools, partly owing to smaller classes and better facilities, partly owing to their ability to pay their way at the university, and to special links with Oxford and Cambridge colleges, fill a disproportionate amount of university places. While this continues, the common secondary school will be faced with sharp competition which will prevent it from developing a broad, human education. To make a unified educational system, with all its advantages for the mass of the people, a practical possibility, the public schools will have to go. Indeed, there is no place for these schools in a democratic system of education.

But will the unified secondary school lead, as is so often claimed, to the "destruction" of all that the grammar schools have stood for, and, in particular, to the penalising of the "brilliant" child? On the contrary, one of the main defects of the present educational system is the treatment it accords to the early developer. The child who early shows promise, who manages to jump the various hurdles that straddle the road from junior school to university, is rushed through his courses at a high speed, inevitably keeping to a narrow and closely defined path. Concentration on the scholarship at ten is followed, admittedly, by a year or two of more general education in most grammar schools; but in others the child has to make a choice between various specialisations on entry, in other words he must opt for classics, science or modern subjects at the age of ten or eleven. As soon as possible, usually at fourteen or fifteen, he drops most of the subjects not essential to him for future examinations, even such important subjects as history, geography, and foreign languages. At the age of sixteen the young scientist's curriculum may, and frequently does, consist of nothing but pure and applied mathematics, physics and possibly chemistry, leavened only by a couple of periods in English and scripture with possibly a weekly talk on "philosophy" by the headmaster. At the same time the exigencies of the examination syllabus require a narrow concentration on the subject matter in the main fields of study chosen. Anyone who has had some experience of teaching in grammar school sixth forms knows that this system not only puts a tremendous strain on young people, but also fails to educate them in any true meaning of the term. The teacher sighs for more time and leisure with his pupils, free from the care of decisive examinations ahead. He realises with dismay that his pupils often go on to the university ignorant in many important respects. His forecast that many of the children are being tried beyond their powers seems to be borne out by the relatively high proportion of nervous disorders among university students and the high suicide rate at the universities.[1]

For this state of affairs the universities themselves are, to some extent, responsible; their entrance requirements must be broadened if the schools are to be freed to give a general education to all their pupils. But in the comprehensive school as outlined here, the early developer would not be forced ahead, learning more and more facts in an ever narrowing context. He would be given the chance of developing more evenly, with a more general background and a greater width of study, and with more time available to devote to his own interests, music, drama, painting, or whatever they may be. But, of course, no school can contract out of a fundamentally competitive system. Although the establishment of a few common secondary schools is certainly a step forward, only if comprehensive schools are established throughout the country can the present pressures be relieved, and these schools enabled fully to prove their worth.

The final objection to the comprehensive school is based on the supposition that these schools must be of enormous size; that is, even bigger than some of the better known secondary grammar schools such as Manchester (1,350), Bristol (1,043), Bradford (975). Some

---

[1] For instance, Dr. Parnell, until recently Physician in charge of the Student Health Survey at the Institute of Social Medicine at Oxford, has reported that the suicide rate at Oxford University is "far higher than for any other class of similar age, military or civil, in the country." He also found, in a three-year survey, that seventy-six undergraduates were absent from the University for a full term on account of mental illness or nervous breakdown. Cf. *Times Educ. Supp.*, April 3, 1953. See also Report of Home Universities Conference, 1951.

people hold that this is necessary if comprehensive schools are to provide a wide variety of highly specialised teaching in the sixth form.

But if, in the new comprehensive school, the emphasis is put on a common education this argument no longer carries much weight; the aim must be to reduce the high degree of specialisation which is, in any case, educationally undesirable. Even under present conditions, comprehensive schools need not be large. The Scottish "omnibus" school, a form of common school, often has only 400 pupils, or even less, and is still able to provide for sixth form study and to prepare children effectively for the university. The Scottish Advisory Council on Education in Scotland proposed that such schools should normally number about 800.[1] In England, one local authority at least has plans for comprehensive schools of 600 and less. Certainly the L.C.C. schools are large, but the main reason for this lies in the difficulty of procuring sites in a huge conurbation. Under normal conditions there is no reason whatsoever why the comprehensive school, as outlined above, should be any larger than many existing grammar, secondary modern and all-age schools.[2]

Secondary Education for All

Some of the more usual objections to the comprehensive school have now been considered. But the underlying argument is, of course, that the majority of children are not capable of profiting from a systematic secondary education. Whatever form this argument takes, whether it is a denigration of the average working-class child, who has never been given a chance to prove his powers, or a defence of the "brilliant" child whose race to the front would be impeded by the presence of slower contemporaries, it will be found to depend upon the theories drawn from intelligence testing; theories which have been derived, in part, from the very limitations of the present educational system.

These theories, it has been admitted, were first evolved because "the immediate needs of applied psychology call for working hypotheses and some practical device for determining the key-characteristics of individuals".[3] Psychometrists themselves are fully aware that the mathematical techniques of research used to isolate intellectual "abili-

---

[1] *Secondary Education.* A Report of the Advisory Council on Education in Scotland, 1947, 39, 40.

[2] For a full discussion of this question, see Lady Simon, *Three Schools or One*, 1948, 77–83.

[3] Burt, *The Factors of the Mind*, 12.

ties" result in "crude distinctions", and that they may eventually turn out to be "a mere makeshift—a temporary expedient which we may conveniently exploit while awaiting a more refined experimental technique."[1] It is on the results of research described in this way that the theories criticised in this book are based; yet these theories are, in the last analysis, the *only* justification of the divided educational system.

Thirty years ago, when the Labour movement first put forward the demand for secondary education for all, it rejected with contempt the idea—concretely embodied in the school system—"that the mass of the people, like anthropoid apes, (have) fewer convolutions in their brains than the rich".[2] Today this idea, an idea as old as class society itself, has been given new currency in a form which is far more difficult to challenge; it has been forced on the public as an inescapable scientific truth.

It has been the object of this book to show the failure of intelligence testing to establish itself as a science. Educational administrators and teachers are beginning to be seriously concerned, not only about the fairness of the selection system but also about the effect of testing on education; parents have also been growing increasingly restive. This general concern has not hitherto been translated into a general demand that selection be abolished because the nature of tests has not been clearly grasped. Some directors of education do not understand what exactly tests are, and how results are worked out; nor do members of education committees, though they assure parents, in perfect good faith, that the particular system adopted in their area is the fairest and most objective that can be devised, adding, no doubt with truth, that an enormous amount of time and money has been spent to ensure that this is so.

The real truth of the matter is that there is no fair or objective method of selection at ten, and that the present system results not only in individual heartbreak but also in disastrous wastage of ability from the social point of view. Moreover, the theories based on "intelligence" testing, theories which preach the limitation of human powers, the decline of "intelligence" and the helplessness of men in the face of their inherent defects, stand like a barrier in the way of real educational advance. These must be rejected, and with them the divided system of education which they serve and justify.

Instead, let us recognise that the most valuable capital of society is *people* and that the most important task today is to provide for the

---

[1] Burt, *The Factors of the Mind.*   [2] *Secondary Education for All*, 33.

youth of this country the conditions for healthy, human development and the exercise of ability. One of the most important first steps towards this end—a step which can be taken immediately if we have the courage and conviction—is the establishment of a genuinely democratic system of education.

PART II

PSYCHOLOGY AND EDUCATION[1]

Psychology is essentially the science of the mental processes. Education, which cannot as yet be claimed to be a science, is concerned both with teaching, that is, with the promotion of learning on the child's part, and with what may be called "upbringing", the development of particular mental qualities. Psychology, therefore, lies at the basis of education; or, as James Mill put it in his famous *Essay on Education* (1818) "the whole science of human nature is . . . but a branch of the science of education. Nor can education assume its most perfect form, till the science of the human mind has reached its highest point of improvement."

The chief role of psychology, in so far as education is concerned, is to discover the laws governing child development, in particular the learning process, and so to assist parents and teachers to develop the abilities and qualities of behaviour of children under their care. But even the most cursory examination of the state of educational psychology in this country shows that this task is not today regarded as the main aim. Though some investigation of the learning process does take place, current educational psychology concentrates chiefly, not on revealing the laws governing the mental processes as processes, but on measuring and classifying discrete mental "abilities" by the superficial method of using mental tests. This method of approach excludes any attempt to explain how it is that a particular ability develops. It attempts only, as it were, to take a snapshot of this ability at a particular moment or series of moments, and can then only explain its formation in vague terms as resulting from the interaction of "heredity" and "environment". The psychology based on mental testing is, therefore, basically static and external. It cannot explain the inner processes that result in human change and development and so it ignores them. Consequently it does not set out to be of any assistance to the teacher or parent concerned with creative education. It turns its back, as it were, on all the more complex problems of teaching and learning.

This psychology has now, for a considerable time, dominated

[1] First published in *The Marxist Quarterly*, Vol. III, No. 4, 1956.

both the theory and practice of education. It has attained this position because it justifies the selective character of secondary and higher education in this country, because, on the basis of highly questionable statistical investigations and equally questionable theoretical propositions, it has asserted that the majority of children lack the necessary ability to profit from advanced education. Leaving aside the effect of this doctrine on the structure of the school system, it is clear that it has had an extremely deleterious effect on educational theory and practice. Every child, teacher, parent and administrator is affected by these psychological conceptions which operate to restrict, rather than to assist, the development of education.

Nevertheless, there have been some important new departures in the schools and, with them, a growing criticism of the theories based on testing. Much of this criticism has been irrefutable and, as a result, the psychology of mental testing is beginning to crumble. Attempts have been made to reformulate theories but without much success. All that has emerged are more complex and tentative definitions of, for instance, "intelligence", which fail to carry conviction as compared with the dogmatic assertions of the 1920s and 1930s. It remains true, however, that mental testing will continue to exercise a negative influence on education as long as there is no alternative educational psychology to take its place. The vital need now is to consider the possible line of development of a positive educational psychology, one that will restore psychology to its proper place in the promotion and development of education. In the past, England has been the home of systematic, materialist psychology, and today we would do well to recall this classical materialist tradition, its later development and enrichment elsewhere and its relevance to the problems of education today.

I

The first attempt to interpret man's mental processes in a systematic materialist way was that of David Hartley in his *Observations on Man* (1749). This book paved the way for the separation of psychology from philosophy and for its study as a branch of natural science, and it had an immense influence not only on philosophy and psychology but also on education. Hartley's theories were developed by the French Encyclopaedists, to whom Marx owed so much; and especially by the great French educational reformers of the late eighteenth century, including the revolutionary period. In this country his book was reprinted in 1775 by Joseph Priestley, scientist, philosopher and educationist, who held that Hartley "has thrown more light upon the theory of the mind than Newton did upon the theory of the natural world". It is a measure of Hartley's influence that as late as 1818, James Mill based his educational theories on Hartley's psychology.

Hartley was concerned to find a materialist, that is a physiological, explanation of the mental processes. The idea that man's mental processes had a material basis, and so were open to scientific investigation, had been advanced nearly a century before by the philosopher Thomas Hobbes, who held that thought was due to motion in the brain substance. Both Hobbes and his successor John Locke believed that men's ideas were derived, through the senses, from the external world. Both held that thought could be explained by a theory of association of ideas (or sensations); that is, that phenomena associated together because they occur simultaneously or successively in the external world, become also associated in man's mind. According to Locke, the most complex ideas were the result of the combination of simple ideas derived from the external world.[1] Besides having this tradition to draw on, Hartley was also familiar with contemporary advances in science, in particular with Newton's work in mechanics and, more important, in optics, and with the fields of physiology and anatomy which were already beginning to cast a considerable light on the functioning of the nervous system.

Essentially, Hartley's associationist theory is based on the supposition that a sense-impression derived from an external object sets up a vibration in the particles, first, in the external surface of the sense organ, then in the nerves connecting the sense organ to the brain, and finally within the brain itself, resulting in a sensation, or idea. Two or more sensations, experienced simultaneously or successively, set up simultaneous or successive (i.e. associated) vibrations. The connections in the brain are such that, if in future one of these sensations is experienced, the vibrations so caused will arouse others that previously occurred in connection with this sensation; these latter vibrations, Hartley held, are the material cause of associated memory images or ideas. By an elaboration of this theory, which provided an explanation of elementary thought

[1] "Even the *most abstruse* ideas, how remote soever they seem from sense, or from any operation of our minds, are yet only such as the understanding frames to itself, by repeating and joining together ideas which it had either from objects of sense, or from its own operations about them." *Essay Concerning Human Understanding*, Bk. II, Ch. 12, Sect. 8.

processes, Hartley evolved a physiological explanation of the development of the most complex (including abstract) ideas. This objective approach, which attempted to lay bare the material causation of thought processes, was the first significant step in removing the aura of mystery which surrounded the mental functions:

"Since . . . sensations are conveyed to the mind, by the efficiency of corporeal causes upon the . . . substance [of the brain]", wrote Hartley, "as is acknowledged by all physiologists and physicians, it seems to me, that the process of generating ideas, and raising them by association, must also arise from corporeal causes, and consequently admit of an explication from the subtle influences of the small parts of matter upon each other, as soon as these are sufficiently understood . . ."

He added correctly that this theory of vibrations was an hypothesis which seemed to explain how ideas were generated and associated, but that "the doctrine of association may be laid down as a certain foundation, and a clue to direct our future enquiries, whatever becomes that of vibration".[1]

The main outline of Hartley's theory may not seem very revolutionary today. When it was first produced, however, and for a long time after, it opened out quite new perspectives, and laid a scientific basis for the theory of human perfectibility, typical of the most forward-looking materialists of the eighteenth century. It did this because it led to the conclusion that an individual's character was determined by his external circumstances. That, in practice, human nature could be changed by changing the environment. When Robert Owen challenged the obscurantists and fatalists of his time with the thesis that "Circumstances make Man", and put forward his vision of the co-operative society with the dominant role played by education as the means to human perfection, he was basing himself on the classical materialist view developed by David Hartley. Indeed, materialist

[1] Again, "The influence of association over our ideas, opinions and affections, is so great and obvious, as scarce to have escaped the notice of any writer who has treated of these, though the word *association*, in the particular sense here affixed to it, was first brought into use by Mr. Locke. But all that has been delivered by the ancients and moderns, concerning the power of habit, custom, example, education, authority, party-prejudice, the manner of learning both manual and visual arts, and etc., goes upon this doctrine as its foundation, and may be considered as the detail of it, in various circumstances".

philosophers had always emphasised the dominant role of education in human development. Hobbes insisted that the human faculties "are acquired, and increased by study and industry; and of most men learned by instruction, and discipline". With the help of speech "the same faculties may be improved to such a height, as to distinguish men from all other living creatures".[1] John Locke, profoundly interested in education, developed the same point: ". . . and I think I may say, that of all the men we meet with, nine parts of ten are what they are, good or evil, useful or not, by their education. 'Tis that which makes the great difference in mankind." Since "the difference to be found in the manners and abilities of men is owing more to their *education* than to anything else, . . . great care is to be had in the forming of children's minds".[2]

The full impact of the first scientific theory of learning on educational theory was felt in this country towards the end of the eighteenth and in the early nineteenth centuries. Priestley developed Hartley's associationism, used it in his ceaseless struggle for materialism against idealism, and applied it to education. Later, James Mill wrote a text-book of materialist psychology in which he took up a position of consistent psycho-physical monism (*Analysis of the Phenomena of the Human Mind*, 1829); time and again he stressed the power of education for human development.[3] But perhaps the clearest expression of the contemporary denial of a fatalist hereditary determinism is to be found in Godwin's *Political Justice*, which appeared at the height of the early period of the French Revolution. Because of its topical significance, it is worth quoting in full:

"How long has the genius of education been disheartened and unnerved by the pretence that man is born all that it is possible for him to become? How long has the jargon imposed upon the world, which would persuade us that in instructing a man you do not add to, but unfold his stores? The miscarriages of education do not proceed from the boundedness of its powers, but from the mistakes with which it is accompanied. . . .

"Education will proceed with a firm step and with genuine

[1] *Leviathan*, Pt. I, Ch. 3.
[2] *Some Thoughts Concerning Education*. Sect. 1 and 32.
[3] E.g. ". . . the power of education embraces everything from the lowest stage of intellectual and moral rudeness, and the highest state, not only of actual, but of possible perfection. And if the power of education be so immense, the motive for perfecting it is great beyond expression." *Essay on Education* (1818), Sect. 4.

lustre, when those who conduct it shall know what a vast field it embraces; when they shall be aware, that . . . the question whether the pupil shall be a man of perseverance and enterprise or a stupid and inanimate dolt, depends upon the powers of those under whose direction he is placed, and the skill with which those powers shall be applied. Industry will be exerted with tenfold alacrity, when it shall be generally confessed that there are no obstacles to our improvement, which do not yield to the powers of industry. Multitudes will never exert the energy necessary to extraordinary success, till they shall dismiss the prejudices that fetter them, get rid of the chilling system of occult and inexplicable causes, and consider the human mind as an intelligent agent, guided by motives and prospects presented to our understanding, and not by causes of which we have no proper cognisance and can form no calculation."[1]

II

At this period, then, psychology acted as a support to education, both as regards intellectual or mental, and general human development. Whatever its limitations, and early associationism did imply a predominantly mechanist interpretation of learning, psychology was a positive science, showing how intellectual development could be fostered by the conscious direction and systematisation of the educational process. All the great educational innovators of the period, Pestalozzi and Herbart, for instance, and their counterparts in this country, built their educational practice on the basis of associationism. The revolutionary upheavals in Europe in the late eighteenth and early nineteenth centuries were ushering in a new world; for a period, the perspective of full human development for men of all classes through education took hold of men's minds, particularly in France and Germany. Education, it seemed, was to become a science.

Associationism continued to hold the field in this country for much of the nineteenth century, and while this position was maintained, the

[1] *Political Justice* (1793), Bk. I, Ch. 4. James Mill makes the same point when he writes: "Enough is ascertained to prove, beyond a doubt, that if education does not perform everything, there is hardly anything which it does not perform: that nothing can be more fatal than the error of those who relax in the vigilance of education, because nature is powerful, and either renders it impossible for them to accomplish much, or accomplishes a great deal without them: that the feeling is much more conformable to experience and much more conformable to utility, which ascribes everything to education and thus carries the motive for vigilance and industry, in that great concern, to its highest pitch." *Op. cit.* Sect. 4.

possibility of developing education as a science remained a conscious objective. With some qualifications, John Stuart Mill held to the views of his father, and republished his book on psychology in 1869 with an introduction of his own. He, too, held that the chief cause of differences between individuals lay in the character of their education, and maintained that any normal child would have been capable of his own (extraordinary) achievements if given a similar education. The leading expositor of associationism in the mid-nineteenth century was Alexander Bain, who combined the interest both in psychology and education which characterised most associationists. His books are still of interest in their combination of physiology and psychology at a new level. In line with the materialist tradition, Bain published his *Education as a Science* in 1879.

Throughout this period, the theory of teaching and its precepts (from the simple to the complex, from the particular to the general, from the known to the unknown, etc.) were based on associationism, as a glance at any of the books on teaching method published during the latter half of the nineteenth century makes clear. Spencer's *Principles of Psychology* (1855) and his *Education* (1861), both extremely influential books, are informed with similar psychological principles. The greatest of nineteenth century continental educationists, Herbart (1776–1841), based his psychology and teaching method on a development of associationism in his theory of the apperception-mass. Significantly rejecting the idealism of Kant and Fichte, the theory of free-will, of instincts and faculties, Herbart saw a systematic education based on a scientific psychology as the means of developing many-sided individuals. It is significant that, when a state system of secondary education began to be developed here at the close of the nineteenth century, a system which *required* a positive theory of learning, Herbart's works were translated and his influence for a time was very great.[1] Even today educational theory and practice owes more to Herbart than is commonly realised. He was, perhaps, the last great bourgeois systematiser of educational theory.

Yet the perspective of education as a science was not realised. During the latter half of the nineteenth century, associationism was subject to increasing criticism, and indeed the mechanism of the classical formulations laid it open to such attack, as Marx had already shown in his Theses on Feuerbach. Similarly, it led to a somewhat mechanical approach to education. It upheld the conception that to

[1] Especially his *Science of Education* translated in 1892.

teach a child it was necessary only to show him things and to talk at him; that every influence to which the child was exposed would leave its mark, as it were, on his brain. Thus learning was regarded as essentially a passive process, and this influence still remains in our schools, especially the grammar schools.

Early associationism was, therefore, incapable of understanding the dialectical relationship between subject and object, between the child and his environment. The child was regarded simply as the passive product of his environment; no room was left for the child's self-movement, his self-activity; the idea of a process of self-change through active interpenetration with the environment was alien to the early materialist philosophers. With the beginning of scientific study of child development, the inadequacy of his conception became increasingly apparent. So the field was clear for idealist theories of the child's inner self-development initially derived from Rousseau, Froebel, Coleridge, Kant and Fichte.[1] Finally, with associationism conducting a rearguard action, there emerged, towards the close of the nineteenth century, the theories of mental testing. Significantly, these theories first made their appearance with the advent of imperialism; they reflected the realities of a stratified, class society, and were admirably suited to provide a "scientific" justification of this relatively static social order.

With these developments, educational psychology took a turn away from associationism, and so from any all-embracing theory of learning. The result has been a decline of coherent educational theory in favour of an enormous variety of eclectic ideas—the firm psychological foundation of education has disappeared, education has no longer a spine, a central support.

III

When classical materialist philosophy and psychology began to be neglected in England, it was taken up anew in the Russia of the 1850s and 1860s. The social criticism of the group of distinguished philosophers and critics who espoused materialism, among them Chernyshevsky, Belinsky and Dobrolyubov, marks the beginning of the revolutionary upsurge that was to break through first in 1905, and

[1] Coleridge called his first son after Hartley, whom he then described as "of mortal kind wisest". Later he devoted a chapter of *Biographia Literaria* (1817) to proving "that Hartley's system . . . is neither tenable in theory nor founded in facts".

later, successfully in 1917. This movement had its impact on scientists, notably on the distinguished physiologist Sechenov, who, in 1863, published his remarkable book *Reflexes of the Brain*. Though Sechenov's theories were necessarily to some extent speculative, he attempted a consistent explanation of human activity, including the highest form of "voluntary" activity, in terms of reflex action, and proclaimed the possibility of an objective science of mind. It was this book that Pavlov acknowledged as his inspiration, and Pavlov's consistently materialist approach to the investigation of mental phenomena places him in the mainstream of development of classical philosophic materialism, and of the early scientific psychology which stemmed from it.

"The most important and incontrovertible old-established discovery of psychology as a science", wrote Pavlov, "is the establishment as fact of the connection between subjective phenomena—the association of words, as the most obvious example, and then the connection of thoughts, feelings and drives to action." It was his own contribution to demonstrate that association arose on the basis of temporary connections established in the cortical cells. Taking up a position of psycho-physical monism, he insisted that there should be no arbitrary separation of the physiological and the psychological:

> "The temporary nervous connection", he wrote, "is the most universal physiological phenomenon in the animal world and in man too. And it is at the same time psychological, that which the psychologists call association, whether it be the formation of combinations from all manner of actions or impressions, or the formation of combinations of letters, words and thoughts. What justification is there for differentiating between or separating what the physiologists call temporary connection and the psychologists association?"[1]

Pavlov, of course, reached these conclusions as a result of his experimental investigations. By establishing that a conditioned reflex could be established on the basis of an unconditioned reflex, he demonstrated objectively for the first time the *fact* of association as the basis of learning, and in his further work on the higher nervous processes, began to establish the laws governing the formation of associations (or temporary connections). We have seen that Hartley postulated the existence

[1] *Scientific Session on the Physiological Teachings of Academician I. P. Pavlov.* Moscow, 1951, p. 126. Pavlov, *Selected Works*, p. 251.

of association, and speculated on its physiological causation on the basis of contemporary science. When Pavlov associated the feeding of a dog with the ticking of a metronome, and succeeded in evoking a secretion of saliva with the latter stimulus alone, he showed objectively that the dog had "learned" that the metronome was the signal for the insertion of food into the mouth, that a temporary connection had been formed between the relevant areas of the brain, resulting in a conditioned reflex.[1] But Pavlov, of course, did a great deal more than establish as fact the physiological basis of association. The discovery of the conditioned reflex was the groundwork of his theory, the basis of his experimental technique. Early American behaviourism seized on this one aspect of Pavlov's work, and attempted to build a system of psychology based on the stimulus-response formula which denied or ignored consciousness. Pavlov opposed this blanket and over-simplified use of the conditioned reflex, just as he constantly criticised the mystique of German gestalt psychology which went to the opposite extreme.[2] He himself used the technique of forming conditioned reflexes in order to investigate the whole functioning of the higher nervous system, and, as a result, was able to formulate important laws governing higher nervous activity.

Perhaps the chief aspect of Pavlov's theory which concerns us here is the stress laid on the interpenetration between the organism and its environment, epitomised in the functioning of the higher nervous system, and therefore the adaptability, or capacity for learning, of the living organism. Pavlov demonstrated that the essential role in this interpenetrative adaptation is played by the higher nervous system in which is embodied, as it were, the whole evolutionary development of the organism:

"The cerebral cortex of the higher animals, according to Pavlov, possesses a coupling, or linking function, that is, the function of

[1] It is important to note that Pavlov held that association, or temporary connection "is a generic concept, i.e. the bringing together of what was previously separate, the union of two points in a functional relationship, their fusion in one association—whereas a conditioned reflex is a specific concept". (*The Pavlovian Wednesdays*, Vol. 2, p. 262. Russian Edition.) The conditioned reflex presupposes a link between the cortical representatives of receptors and effectors (e.g. the eye and the hand etc.). But associations are formed on a much wider scale, e.g. between separate sensory fields of the different cortical areas; they may not be directly linked with an effector, and so may not result in an external movement.

[2] "Gestalt psychology, with its negation of association, is an absolute minus, in which there is nothing positive." (*Ibid.*, Vol. 2, p. 580.)

acquiring, forming, creating, new connections between the organism and its environment, the function of evolving new vital experience, the function of ontogenetic adaptation, which adjusts the organism to the conditions of the environment, and the environment to the requirements of the organism."[1]

Pavlov took his stand as a materialist and a determinist. But he was in no sense a mechanist; on the contrary, his conception both of the cerebral processes, and of the relation of the organism to the environment, is essentially dialectical. His great contribution, in fact, is that while placing the materialist interpretation of mental phenomena on a new scientific basis, he rid it of its mechanism.

The very foundation of a scientific psychology is an understanding of the physiological processes underlying mental phenomena. This is what Hartley set out to provide in the mid-eighteenth century, and what Pavlov was also concerned to achieve at a time when physiology had made important advances and itself begun to border closely on the field of psychology. And, just as Hartley's theories proved an inspiration to those concerned with education, so also Pavlov's theories have a close bearing on educational psychology and on the practice of education in the Soviet Union. Their chief significance for education lies in the emphasis on the extreme plasticity of the higher nervous system:

"The chief, strongest, and most permanent impression we get from the study of higher nervous activity by our methods, is the extraordinary plasticity of this activity, and its immense potentialities; nothing is immobile or intractable, and everything may always be achieved, changed for the better, provided only that the proper conditions are created."[2]

This conclusion, summarising the results of extensive experimental research, demands a return to the positive view of the role of education as it was expressed by Locke, Godwin, Priestley, Mill and Owen, but on a higher level, in the light of new and growing knowledge of the laws governing the cerebral processes. It makes possible a fruitful development of the ideas of the classical materialists. The weakness of the classical view lay in its mechanism, in the conclusion that mental

[1] A. G. Ivanov-Smolensky. *Scientific Session*, p. 78.
[2] "Reply of a Physiologist to Psychologists." *Selected Works*, p. 447.

development was the simple resultant of the impact of external forces on the individual. Educationally this led to the passivity of the child, who "imbibed" knowledge from the teacher. The Pavlovian theory rejects this one-sided interpretation. The relationship of the organism to the environment is regarded as one of "equal-weighted", active inter-penetration. The individual, then, is no automaton; nor, of course, is his behaviour the outcome of some inner forces which function quite apart from his conditions of life and are inaccessible to scientific investigation. His consciousness is formed in his activity, his mental processes depend upon the character of that activity. This is the key to education, to the deliberate formation of mental abilities and the deliberate and conscious encouragement of mental development.

That this is so is suggested by developments in Soviet psychology, which has of recent years been assimilating Pavlovian theory in its bearing on teaching and upbringing. Two examples may be taken: first, a relatively simple case, an experiment by A. N. Leontiev with tone-deaf children. The ability to sing the note heard depends, on the Pavlovian hypothesis, on the formation of the necessary aural-oral connections. For the vast majority of children such connections are formed, without special instruction, in the course of their normal life before they first go to school. In a few cases, however, the circumstances of life are such that these connections are not formed (Leontiev gives an explanation as to why this may occur). Such children are tone-deaf. Leontiev experimented with a number of these children given up by their teachers as quite incapable of reproducing orally the note heard. He set out systematically to form the necessary connections in an ingenious manner. He was successful with all the children concerned.

The second example is based on researches into the teaching of arithmetic. L. S. Slavina experimented with children aged seven and eight who, according to the teachers, were quite incapable of adding, subtracting, or doing the simplest sums. Slavina worked on the hypothesis that the ability to add, subtract, etc. "in the head" is a matter of systematic formation, which must go through a series of stages, beginning with the carefully controlled manipulation of exter-nal objects. She took her pupils back to the earliest stages of addition and subtraction with objects, and then forward by planned stages to that of abstraction, when the pupils were able to make calculations in their heads without the use of objects. She was successful in all cases; when the children were returned to the normal class they were found to be as competent, and in some cases more so, than the others. In other words she showed that the children were not held back by any innate dullness. They had been held back fundamentally because a basic number sense had not been developed in the course of their ordinary lives before going to school, as it had been in the case of the majority of children in the class, and as had been wrongly assumed by the teachers. What was necessary to overcome the apparent dullness, which expressed itself in apathy or hostility to school and to arithmetic in particular, was systematically to form the necessary temporary connections, appropriate to the "missing links", and to develop from there to the stage of abstraction and automatisation.

These and other researches in the Soviet Union point to the conclusion that human abilities are formed systematically through a series of stages, each of which is vital to the establishment of the ability. During this process the earlier stages, often formed on the basis of external action with objects (e.g. in the case of number) become automatised and so "drop out" of consciousness. In other words, the final ability, which appears as the manifestation of some special capacity of the mind, is in reality the product of past experiences, reflected and transformed in the mind of the individual. This theory clearly has an important bearing on the whole question of inborn differences. Summarising a considerable amount of research into this question in the Soviet Union, Leontiev writes:

"The general conclusion to be drawn from this experimental work is that human mental properties, both general and specific, do not represent the manifestation of certain special 'powers', the presence or absence of which can be only stated, but are the product of ontogenetic development. This does not mean that anatomical-physiological differences between people play no part; it simply means that mental properties and peculiarities cannot be directly inborn, that they are always formed in the process of the individual's development and education, and that knowledge of the laws of their formation makes possible the conscious direction of this process."[1]

Fundamentally, it is the acceptance of this approach that underlies the achievements of education in the Soviet Union.

[1] "The Nature and Formation of Human Psychic Properties." *Voprosy Psikhologii*, No. 1, 1955. (Both Leontiev's and Slavina's articles were included in B. Simon (ed.), *Psychology in the Soviet Union*, 1967, pp. 205–212 and 226–232).

IV

Only the briefest of outlines has been given here of the implications of the new physiology of higher nervous activity for education. Naturally, advances in physiology cannot in themselves provide the solution to the complex problems of psychology, and it would be erroneous to think they can. On the other hand, if psychology is to develop as a science, it must be firmly based on physiological findings. Herein lies the importance of the Pavlovian contribution. Other brain physiologists are taking the same road, with the use of Pavlov's and of other methods. Reference should be made here to the work of Professor J. Z. Young, whose researches have led him to the conclusion that the inherited brain "may be largely a blank sheet of possibilities; as it acquires an organisation by social inheritance its powers rapidly become altered", and who believes that "we have a long way to go to find how best to use the time available for teaching. . . . With more careful study and more daring in exploring new methods", he adds, "I believe that we could strikingly improve our power to train brains to convey information to each other. No one avenue holds out so much hope for improvement in the welfare of the human race."[1] Again, one might refer to the work of Wilder Penfield of Montreal, who concludes a recent paper on direct research into the functioning of the brain with the hope that, by such means, physiology and psychology may be drawn more closely together, so that light may be thrown upon the mind of man.[2]

Enough has been said to show that there is a basis for a return to a positive systematic psychology which can take the place of the eclecticism which at present dominates this field, and particularly of the "short cut" of mental testing which, by its very method, evades all the real issues, and so diverts attention from them. But this is not only an academic question. There is an urgent social need for the development of education. Once a new, positive outlook in educational psychology and theory begins to find expression, the full energies and creative initiative of the teachers can be released for education in its true sense; for the development of the abilities of children and the raising of standards in the schools. To promote such an outlook is, therefore, a primary condition for real educational advance.

---

[1] J. Z. Young, *Doubt and Certainty in Science*, 1951, pp. 128–9.
[2] *Proceedings of the Fourteenth International Congress of Psychology* (1954), 1955, p. 69.

SOME CONTRIBUTIONS OF SOVIET PSYCHOLOGY TO THE UNDERSTANDING OF THE LEARNER[1]

In 1956 Piaget visited the Soviet Union and on his return wrote of the great "richness and variety" of experimental work in educational psychology being carried on there. I went to the Soviet Union, for a second time since the war, in September last year, specifically to have discussions with educational psychologists and to see something of the experimental work. This visit was made in connection with a collection of papers on educational psychology in the Soviet Union now being prepared for publication. Although a teacher rather than a professional psychologist, I have for some time been following developments in Soviet psychology from which, I believe, we may have something to learn. It was during my previous visit in 1955, invited to see schools as a guest of the Academy of Educational Sciences, that I first became fully aware of the extent to which psychological theory underpins educational practice in the Soviet Union. For the inquiry revealed the close collaboration between psychologists and educationists in wide-ranging research into learning and intellectual development. It became clear to me that Soviet psychologists are making a well-ordered and disciplined attempt to penetrate into the processes of human learning and that this is regarded as one of the major fields of application of the science of psychology, one to which all the leading Soviet psychologists have made definite contributions.

What is the main feature of their approach to the learner and the psychology of learning? Here, I think, everything hinges on the fact that research is primarily into human learning. I will try, very briefly, to summarise what this implies.

Soviet psychologists accept, of course, that there are features common to all learning, whether of animals or human beings. But they hold that what are decisive in defining different stages or qualities of learning are not the features that are similar but those that differ. The specific characteristic of human learning is that it takes place primarily by means of language, in social intercourse, in a man-made setting

[1] Based on a paper given in the Symposium "The Teacher and the Learner" at the Annual Conference of the British Psychological Society 1962, and first published in the *Bulletin of the British Psychological Society*, No. 49, October 1962.

which itself incorporates the achievements of human development.

This means that the whole framework and course of human learning differs from that proper to the animal world. It is impossible to consider human learning as the simple product of an interplay between heredity on the one hand and environment on the other. While animals learn only through individual experience, the human child learns through joint practice and speech with other human beings; it is by means of the language he acquires, the tools he learns to handle, and so on, that the achievements of the human species are embodied and handed on. Hence the key importance of education as the means of ensuring that this social inheritance is mastered by the child; which has, therefore, a decisive influence on the child's whole mental development.

This approach will be familiar to many from the lectures and writings of Luria, who also makes clear the extent to which Soviet research has concentrated not only on what might be called external evidence of learning but also on investigation of its inner mechanisms. It is not merely a question here of the summation of simple units of learning—temporary connections or conditioned reflexes, as it were, strung together—but rather of the formation of complex functional systems formed in the course of life which underly qualitative changes in mental processes. To quote from a recent paper of Luria's not yet published here:

> "It is now generally accepted that in the process of mental development there takes place a profound qualitative reorganisation of human mental activity, and that the basic characteristic of this reorganisation is that elementary, direct, activity is replaced by complex functional systems, formed on the basis of the child's communication with adults in the process of learning. These functional systems are of complex construction and are developed with the close participation of language, which as the basic means of communication with people is simultaneously one of the basic tools in the formation of human mental activity and in the regulation of behaviour. It is through these complex forms of mental activity . . . that new features are acquired and begin to develop according to new laws which displace many of the laws which govern the formation of elementary conditioned reflexes in animals."[1]

[1] *Voprosy Psikhologii*, 1962, No. 4.

It is within the framework of this general outlook (very summarily described here) that research into the learning process takes place.

The collection of papers now in preparation[1] includes a very long article by Bogoiavlenski and Menchinskaia covering the whole field of research into the psychology of learning over the years 1900 to 1960, though concentrating particularly on the last two decades. Here the evolution of this outlook, as well as the specific forms of research it has led to and the methods of research developed, are described.

Great emphasis is laid on the pioneering work of Vygotski in the early 1930s, as also on the theoretical discussion initiated by Rubinstein on the relation between consciousness and activity. Vygotski rejected the view that mental characteristics are a simple manifestation of inborn properties—which develop in the course of maturation independently of learning—as also the behaviourist approach. He set out to study the characteristics of thinking as it develops in the process of learning, rather than through what are described as the methods of "artificial experiment"; in so doing, he "placed the question of the formation of concepts on a new footing" since, under conditions of systematic teaching, "all the new stages of generalisation rest on generalisation at preceding stages". As a result of his researches Vygotski reached the conclusion that "intellectual development in the process of learning marks a change to qualitatively new levels of thought—and this opened up new perspectives for research into the learning process". Thus, in the 1930s, psychologists began increasingly to turn their attention to investigation of the changes that take place in mental processes under the influence of teaching and education. In so doing they were forced to seek new methods of research, and began to develop the experimental method known as the "teaching experiment" or "natural experiment", which is carried out with a class or with groups of children more usually at a normal school, a point to which I will return.

Rubinstein's proposition that "mental processes are not merely manifested but formed in activity" began from the mid-30s to take "a central place in Soviet psychological theory, acting as a stimulus to research into the development and formation of mental processes in changing conditions of activity". As a result the distinct sphere of the psychology of learning was clarified. "Study of activity *as a process* took a key place, and psychologists advanced the view that genetic methods of research are of key importance since they allow for study of this process in normal conditions of learning." Hence the conscious

[1] Published as *Educational Psychology in the U.S.S.R.* in 1963.

adoption by Soviet psychologists of the developmental, or genetic, as opposed to the static, or psychometric, approach. Evidently such research is closely linked to the practice of teaching, since research results obtained from normal school conditions can be directly utilised in the schools. In this connection it is worth stressing that educational psychologists in the Soviet Union do not attempt to take the teacher's (or, more strictly, the pedagogue's) place in guiding the whole educational process in the school. It is held that educational psychology must rest on pedagogics and have the aim of aiding the teacher "by working out the scientific foundations for the rational organisation of this process". In effect, much of the work in the psychology of learning has the long-term aim of improving methods of teaching—and the planning of the content of education—in order to facilitate learning and achieve higher levels of efficiency in the mastery of knowledge.

Summarising so far, one might say that the Soviet approach is characterised first by its emphasis on human learning; second, and following from this, by the stress laid on the role of speech in mental development—an approach that received considerable impetus from Pavlov's theories concerning the second signal system; third, by adoption of a developmental, or genetic, approach; and finally in this context by the qualitative methods of research employed. The latter is an important point to stress: researches are carried out longitudinally, as it were, with individuals, groups and classes, sometimes over a considerable period of time—from 2 to 3 up to 7 or 8 years. In this connection another point made in the article already quoted should be brought out—that research into the psychology of learning, though primarily concerned to discover the common characteristics of the process of human learning, is also directed to discovery of the individual differences in this process. It is worth adding that while, in the period 1936 to 1950, research tended to concentrate on the psychology of learning different subjects and skills (that is, on the partial laws specific for the mastery of a specific content) and a large number of monographs were published on, for instance, the psychology of learning reading, spelling, grammar, arithmetic, and so on, since 1950 attention has been progressively turning to the learning process in general. The broad outlines of a learning theory, it is held, are now beginning to emerge.

What has been said may, perhaps, best be illustrated by giving some examples of the kind of research now being carried out; this will help not only to illuminate the general approach but also to show the kind of problems in which Soviet psychologists are interested, and some of the methods used.

Research which raises important questions of teaching method is that on which Galperin bases his theory of the formation of mental actions (outlined in *Psychology in the Soviet Union* (1957)). The approach is a genetic one. "At the present stage of psychological research," writes Galperin, "the best way of finding out about the structure of a mental action is to study it in the process of formation; indeed there can be no true understanding of mental actions without study of this process."

Galperin's conclusion is that mental actions, of the kind which are or should be carefully taught and mastered in school, are formed through a series of stages beginning on the plane of actions with material objects. At the final stage, when the action has been transposed to the purely mental plane, the intermediate stages gradually drop out of consciousness and are not open to introspection. In other words the action, which appears at the final stage as something given or even inborn, is, in fact, the final manifestation of a series of processes which have their own history—which are, therefore, the resultant of an historical formation.

What are these stages? Galperin educes five:

1. First, the child builds up a preliminary idea (or concept) of the action as seen in the external action of another person—the teacher who demonstrates the action. (This is really an orienting phase.)

2. The second stage is mastery of the action using objects—when the child makes himself familiar with the action in its external material content, i.e. counts with objects using his arm and hand as it were as an instrument, so discovering the objective concrete content of the action for himself.

3. Third, the stage of mastering the action on the plane of audible speech—by speaking aloud; for instance, counting with the help of objects. Here the action is freed from the necessity of manipulating objects (the objects are there but the child does not manipulate them). This stage, therefore, represents an advance to action with concepts. The material foundation is changed: from being objective it becomes linguistic, verbal; from an action with things it is transformed into an action with concepts, a genuinely theoretical action.

4. Fourth, the action is transferred to the mental plane. At this stage the child is taught to count, first in a whisper, then in the head. Of course at this stage the child continues to use language and sensory

images, but the more habitual the action becomes, the more automatically it takes place. "It is not really an action any longer," writes Galperin, "but a flow of concepts about it."

5. Finally, the action is abbreviated, compressed and consolidated, so assuming, as he puts it, "that purely 'mental' aspect revealed in introspection which has so often been taken as its real nature". At this stage the former processes—action with objects, speaking aloud and so on—drop out of consciousness; the action is fully automatised.

Galperin's findings are actually a great deal more complex than this; a variety of reasons why the final stage may not be effectively reached by children can be isolated (Galperin produces eight) and these provide a way into diagnosing remedial measures. Such measures have been effectively applied by Slavina and others, i.e. the systematic remedying of particular deficiencies by going back to ensure proper formation at each stage. This general approach, which Leontiev has also done much to develop and make known, has a wide relevance to teaching whatever the content of knowledge—or, more precisely, whatever the mental actions to be mastered.

An illustration of the kind of research that these findings lead to is the project directed by Elkonin, of the Institute of Psychology in Moscow, who is investigating the intellectual capacity of children aged 7 to 11. Holding the view that the intellectual potentialities of children are determined largely by the content of education and the methods by which this is taught (and this is a widely held view of Soviet psychologists), Elkonin and his colleagues have, over a number of years, through experimental work on the teaching of reading, mathematics and grammar, worked out new syllabuses and methods, some of which are based on systematic application of the theory relating to stages in the development of mental operations and the functional systems underlying them. Elkonin claims that the preliminary results of this experiment, now in its third year, indicate that certain concepts or ranges of concepts, previously held to be beyond the capacity of young children, and the mental operations leading to and arising from mastery of these concepts, can in fact be formed at this age. As a result, Elkonin believes that the methods and syllabuses used in the normal schools in the Soviet Union do not fully develop and utilize children's intellectual capacities, and in some cases even inhibit this development.

There is no space here to give details of the interesting methods adopted to teach reading and grammar, but in the field of mathematics Elkonin is investigating the extent to which children aged 7 to 8 can assimilate generalised relationships between quantities expressed in algebraic formulae *before* studying number—which is, of course, only a specific case of such relationships. What I would like to turn to, however, is the actual research method. In this particular instance a team of six psychologists is based on an ordinary school and experimental work conducted with a class as a whole, a parallel class in the same school acting as a control. The work is, so far, after three years, being conducted with the first, second and third classes; similar work is also being undertaken (in parallel) in two other schools, one in an industrial city, the other in a rural area.

The actual method used is as follows. Every lesson given to the class in the experimental subjects is fully planned and written out beforehand. The script of the lesson contains every question, action and statement to be made by the teacher, together with every response expected from the children. This is, in fact, only the final stage in the collaboration between psychologist and teacher: both first discuss the full programme of lessons, then each group of lessons, and finally each particular lesson which is worked out in detail as I have described. The purpose is to ensure the full, systematic control of the educative process which the psychologist must aim for if the child is to be brought *systematically* to the formation of the concepts and mental actions required.

The teacher then gives the lesson; in the lessons I observed the teaching was very effective, involving, incidentally, a considerable interaction between teacher and pupil. The psychologist attends each lesson and makes a complete record of everything that occurs, marking the points of difficulty or failure so that, if necessary, part of the lesson can be repeated. This procedure is used in every lesson given to the experimental classes in the experimental subjects. It might appear this would deaden the initiative of the pupils: there was, in fact, no sign of this; the children were lively and seemed to be acting quite naturally.

This particular experiment is scheduled to last another five years, the original group of children being taken up to the eighth class (when they will be aged 15). The research is seen as having both a theoretical and a practical significance: if the methods adopted (and the changed content or syllabuses) are shown to be successful when tried out on a much larger scale, some of these may be introduced into the general schools.[1]

[1] As in fact they have been as part of the curriculum reform now being carried through in the U.S.S.R. (Ed. 1970.)

The theoretical significance of the research refers to the light it throws on children's capacities—on the specific features of the process of the assimilation of knowledge and on the psychological principles involved in the construction of new methods and syllabuses. This group is now producing a considerable amount of published work giving the research results.

I have cited Elkonin's research methods in some detail for the light they throw on the general approach to research into the psychology of learning, as well as on the methods used. We may now turn to another long-term research project, that under the direction of Krutetski, of the Institute of Psychology, into the nature and structure of mathematical, design and constructional, and literary abilities. The former is, perhaps, of most immediate interest. I should, however, make the proviso that this work should not be seen in isolation, as a sudden turn towards a crucial problem, as it were. Rather it is one aspect of a many-sided attack on the problems of the formation of abilities and the learning process. To see it in context one should be familiar with the research of Teplov's team, which has worked for many years on the borders of psychology and physiology in investigating typological properties of the higher nervous system which, it is held, constitute the inborn (but not necessarily hereditary) basis of individual differences as regards both temperament and abilities; with Leontiev's work on the formation of functional cerebral systems; and with the extensive researches of Menchinskaia and others into the psychology of learning mathematics and the components of mathematical ability. It is against this background that Krutetski is studying the formation of mathematical ability with the aim of analysing the actual process of mastery of knowledge, skills and habits and so the structure and components of the ability.

For this purpose Krutetski works with four groups of children. One is made up of children found to be especially gifted in mathematics, selected from all over the Soviet Union, and chosen at the age of $3\frac{1}{2}$ to 4—these children are now aged 9 to 10. The group is not brought together, but data are systematically assembled about their development. The second group consists of children of above average abilities—in the sense that in the normal, unstreamed class (as all classes are in the Soviet Union) there may be one such child. The third group comprises children of average ability, the fourth children characterised by their teachers as "incapable" in mathematics.

Research is carried on with all these groups but particular importance is attached to the latter since, as Krutetski has put it, in order fully to understand the nature of an ability it is necessary closely to study the nature of incapacity—and, in the process, actually form the abilities lacking. In fact this latter group, taught by methods worked out by the psychologists on the basis of previous research, have in all cases mastered the course at secondary school level. Research with this group has concentrated on a number of specific issues, particularly on the relations between what are called the "visual-image" component of thinking on the one hand, and the "verbal-logical" on the other. The aim here is to discover whether the predominance of the "visual-image" component is one of the causes of relative incapacity in mathematics. Actually the research task was rather more complex than this, and was concerned not only with the interrelations between the two components of thinking but also the level of development of each. I do not propose to summarise the results here—the relevant paper will shortly be published[1]—it is rather the overall approach to which I wish to draw attention, since here we see again the developmental approach typical of Soviet psychologists, together with the qualitative assessment of individual children's thinking in the process of problem-solving and the acquisition of knowledge.

An auxiliary method used is the evaluation—against the background of research findings as to the psychological prerequisites for the mastery of particular concepts or mental operations—of the actual methods of teaching used by an outstandingly good teacher. One example of this is an analysis of the work of a teacher who was particularly effective at teaching problem-solving in mathematics as compared with "doing sums"—or operations with numerical facts. The particular paper I have in mind, after analysing the psychological prerequisites for successful problem-solving—the mastery of a wide range of concepts, both concrete and abstract, reflecting quantitative relations; ability to perform complex analysis of the data given in the formulation of the problems and so on—goes on to describe in detail the actual methods by which these concepts are formed, as well as the actual methods of analysis of the data of problems developed in the classroom.[2]

Some interesting points emerge, particularly the systematic methods used to form elementary number concepts through the use of a wealth of concrete material; the care taken to make the transition from real objects to their two-dimensional visual representation (in the form of

---

[1] *Educational Psychology in the U.S.S.R.* (1963), pp. 214–232.
[2] *Ibid.*, pp. 180–191.

pictures and so on) to the point where the children are led to operate with images and so on to abstraction. In order to develop the conscious use of imagery at this stage a form of "visual dictation" is used in which the children draw concrete objects from memory. The aim of such dictation is to consolidate the relation between word and image while at the same time teaching pupils to reproduce a clear visual image from memory, so making their imagery more precise (and stabilising both concrete concepts, for instance, the number of bricks or hens drawn, and abstract concepts, e.g. "on the left", "on the right", "above", "below"). This example is only one very small part of the analysis of this particular teacher's work, which is fundamentally directed to developing, in the children's minds, complex forms of analysis and synthesis. The effectiveness of the teaching of this particular teacher was shown in the results of experimental tests in problem-solving set both to her class and to three parallel classes which covered the same ground, in two of which experienced teachers were teaching whose methods are also submitted to analysis.

This leads on naturally into research into the learning of particular subjects, and here we may take as an example some recent research into the teaching of certain concepts in physics carried out by Fleshner. This research was concerned generally with investigating pupils' ability to utilise in practice (that is, creatively) knowledge gained in class—an aspect of learning that is now being given very considerable attention.[1] I will describe the content of the research shortly; the method used (with children aged 12 to 13) was as follows:

(i) Observation of normal lessons in school to discover the educational conditions in which children mastered the relevant section of the course, with the aim of establishing the difficulties that arise.

(ii) Experimental checks with individual children to discover the specific features of the application of knowledge to different problems—problems which involved both textbook (or abstract) tasks, and practical (laboratory) tasks.

(iii) Arising from this, the formulation of hypotheses as to more effective ways of organising the teaching, followed by teaching experiments to verify these.

(iv) An auxiliary method used was the psychological analysis of the work of an outstandingly successful teacher, together with indi-

[1] *Educational Psychology in the U.SS.R.*, pp. 198–213.

vidual experiments with pupils of her class, involving conversations with pupils and analysis of their work.

This particular research took place during two academic years, with forty pupils from three schools selected according to their degree of proficiency in physics. Three groups of pupils were selected, classified as proficient, medium and weak. Two control groups were also used, the first consisting of pupils studying the normal school course in normal conditions, the second consisting of the pupils taught by the highly qualified and successful teacher mentioned earlier.

The first stage of research was concerned with the formation and application of the concept of density. Briefly it was found that the usual method of presentation in school, together with the formulation of certain rules, hindered the formation of this concept, and that the proportion of successes was greatly increased when certain changes were introduced in the method of exposition.

The second stage of research concerned the interrelation between new and old knowledge. Researches in the learning of various subjects have shown that, in some cases, earlier knowledge facilitates the acquisition of new knowledge, in other cases it makes it more difficult. The concept children have already formed of "volume" and "weight" (in their normal, everyday life outside school) were analysed, and it was found that although the "everyday" concept most children have formed of "volume" does not conflict with its physical meaning that of "weight" does, and that this earlier acquired concept inhibits the mastery of the physical concept "weight".

In this research the first stage was to discover the actual content of the children's concepts of weight. This was done through conversations with individual pupils with, incidentally, most interesting results. They showed, for instance, that many children associated weight only with things that could be put on a pair of scales—in their view, for instance, a house could not have weight because it cannot be so weighed. The idea of weight as the force with which an object is drawn to the ground was quite foreign to them. The conclusion followed that it was necessary actively to reorganise the children's concept of weight so that it coincided with the physical meaning (this conclusion, incidentally, was at variance with the usual methodological advice). The new concept of weight was then taught. Some ten weeks later individual tests were carried out in order to discover the specific characteristics of the application of this concept. It was found, in particular, that in a high proportion of the subjects (55 per cent) the new knowledge taught had been ousted (or supplanted) by the old, and this was underlined in subsequent conversations with many of the pupils. In fact the practical (laboratory) tasks undertaken were now, in many cases, actually done worse than before.

From this it was concluded that systematic counterposition of the new and the old knowledge was a necessity—a clear-cut differentiation between the two meanings of the term "weight". The value of this method has in fact been consistently shown in educational research in many subjects. New lessons were therefore worked out on this basis and given. Experimental checks showed that in the new conditions the great majority of the pupils, including the weaker ones, now preserved the new knowledge about weight after a protracted interval and easily applied it to the solution of practical tasks.

This is, as I have indicated, only a part of a larger research project, which included at later stages a comparative analysis of the process of performing verbal (or abstract) and practical laboratory tasks and research into the processes of abstraction in the application of knowledge.

The significance of systematic research of this kind, not only in physics but in the other subjects in the curriculum, is sufficiently evident; always provided that its results become the property of the teachers and are applied in practice in the schools.

I have given four examples of the kind of research being undertaken by Soviet educational psychologists: that by Galperin into the formation of mental actions; by Elkonin into the intellectual development of young children; by Krutetski into the development of a particular ability; and by Fleshner into concept formation in a particular subject. The outlook that informs it is clear—education does not simply bring forth that which is already there; education is seen as having the function of adding to, of developing the child's intellectual capacities; and, incidentally, the intellectual capacities of all the children. Soviet psychologists are, in fact, very concerned with the development of creativity—with promoting the capacity for independent work on the part of the children. It is possible for translation of the key word, *obuchennie*, to lead to misunderstanding, since this can be rendered as teaching, learning, or training. If the latter course is taken—as by Brozek in his otherwise very effective and lengthy review of Soviet psychology in this year's *Annual Review*—the phrase "psychology of training" results for what should be "psychology of learning", and currency is given to the stereotyped view of Soviet psychology popularised by Sargant in the Sunday papers and *The Times* a few months ago: that Soviet psychologists are simply concerned with crude forms of conditioning. I hope I have shown how far this kind of interpretation is from the truth—the extent to which Soviet psychologists are concerned with a qualitative assessment and the degree to which they are concerned with conscious learning. Their overall approach, as they see it, is well summarised in an article by Kostiuk, Director of the Institute of Psychology at Kiev: "In our schools", he writes, "the task of teaching is not confined merely to transmitting certain knowledge to the pupils, to forming a certain minimum of skills and habits. The task is to develop the pupils' thought, their abilities to analyse and generalise the phenomena of reality, to reason correctly—in a word, to develop their minds as a whole."[1]

The successes of Soviet education, now generally admitted, owe much, in my view, to the general direction and character of the work of Soviet psychologists in this field, and to its close connection with education and the practice of teaching.

[1] *Educational Psychology in the U.S.S.R.*, p. 39.

SECONDARY SCHOOL SELECTION:
A REPLY TO THE INTELLIGENCE-TESTERS[1]

Criticism of the fundamentals of intelligence testing from a Marxist point of view began in 1949. There followed discussions and conferences on the relation of this question to educational policies and efforts to secure educational advance. *Intelligence Testing and the Comprehensive School*, published in 1953, subsequently summed up the analysis made of testing and selection in popular terms.

This book had its effect on the mounting revolt against the 11 plus examination, and has now drawn an answer from psychologists concerned with constructing and administering tests—*Secondary School Selection*, edited by P. E. Vernon. But before considering this it is worth recalling earlier reactions. It must be remembered that in the late 1940s mental testing and selection seemed to be more firmly fastened on the schools than ever before. Indeed, a leading educational psychologist expressed a general view when he said that psychologists had the answer to all the major technical problems involved in 11 plus selection and the tools for solving any fresh ones which might arise; "the general effect of all this was a fairly widespread feeling of confidence, if not of complacency" (p. 27). How, in this situation, was the case against testing received?

The first notices showed that it could not be ignored. *The Times Educational Supplement* reviewer (15.1.54), characterising the book as "a formidable indictment of the theory and practice of intelligence testing", concluded that "the case stands up"; that, therefore, the arguments advanced "should draw a reply from the defence, and the reply should be couched in language as comprehensible" as that of the prosecution. In the *New Statesman* (27.3.54) Mr. John Garrett, headmaster of Bristol Grammar School, wrote that the case "deserves respect and demands an answer"; in the *New Era* (organ of the New Education Fellowship, January 1954) Mr. James Hemming said that the book showed "with devastating force that what is left of the theory of tripartitism is a mess of unreality, injustice, distortion and pretence".

Psychologists—or rather psychometrists, that is those concerned

[1] Reprinted from *Marxism Today*, January 1958.

primarily with mental measurement—reacted somewhat differently. Dr. A. F. Watts, then consultant to the National Foundation for Educational Research, sweepingly condemned the arguments as misleading and remarked that it was a pity that educational discussion should be brought down "to the tub-thumping level of back-bench party politics"; the main thesis of the book was "too silly to merit rational discussion, except perhaps in the pages of a journal devoted to psychotherapy" (*Journal of Education*, March, April, 1954). Dr. Stephen Wiseman, writing for the *Labour Teacher* (organ of the N.A.L.T., June 1954) professed to find a "grave and fundamental error" which "makes the whole content of the book suspect and does the Communist case more harm than good", though when challenged he did not substantiate this point: he concluded, "it is a pity that the book does its job so badly".

On the other hand, Professor P. E. Vernon, professor of educational psychology at the University of London Institute of Education, took a different line. The author, he said, "has taken the trouble to study the technicalities of his subject far more thoroughly than most propagandists . . . and his distortions are remarkably few. He has made a serious case and deserves a serious answer." Apart from this, the time was ripe for "psychologists to get together and attempt to decide how far their instruments are doing harm, and how they could be better employed". Evidently these suggestions, advanced in the *British Journal of Psychology* (June 1954) were taken up, for now, three years later, there comes this survey of testing and selection and attempt to meet "left-wing critics", or what is sometimes inaccurately described as "the left-wing egalitarian point of view". The authors of the report, issued under the auspices of the British Psychological Society, are a group of fourteen, including professors of education and leading psychometrists (of whom one is Dr. Wiseman), who met under the chairmanship of Professor Vernon. Here, on the face of it, should be a very serious answer indeed.

In fact the survey marks an attempt by psychometrists to put their house in order in face of sharp theoretical criticism, the practical failings of testing and growing public objection to the whole business of selection. For a long time there has been confusion of thought and divergence of views on such fundamental points as whether a child's Intelligence Quotient normally remains the same and whether "intelligence" is innate; these can no longer be passed over in silence, they have been exposed for all to see and must be resolved. Indeed, since

1952, when it became clear that a child's I.Q. could be considerably raised as a result of coaching, there has been open contention among psychologists, and a growing revolt against the original sweeping theories, particularly among those concerned with experimental psychology. In this situation some psychometrists, as the reactions given above suggest, have been for admitting the justice of criticisms and consolidating the ground on the basis of less far-reaching claims; others have objected to this departure, attempting rather to ridicule criticism and confuse laymen with technicalities in order to hold the old front. It is freely admitted that there were, and remain, some divergences; these, in fact, give rise to contradictory theses in different chapters of this report. But on the whole it seems that the first school of thought, strengthened as it was by the force of popular protest and pressure, has won a victory. Thus, referring to "left-wing" and other radical critics[1] of testing and selection, the report states "we accept some of their arguments, and will attempt to supply reasoned answers to others" (p. 35).

These answers, designed to establish a new base for operations, may be considered under the headings of theory and practice.

I

CONSIDERATIONS OF THEORY

What were our main theoretical criticisms of "intelligence" testing? Leading psychometrists claimed that they had constructed tests which confirmed the existence of, and accurately measured, an innate quality of mind—"intelligence". This, they maintained, was the key mental quality which determined all intellectual achievement. Since it was inherited at birth and could not be improved, a measurement taken at an early age could accurately predict the future level of intellectual development of any child. Hence streaming and selection of school children according to their "intelligence" were socially and education-ally necessary.

Marxist critics pointed out that these claims rested on a series of circular arguments and unproven assumptions. There was no scientific evidence whatsoever that tests measured an innate quality of mind; on the contrary, even internal evidence derived from testing showed that a child's I.Q. did not normally remain constant but changed. Equally

[1] E.g. A. W. Heim, *The Appraisal of Intelligence* (1954).

there was not, nor could there be, any objective criterion of "intelligence". In fact, when a test constructor set out to make up a test composed of a series of questions he had no scientific terms of reference to guide him; all he could do was to choose the kind of questions which he himself *thought* were good tests of what he *thought* was "intelligence". Thus the very statistical techniques used embodied certain assumptions about the nature and distribution of "intelligence" for which there was no scientific justification. Most of the facts supposedly established about "intelligence" were, therefore, not scientific findings at all; they remained nothing but assumptions inserted into the tests by the constructors at the outset and then held up as new discoveries at the end. Since tests had been constructed in this way within the framework of a class-divided educational system, the whole conception of "intelligence" was class-conditioned; inevitably, therefore, "intelligence" test results indicated that the middle class tends to be "intelligent" while the working class tends to be stupid.

How are these points met in the chapter dealing with "intelligence" tests? The writers profess their intention "to set out the arguments for, and the weaknesses of, intelligence tests rationally and impartially, guided by the evidence of scientific research rather than by traditional theories or by appeals to casual observations, hunches or (so-called) common sense" (p. 88).

But they find it difficult to live up to this. In fact, most of the "scientific research" referred to is based on the use of tests which for the most part inescapably include and give expression to traditional theories; theories which, it is clear, have by no means been rejected outright. But, while failing to admit their own partiality, the writers persistently impute bias to their most radical critics by labelling them "left-wing"; so obscuring the essence of criticism which shows objectively the *unscientific* assumptions and procedures of psychometry.

Nevertheless they are forced to concede the major points at issue. Thus, after stating that "the main object of introducing intelligence tests was ... to provide an objective assessment of ability", the writers admit that "there is no ... external criterion of intelligence", that therefore tests are made up of "items (which) *appear* to psychologists to involve intelligence" [my italics.—B. S.], and that the definition of intelligence can be anything which happens to be convenient—"Our tests can emphasise any aspect of intelligence that we wish" (pp. 96–7, 100).

The corollary of all this, of course, is that the "intelligence" measured by tests can no longer be claimed to be an innate and absolute quality. Though it is nowhere clearly stated that the whole practice of mental testing has for decades been informed by fallacious assumptions, it is inferred that there is no way of producing an objective—that is a scientific—measurement of innate mental powers.

Further, it is admitted that assumptions which are of crucial importance both to the construction and application of tests remain unproven and are upheld solely by the use of certain statistical techniques. But this admission is so damaging that, even while making it, the writers are forced to cover up the issues and give a false impression of the criticisms made. It is worth examining in some detail how this is done, for this is an essential aspect of the attempt to firm up anew the tottering foundations of psychometry.

The conclusion drawn from testing which has the most far-reaching implications is that "intelligence" is always normally distributed. This means that in every population—whatever the differences in social and educational background and the changes in social living that may take place—there is always a given (small) proportion of highly intelligent people at one end of the scale and an equivalent proportion of very dull people at the other; the majority of the population are strung out between these two extremes, tailing off through the moderately clever at one end and the moderately stupid at the other to the two end points of genius and idiocy.

Until recently psychometrists claimed that this conclusion had been established *scientifically* as a result of mass testing. Marxist critics pointed out, however, that this finding was simply the outcome of using the particular statistical technique known as the "normal curve". All tests are so constructed that the results *must* fall into this pattern; indeed, a test which does not produce this pattern is considered to be a "bad" test of "intelligence" and so never put into use. Inevitably, therefore, all tests currently used give the same pattern of results but this proves absolutely nothing at all about the existence of "intelligence" in human beings. What it does show, on the other hand, is the ramshackle nature of the whole edifice of psychometry.

Now this is not an easy argument to refute. The point is that, if tests are to be constructed for general use, then it is absolutely necessary to assume that "intelligence" is normally distributed because this is the only way of providing an "independent" yardstick. Once this yardstick is assumed, it is always possible to argue that all tests which produce results conforming to it are measuring the same "thing"—i.e. that they are all really measuring "intelligence". Whatever the cost, then, the dogma of normal distribution must be retained.

So when dealing with this question the authors of the report first throw up a heavy smokescreen. "Left-wing critics", they write, "rebel against the implication that there is, *and always must be* [my italics.—B. S.] a limited proportion of the population with high intelligence." After implying in this way that their critics have an emotional bias against a scientific finding, the writers then admit (so blandly that the uninitiated would never guess the significance of the point conceded) that the rebellion was absolutely justified; that, in effect, this is not a scientific finding at all but merely a useful assumption upheld by a statistical technique. "It is true that no conclusive proof that intelligence is so distributed can be adduced, and that the distribution of the scores of I.Q.s we actually obtain from most tests approximate to the normal type *simply because of the manner in which tests are constructed*" [my italics.—B. S.) (pp. 91–2].

But then, instead of going on to admit that no conclusions can be drawn from such a procedure—let alone far-reaching social conclusions (for such have already been dogmatically asserted)—the writers then attempt to argue that it is justifiable nevertheless to accept the dogma of normal distribution, that this is a "reasonable" assumption. This they do by reproducing three different arguments all of which have long since been disposed of as irrelevant. (1) Physical traits, they say, like height, tend to be normally distributed so why not "intelligence"? But science does not recognise this kind of argument by analogy, and and anyway it can just as well be argued that other physical traits, such as weight and hair colour, are *not* normally distributed. (2) Next they try a purely technical point, that I.Q.s obtained by the Mental Age scoring system do not assume a normal distribution in advance but do give something like it. This has been refuted elsewhere on technical grounds. Here it is sufficient to note that, in the very next paragraph of the report, the Mental Age scoring system (whose serious defects have been analysed earlier) is dismissed as quite "outmoded"; indeed, it is explained, it was only intended for use with backward children and never supposed to be suitable for the ordinary child or the general population! (3) Finally, "common observation suggests that the very bright and the very dull really are relatively rare". This alone, after the specific rejection of appeals to "so-called common sense", indicates a sloppiness of thought which is the reverse of scientific. Yet these are the *only* arguments advanced in favour of a key assumption and technique in what is held to be a genuine science.

In fact, the argument that "intelligence" is always to be found in fixed proportions in any population hinged on the belief that it is an innate and unchangeable quality. Once psychometrists admit (as they now appear to do) that "intelligence" can be improved by education, then it is impossible to argue that it must inevitably be distributed among people according to an unchanging pattern. On the contrary, everything depends on the extent of educational and social opportunity. A society which demands much of all its members in terms both of theoretical knowledge and practice, and which accords value to the most varied kinds of activity, will not look like a pyramid with only a few intelligent people at the apex thinking for the rest. In such a society intelligent behaviour will be evaluated, not merely in abstract and academic terms, but in terms of the social tasks set and the measure of success achieved in these infinitely varied activities. Who are the psychometrists to lay down what future tasks humanity will set itself, whether or not these will be successfully fulfilled and by how many people? The trouble is they cannot see things in this light. They are imprisoned within a restricted field of study and reduce the rich and various material of social life to this measure. In effect they can only think of human intelligence in terms of success in the present General Certificate of Education examination under existing competitive conditions.

This is again demonstrated in the discussion of "I.Q. and social class" (pp. 108–10). This opens with the statement that "the complaint of left-wing writers that intelligence tests reflect class differences is irrelevant". And why? Because "most of the abilities we wish the tests to predict are also affected by social class". Of course. In other words, all the psychometrists' ideas about "intelligence" and the ways in which it is manifested are socially conditioned, in a class society class-conditioned; which is precisely what Marxist critics, very relevantly, have pointed out. Thus, on the usually accepted criterion of "intelligence" it can be shown (there is a table as illustration) that "large employers" rank high and "skilled manual workers" low. But it is perfectly possible to construct tests which reverse the position of these two classes—as indeed has been done. Such tests, however, are rejected by psychometrists as "not valid" since the results differ from their own.

The point is, of course, that formerly psychometrists claimed that their tests measured *pure* "intelligence" (virtually uncontaminated by environmental influences, educational or social); then they affirmed that the middle class tends to be highly intelligent in this absolute sense while the working class tends to be dull. They have been forced to abandon this position and to recognise that, in general, test results reflect class differences. All they can argue now, therefore, is that "intelligence" tests when used for selection may reflect class differences *less* than other sorts of test in individual cases. In the light of this, they suggest, "it would be more logical for left-wing critics to welcome rather than decry them". But this is a strange morality. We should accept an unscientific and anti-educational procedure because it may sometimes operate in favour of individual working-class children and enable them to get to grammar schools! Must we suppose, then, if this is their way of looking at things, that psychometrists "logically" uphold "intelligence" tests because they show professional workers to be highly intelligent and provide psychologists with a career?

These are bankrupt arguments. In fact, throughout this report, position after position has to be abandoned. Once it is admitted that tests in use do not test "intelligence" as formerly understood, it becomes necessary to suggest that they measure "academic aptitude" instead. But since they were constructed in an attempt to get at the essence of "intelligence" it must also be recognised that they are full of inconsistencies. Clearly, then, it may be necessary to start again from the beginning and simply try to construct tests which measure "intelligence for grammar school work". Here, yet again, is evidence of the extent to which testing depends on the present set-up. Without the present selective system of education it would be impossible to suggest even this socially conditioned criterion of "intelligence" as a basis for differentiating children.

Nevertheless, in spite of all this relative thinking, an attempt is made to affirm that "facts" gained from research point to a genuine "psychological theory of intelligence" (p. 106). What is this theory? It is significant that no appeal can be made here to any genuinely psychological enquiry in this country about *how* children learn, and how, therefore, they can best be educated. Instead, there is recourse to a theory advanced by the Canadian psychologist, D. O. Hebb, in an interesting but highly speculative book, *The Organisation of Behaviour*, published eight years ago. This book was little noticed in this connection at the time but now appears to provide a solution to a dilemma, an answer to unanswerable criticisms, and it was first popularised here by Professor Vernon in 1955. Briefly, the solution is that there are two "quite different *meanings* of the *word* intelligence" [my italics.— B. S.].

Now words do not just spring up and acquire meanings on their own. This is just another way of saying, in the philosophical terminology now fashionable, that it is proposed to advance yet another, purely arbitrary and speculative, interpretation of "intelligence". And this, of course, is what follows. There are, it is suggested, two different intelligences: Intelligence A, which is "innate potentiality or endowment"—this is purely hypothetical and cannot be measured—and Intelligence B, built up on the former "through interaction with the environment". It is Intelligence B, the psychometrists affirm, which we call intelligence in everyday life and "which our tests represent more or less effectively" (pp. 106–8).

This last conclusion is quite inacceptable on the basis of the psychometrists' own case. What they are concerned to measure, on their own admission, is not everyday intelligence but capacity to pass certain examinations after a course in an English grammar school of a particular (and not always educationally desirable) type; and this is quite another thing. But it is important to recognise what is involved in accepting Intelligence B, because this is the new position on which a stand is henceforth to be made. In the first place, it should be said that this definition rests chiefly on the basis of what can only be described as some very sparse experiments, not this time with children and I.Q.s but chiefly with blinded rats. Almost any conclusion could be drawn from these, though it is doubtful if any would really be relevant to human education. The conclusion actually drawn, however, is one that is badly wanted; namely that innate powers and acquired knowledge become inextricably interconnected from birth to make up educability, and that it is *the very early years that are absolutely decisive* in this connection. Thus, even at the age of five,

"The level of concept development and thinking shown by a child . . . largely determine his capacity for further intellectual growth. Improved education or improvements in personality adjustment may alter his educability, but do so to a marked extent only in exceptional cases. Similarly on entry to secondary schooling, the I.Q. tests do give a fair indication of capacity for acquiring advanced education, not because this capacity is truly inborn, but *because it has become more or less established* in the previous 11 years" [my italics.—B. S.] (p. 108).

So, deprived of the argument that the "intelligence" they measure is fixed at or before birth, psychometrists find a new theory; that "educability" becomes fixed, for the vast majority of children, from the age of five. In the light of this new theory they can affirm that it is a very good thing that their "intelligence" tests measure environment and education instead of (as was once hoped) only innate powers; for if they did measure only Intelligence A they would be bad predictors of grammar school success! (p. 108.)

It is almost incredible that arguments so doctrinaire should attempt to pass muster as scientific. But there it is. This is the kernel of the case for the defence. It is a theoretical standpoint which is, of course, *of the same order as*, though much weaker than, the one which psychologists have been forced to jettison. It, too, must soon go the same way.

II

PRACTICAL CONSIDERATIONS

Besides criticising "intelligence" tests from a theoretical angle, Marxists, together with many progressive educationists, showed the devastating effect of testing on the schools. They argued that there can be no real educational advance until the practice of testing, streaming and selecting is set aside together with the theories which uphold it.

In an earlier chapter of this report, evidently written by another hand, some of these arguments are seriously discussed. Here a genuine attempt is made to approach the question from a social and educational point of view and the nature and outcome of the discussion is, therefore, rather different. In this case the psychological standpoint which informed all the recommendations from the Hadow Report (1926) onwards, for segregating children in different schools and in A, B and C streams within schools, is overtly rejected. "Few nowadays would subscribe to the statement made in the Spens Report . . . 'that, with few exceptions, it is possible at a very early age to predict with some degree of accuracy the ultimate level of a child's intellectual powers' " (p. 42). The question of streaming and selection is, therefore, considered afresh.

On the whole, the chapter honestly stresses the dangers of streaming, accepting the arguments we advanced. "Children who are relegated to a low stream, to suit their present level of ability [we would write: attainment.—B. S.] are likely to be taught at a slower pace; whereas the brighter streams, often under the better teachers, are encouraged to proceed more rapidly. Thus initial differences become exacerbated . . ." In general, therefore, the authors agree with us that ". . . the 'freezing' of abilities through streaming is to be deplored", and, though hedging their conclusions around with qualifications, they appear to come down against streaming and differentiation below the age of thirteen. Segregation into different types of secondary school is similarly deprecated. "Any policy involving irreversible segregation at eleven years or earlier is psychologically unsound, and therefore . . . in so far as public opinion allows—the common or comprehensive school would be preferable, at least up to the age of thirteen" (pp. 43-4, 53).

Now these are very important concessions and should be welcomed as such: they can be used to strengthen the struggle against streaming and for the comprehensive school. But two important reservations must be made. Firstly, this standpoint is at variance with the one outlined earlier, which attempts to infer that diagnosis of children's "abilities" is both possible and desirable from the age of five. This dichotomy appears throughout the report, the conservative view coming out particularly strongly in the chapter "The Validity of Selection" where it is argued, once more, on the basis of highly questionable statistical techniques that selection as practised today is highly reliable and accurate. In other words, the more progressive psychologists have as yet only a limited foothold, while a strong rearguard action is being conducted.

The second point, which follows from this, is that the whole sense of the report is to advance plans for maintaining the practice of testing at all costs, come what may. In short, if selection should go then the psychometrists propose to assert their domination over education in a new way by directing streaming and classification *within the comprehensive school itself*.

Now the Labour movement is concerned to develop the comprehensive school precisely in order to abolish selection at ten and provide the conditions for a real secondary education for all. Implicit in this approach is the radical reduction of streaming both in the junior and secondary (comprehensive) schools with the aim of ultimately abolishing it altogether. For instance, Miss Margaret Miles, the head of a large London comprehensive school, in a recent broadcast, strongly opposed the idea of "the division of the school into labelled streams", urging that this does not make "the right use of the continuing opportunity the comprehensive school offers". Children should be arranged in parallel (i.e. unstreamed) groups "pursuing a common curriculum for as long as possible".

But what does the report say on this issue? "We venture to point out that no one, except perhaps a few left-wing enthusiasts, intends to eliminate ability grouping [streaming.—B. S.] in such schools." And they follow this up with an agreed conclusion that psychologists "should uphold their claim to diagnose the most suitable form of schooling for not all but a great majority of the children . . ."—in particular, they must be consulted on the "proper allocation" of pupils "to streaming within comprehensive schools"; "if comprehensive schools become general, psychology will have at least as much to contribute to the technique of diagnosis and guidance within such schools as it has to the more restricted aim of accurate selection" (pp. 49, 169).

Now if it were a question of a genuine *educational* psychology concerned to elucidate the inner mental processes involved in learning, the social and emotional aspects of learning, and the practical problems of teaching, then the schools could only profit from any advice proffered. But at present, and obviously in this context, psychology means psychometry—the classification and grading of children by the use of mental tests. This form of activity has nothing whatever to do with the real problems involved in teaching and learning; indeed, by its very nature it operates to *obscure these problems*. It is precisely on the basis of psychometry that psychologists have given what they now admit to be consistently *wrong and harmful* advice, both to educational legislators and to teachers, for over three decades. This advice has helped to maintain in being an obsolete educational structure, has provided "scientific" justification for blighting the prospects of innumerable children, has reduced the efficiency and dulled the enthusiasm of thousands of teachers. One might expect a little humility in the light of this record. But no; instead psychometrists assert their right to continue giving "guidance" using the old techniques, which clearly means a free hand to push outworn ideas and methods on the new schools. To stream *as a question of principle* within the comprehensive school, instead of seeking ways to overcome it by investigating the very real problems of teaching and learning, is to give a new impetus to the very practices and outlook which the comprehensive school is designed to overcome.

It is clear enough, then, that the struggle against testing is by no means over. Communists, of course, are not so simple as to believe that, because a theory has been shown to be untenable, it will forthwith be abandoned—especially in a field so remote from the exact sciences as psychology is at present. In addition it must be recognised that testing has been deeply entrenched in the schools. It is on this basis that the psychometrists, together with the effort to reformulate exploded theories, insist on the practical convenience of testing. So the writers of this report claim that "our tests are extremely useful"; but they do not stop to ask—to whom? Certainly not to the working class. And it is worth noting here that the new developments in the Soviet educational system, whose achievements are now generally acclaimed, effectively began twenty years ago when the psychometrists were excluded from practising in the schools and offered an opportunity to retrain as teachers. One of the reasons given for this, besides the harmfulness of their theories, was that the teachers and teaching should be put at the centre of the picture, and that the schools should not be run for them by psychometrists. In the same way, British teachers, especially those in comprehensive schools, need to make their own decisions about the school's internal organisation and structure, instead of submitting to "guidance" from outside.

The writers of this report are not, of course, consciously propounding false and harmful doctrines for purely subjective reasons. As professional workers they see it as their job to serve society and its educational system and for the most part they simply do not recognise that to do this unquestioningly in a class society is simply to foster class ends. However, the contradictions are so obvious that attempts to establish this standpoint lead to a rich confusion of thought. Thus, at the very outset of this report the writers affirm that they are concerned "with the techniques that can best be employed given the present set-up. It is not our function to suggest reforms in matters of educational policy . . . " (p. 13). Later they suggest that "the majority" of psychologists "would probably gladly abolish the selection system if there were a practicable and just alternative", but only in order specifically to reject the views of "many" psychologists who so object to the use of psychological tests in selection that they "have gone so far as to advocate that their profession should 'contract out', and refuse to have anything to do with procedures that have such harmful effects on children's educational and emotional development" (p. 35). This attitude, it is affirmed, is mistaken; psychologists have done much to bring about improvements and can do more. To improve the existing system with a view to making it work better is, one gathers, a sound and politically neutral thing to do; whereas to contribute towards any radical change is mistaken and political. This argument is, of course, typical of the traditional Conservative attitude to social change, as is the remark that "many people might subscribe to the Labour Party's desire to abolish selection of [*sic*] 11 plus, if that were possible. But to assume that it could be done by a stroke of the pen is quite unrealistic. Rather we must think in terms of a programme of gradual change . . ." (p. 14). This, of course, is as much a political standpoint as is the policy of the Labour or Communist Party.

For the Labour movement the lesson to be drawn is clear. It is mass support for an extension of educational opportunity that can be decisive. Much more can, and should, be done to explain all the issues to the people and so to give real leadership to the present scattered and largely instinctive revolt against educational inequalities and frustration, both on the part of teachers anxious to give of their best and parents whose hopes for their children are shattered. The force of popular determination, and the measure of informed criticism there has been, have already led to the defeat of the most reactionary views, and to a retreat all along the front of the part both of psychometrists and those who formerly supported the tripartite system. It is only necessary to bring the theory and practice together, to inform the popular struggle and raise it to a new level, for this retreat to become a rout.

INEQUALITIES IN EDUCATION[1]

It is now clear that the main inequalities in British education today are due to three factors: differences in social class, in sex, and in geographical location.

If you happen to have had the luck to have been born a boy in Cardiganshire, your father being in the professional (or managerial) class, your chance of achieving full-time higher education would almost certainly be about 80 per cent—that is, of every 10 children in this class, eight would achieve higher education. If, on the other hand, you were born as the daughter of a semi-skilled or unskilled worker living in West Ham, your chance of reaching full-time higher education would probably have been less than 0·5 per cent. I say "probably", because these figures are not based on a survey of the actual situation in these two areas as far as class and sex differences in opportunity are concerned; the assumption I have made is the not unreasonable one that these differences are the same in these two areas as they are in the country as a whole.

These figures quantify the extent of differences in opportunity at their extremest points; they show that the Cardiganshire middle class boy has roughly 160 times as much chance of reaching full-time higher education than the West Ham working-class girl; and this when the country has, in a formal sense, committed itself to a policy of equality of opportunity.

To make clear how these differences operate, I want to analyse the situation in relation to the three variables I mentioned earlier, starting with regional or local variations.

Of all the counties and county boroughs in England and Wales, Cardiganshire, in 1960, had the highest proportion of 17-year-olds at school—27·9 per cent compared to the national average of 9·5 per cent. Over a quarter of the age-group stays on to the sixth form. (It is worth noting in passing that this is a higher proportion than even obtains entry to grammar schools in many areas.) In this county, just under 25 per cent obtained entry and took up awards in full-time higher education. This figure approaches the proportion in parts of the

[1] Address given at the annual conference of the Confederation for the Advancement of State Education, 1965.

United States and is equal to or above the proportion in the U.S.S.R., Canada, and other countries where higher education is a great deal more widely available than it is here. It is worth noting that the top places among local authorities in the country as a whole are taken by five Welsh counties, including Anglesey, the proportion going on to higher education varying from 16·2 per cent to 24·9 per cent, although one English city (Oxford) is among them, while three English counties approach them with over 14 per cent going on. This is not, then, only a Welsh phenomenon.

In West Ham, on the other hand, the proportion of 17-year-olds at school is 2·9 per cent. The percentage of the age group entering full-time higher education is only 1·7 per cent (in 1960)—between one-fourteenth and one-fifteenth of the position in Cardiganshire. The five county boroughs with the lowest proportion of the age-group going on to higher education are: West Ham, West Bromwich, East Ham, Smethwick and Salford. These are all cities where the population is predominantly working-class.

Attention has been drawn recently to the wide variations that exist in educational opportunity between the North and the South of England. Recent statistics show that the proportion of 16-year-olds in maintained schools (as a proportion of 13-year-olds in these schools three years earlier) is given as 15·3 per cent in the "Northern" region and 18·3 per cent in the East and West Ridings of Yorkshire, as compared to 28·1 per cent in the Metropolitan region and—the highest —28·6 per cent in the South Eastern region: a variation covering regions as a whole, and therefore millions of people, of nearly two to one at the extremes.

How do we interpret these enormous variations?—because they are enormous. Does it mean that the Welsh in general, and the youth of Cardiganshire in particular, are innately more intelligent than the young people of West Ham, Smethwick and Salford? Hardly. Indeed it could be argued that the children of Cardiganshire are more likely to be affected by what used to be known as "rural idiocy" than those of West Ham, whom common observation suggests fully share the life, vitality and native wit of Londoners generally.

Of course we no longer accept such reasoning; that is one of the advances that has been made over the last decade. The regional and local differences have to be explained in social and historical terms. The level of educational provision in Wales, and Welsh attitudes to education (perhaps particularly in the rural areas) reflect a complex set of national, social and economic circumstances. For decades, grammar school provision in Wales has been far ahead of most of England; already in many of their counties (not only Anglesey) these have developed into full systems of comprehensive schools now sending on an increased proportion of the age-group to higher education. The provision of educational facilities on this scale is partly a reflection of the demand for education, and partly a cause itself accelerating it. The more meagre facilities in the English county boroughs at the bottom of the table also reflect the social and economic circumstances of these areas.

Now I want to give you the result of one calculation I have made. There are now 216,000 full-time students in higher education in Great Britain. Suppose the rest of the country caught up with Cardiganshire (as it was in 1960—it will be further ahead now) and, over the country as a whole, 24·9 per cent went on to full-time higher education; how many young people would be studying at our universities, technical colleges and colleges of education? The answer is 787,500. The Robbins target for *1980* is 507,000.

What is the conclusion? Obviously, that regional or local variations in educational opportunity are very great indeed. We have not known their full extent until recently, because we have not had the facts. Knowledge of the extent of these variations should strengthen our determination to bring about a radical change; particularly so far as the more deprived areas are concerned. Above all, these variations challenge fundamentally any conception that we are anywhere near scraping the barrel, as far as children's abilities are concerned. Only the proverbial ostrich can maintain this thesis in the light of the *facts* now available.

A great deal of attention is being given today to what is called the sexual revolution. I hope I won't be considered too much of a reactionary if I say that some of the energy going into liberating us from age-old inhibitions might usefully be spent on the more fundamental question of the actual social position of women in our society; above all, of achieving a genuine equality between the sexes which involves opening up to women real opportunities for participating fully in the social and economic life of the community on terms of equality with men. I am constantly amazed that so little attention is devoted to this aspect.

In 1961 nearly three times as many men entered universities as women; for full-time study at technical colleges, four times as many.

Only the colleges of education have a preponderance of women over men. Opportunities in certain fields requiring higher education are very restricted. There are nearly four men preparing as doctors for every one woman; the same proportion holds for pure science at universities. The most striking figure is perhaps that for the technological faculties of universities where there are 32 men for every woman.

If we look further back we find that girls tend to leave school earlier than boys; of boys and girls with five or more O levels, ten boys stay on to 18 to every eight girls. 51 per cent of these boys get three or more A levels, as compared with only 34 per cent of the girls. Yet no one claims today that there are innate differences in intelligence between the sexes. It is not only, as the Robbins Committee say, that "one should not forget that the reserve of untapped ability is greater among women than men", it is that *severe inequalities exist between men and women as regards educational opportunities generally.*

Must this always be the case? We should note that while the proportion of boys and girls getting two or more A levels has "risen steeply" over the last few years (Robbins), yet "the differences between the proportions between boys and girls has been hardly reduced". In other words, no serious tendency is being shown towards a diminution of these inequalities. Yet there are countries where the situation is very different, and of these the Soviet Union is certainly the most striking. In 1960–61, 43·5 per cent of students in higher education in the U.S.S.R. were female, as compared with about 33 per cent in Britain. More remarkable is the fact that nearly 30 per cent of the students following technological courses at university level in the U.S.S.R. were women, as compared with under 2 per cent in England and even less in the United States. Women play a leading part in the engineering industry and in technical education in the U.S.S.R.—in the medical profession, scientific research and administration. Clearly, then, this question can be solved, although a full solution requires rather fundamental changes in the whole position of women in society.

We should, then, note this factor as one of the major causes of inequality in education. In directing attention to it we need to ensure that everything is done to improve educational facilities for girls, in particular in science and technology; recognising also that there is urgent need to provide the kind of conditions which will make it possible for women to develop and use their skills and talents in the service of the community.

Having said this, there is no doubt that the most important, the most pervasive and intractable, of the three factors leading to inequality is the class factor—this because it is all-inclusive, affecting everyone wherever they live and of whatever sex. An enormous amount of evidence has been gathered over the last decade and more highlighting class inequalities and making clear how deep-seated and enduring they are.

Here are some of the crucial facts. The Robbins Report showed that 45 per cent (or nearly half) of those from higher professional families get into full-time higher education; 10 per cent of those whose fathers are in clerical jobs, 4 per cent of children of skilled workers, and only 2 per cent (or one in 50) of children of semi-skilled or unskilled workers who comprise, in fact, about 22 per cent of the total population. As we would expect, the differentials are much sharper for girls than for boys.

These figures are the crucial ones because they deal with the end of the educational process. We find that, although the working class as defined for these surveys contains about 80 per cent of the population, only 29 per cent of university students come from this section of the community—in Oxford and Cambridge the proportion is far less. We have statistics showing how at each stage middle-class children gain as compared with those from the working class: for instance, Douglas has shown that children from poor homes "tend on the whole to get to the less good primary schools, and having got there are more likely to get into a low stream". From this point onwards, says Professor Moser, "disadvantages reinforce one another". Those in low streams tend to deteriorate—those in upper streams to improve. The chances of both groups at the 11 plus stage are, therefore, already unequal and this is reflected in the results. There are wide differences between L.E.A.s, as has been noted, but, says Moser, "even within the L.E.A.s, the selection process at 11 operates in favour of the middle class child, far more of whom at any given level of ability get into grammar schools". Hence a further widening of differences both in opportunity and attainment—those getting to grammar schools tend to improve their performance, those in secondary modern schools to deteriorate even if just as able. Those in grammar schools tend to stay to 17 and beyond, to take O and A levels; those in secondary modern schools (who are predominantly working class) to leave at 15. Even within the grammar school the differences are striking. As Jean Floud has pointed out—there is something about the grammar school which alienates the working-class child; it is too often unable to hold him or her. Jackson and Marsden analysed this process of alienation in their book *Education and the Working Class*.

I have said the class factor is deep seated and enduring. Moser makes the point that these inequalities "have remained remarkably persistent . . . over the last 10 to 20 years". He gives several examples in illustration. Here is one: "The percentage of entrants to grammar schools from the working class has actually *fallen* over the last 15 years." At this crucial hurdle then, opportunities are becoming more unequal. Perhaps I may quote one more expert—Mr. Furneaux (who wrote *The Chosen Few*, a study of selection for the universities). He referred recently to "the extraordinary stability in the picture of differentials in social class attainment, not only over the past 10 years but over the past 15 or 20". "In fact", he adds, "we have a social class structure which, as things stand, is virtually self-perpetuating." He concludes "unless we have done something about initiating social change then we shall be in the same position in 50 years' time as we are now".

I have discussed the three main factors leading to inequality. Naturally, there are many others since this is a very complex question indeed; but these are the crucial ones. What can we do about it?

First—should we do anything at all? Perhaps this is a matter for the individual conscience; but I think the answer must be, yes. The present position is neither socially nor morally justifiable. We must find the way both to develop and to use the abilities of the children— to break out from our present crystallised educational structure; this is a matter of national survival, particularly if one takes the long view. Morally, the situation is unacceptable, since the discrimination against working-class children operating partly through the educational system does not meet even the most elementary requirements of social justice.

Secondly—let us be clear that our objective should be equality— not equality of opportunity. The two concepts are different. Equality of opportunity has served its day as a slogan for educational advance. The 1944 Act was supposed to have achieved equal opportunities for secondary education, or, more precisely, equal opportunities to achieve unequal things—a grammar school education or a modern school education. But for a whole number of reasons, based chiefly on the deep-seated influence of social class, the competitors never line up equal. Some are already miles behind before the starting gun goes off, others far ahead, and these differences, as we know, are partly the

product of the educational process itself—the outcome of streaming
and so on. Equality of opportunity is today an élitist concept—
presupposing an élitist society; the central democratic notion must be
that of equality. Hence the title of this Conference—Inequalities in
Education—is in my view a correct one.

What does this imply? It implies, as Professor Hilde Himmelweit
and others have said, that we begin to see education as concerned with
compensation—as an instrument designed deliberately to overcome
differences rather than exacerbate them (particularly those differences
due to deprivation). It implies also that we break right away from the
present selective system of education concerned largely with the production of a docile élite; that we build a genuinely open and democratic
system of education in which each child is regarded as of equal value
with a unique personality, and every effort made to develop the capacities of all children.

What should be done? In my personal view, we cannot overcome
class differentials while we remain essentially a class society. Education
alone cannot bring about fundamental social change. Nevertheless
every effort must be made to modify these differentials. I suggest first,
that it should be ensured that working-class areas (for instance, those I
mentioned earlier) are given priority in rebuilding schools, perhaps also
in staffing and equipment. Such an effort would have to be carried out
as national policy, though working of course through local authorities.
Much of our effort to date (based on existing priorities) is in fact by-
passing the very areas that most need attention and resources.

Secondly, we need to structure the schools so that they are genuinely
open—that is, we need to break down the artificial barriers to advance
that we have erected during the last 20 or 30 years when the aim of an
élitist education was being pursued with undivided enthusiasm. The
particular barriers I am thinking about are those embodied in the
practice of streaming and selection.

There is now a serious move away from what became a really vicious
system of streaming in junior schools a few years ago. In their evidence
to the Plowden Committee, the L.C.C. made clear that this movement
is rapidly making headway all over London. In Leicestershire, the
Director has reported that, with the abolition of the 11 plus where
comprehensive schools have been established, hardly a junior school
continues to stream, and stresses the liberating effect on the whole
ethos and character of the schools. Jackson and Douglas have shown
beyond doubt how this practice discriminates against the working-class

child. In Sweden, as a result of research conducted over many years, streaming has been made illegal before the age of 15 or 16. I am sorry if I appear dogmatic; but it is difficult to contemplate with patience a practice which may determine a child's whole future at the age of 7, which inculcates a sense of failure and inadequacy among a substantial proportion of our youngest citizens, a sense of failure constantly reinforced and extraordinarily difficult ever to overcome. I was delighted to see a report in *The Times* recently that parents are at last beginning to take a hand in this matter, as surely they have every right to do— a group of parents in Darlington refused to send their children to a streamed school.

Then, as many authorities are now doing and as is now government policy, we must develop the common secondary school and so put and end once and for all to the 11 plus. The common school is not a panacea which will finally solve all the problems of inequality. But insofar as, by definition, it is a school which takes in all the children in a given locality, it provides the conditions where all children can be treated alike as *children* and not as types; and in which they can be treated equally. Of course we have very few comprehensive schools which meet this definition—parallel with these in most cities and counties there exist various types of selective school as well as the independent, so-called "public" schools. While this separatism continues there cannot be a system of genuinely common schools. Nevertheless many authorities are moving in this direction.

But it is argued—for instance by the *Times Educational Supplement*—comprehensive schools are themselves streamed, sometimes rigidly, so that selection takes place within them as sharply as in the tripartite system. The description of the school circulated with your papers gives a picture of a school that apparently operates a rigid system of streaming. But in my view the comprehensive schools will, as they gain confidence, move away from streaming just as junior schools have done, and I hope that parents will assist them in this. I will stick my neck out and say that I think it will be shown, over the next few years, that streaming is as educationally deleterious in the comprehensive school as it has been shown to be in the junior schools over the past years—by empirical evidence. Research into this is only just beginning here. The last number of *Forum* carried a long article by Mr. Thompson, head of the Woodlands Comprehensive School, Coventry, which on the basis of a mass of statistical information (covering three years' research) showed the bad effect of streaming the first year in his school;

as a result he has now *entirely* unstreamed the first year and is modifying streaming in the second and third years as well. His experimental work is continuing and the school will be reorganised on the basis of the results. There are today quite a number of unstreamed secondary modern schools—and of unstreamed grammar schools. The problem as regards the comprehensive school is perhaps greater, since these schools take in children across the whole range. But I believe this movement is bound to develop.

This is what I mean by opening up the school—breaking out of our rigid and crystallised structure. And I believe the common school should be able to retain the enthusiasm and interest of working-class children more easily than the grammar school, with its particular inherited middle-class ethos and inevitably narrow curriculum and direction. The transition to comprehensive education will certainly upset the Robbins targets for the expansion of higher education by 1980; it was one important factor they failed to consider, so rapidly have things changed.

I said the comprehensive school was now government policy, and so it is. But what we need to watch are the actual actions of the Secretary of State rather than words spoken or published (in, for instance, Circular 10/65). Naturally one can only welcome the acceptance of a comprehensive school policy by the government— it was, after all, promised in the election manifesto. But what has happened? The Liverpool scheme, which in my view, in its main outline, was a good one, has been postponed as a whole (though some projects can go ahead), largely on the argument that to group schools some distance apart to form comprehensive schools is not satisfactory. But this, of course, is a practical way of making a rapid transition to the all-through comprehensive school, used by many authorities that have these schools now. London started many of its schools in two or even three buildings, sometimes quite far apart. I visited some of these 13 years ago. The problems were difficult, but they were overcome and what stands out in my memory is the enthusiasm of the teachers, heads and assistants, as well as the children about their pioneering role. With effective organisation it does not mean that children and teachers spend their time moving from one building to another. London still has 20 or 30 schools in this situation. It is not ideal, but it is a necessary stage in the transition. Manchester's plan also utilises this method.

While Liverpool has been told to go away and think again (and so also Luton) schemes which, in my view, have nothing in common with the comprehensive idea have been accepted and passed by the Department. In the case of Doncaster and Cardiff, the parents are to choose when their children reach the age of 13, whether they wish them to stay at school until the age of 18 and sit A levels or not. If the answer is yes, they go to the "grammar" schools, if not they remain at the "modern" schools. This introduces a new factor of social selection which may well be worse than the strictly tripartite system. We have an enormous mass of evidence, collected by official committees and others—all fully available to the Department of Education and Science—which indicates clearly that, while middle-class parents will tend to choose that their children remain in school until 18, working-class parents will not. And for a number of very cogent reasons. If one set out to turn the public system of education into one which was primarily socially selective, no better means could be devised. It seems to me scandalous that such schemes should be brought into being under the "umbrella" of a policy for comprehensive education.

What the genuine comprehensive school can be is a really popular educational instrument, a neighbourhood school that channels the interest and concern of a whole district, above all of parents; a centre that can release something of the potential creative energies of ordinary people, now too often suppressed. Education in this country has always been imposed from above, never created from below—as was pointed out 25 years ago by Sir Fred Clarke in his noteworthy book *Education and Social Change*. But the transition to the common secondary school does bear the marks of a popular movement, a grass roots movement, developed from below. If the schools so created can establish close relations with the life and vital interests of the locality; if they can be made responsive to its requirements and outlook—and many comprehensive schools are attempting just this as a foundation for their work —then it seems to me that we should begin to overcome the problems of inequality, both in relation to class and to sex as well as contributing towards the enrichment of social life generally. For comprehensive schools should evidently be coeducational, institutions in which boys and girls have like opportunities, sharing similar facilities covering the whole range of the humanities, sciences and technology. In all this parents have a crucial role to play as well as teachers, and a better opportunity to do so, for comprehensive schools rarely—like some others—keep parents at arm's length.

Professor Moser has called for a National Plan for Education, worked out on a 10-year perspective, covering the whole field of education including the universities, and with clearly defined criteria such as the achievement of equality. Of course, he is right. We must plan in this way if we are to develop our resources, if we are to get the priorities right and really tackle the main problems revealed in the information which is now to hand. This implies keeping a close eye on national planning and ensuring that the rate of growth of educational expenditure shows a continuous upward curve.

I believe that this Conference is planned as a stage in the formulation of a National Charter of Education by the Confederation. I have seen the conference documents and have been extremely impressed with the work that has already been done. I believe that this Confederation would be doing a first class job if, in drawing up such a Charter, and in popularising it, it could focus specifically on the major inequalities and the wastage arising from them and work out a clear programme.

We would then have a focus around which those really concerned with the national system of public education could mobilise themselves, both locally and nationally, and arouse public opinion to ensure its implementation. We are moving into a new phase in the fight for education in this country, and we should recognise it. May I offer my best wishes for the future success, and particularly, for the growing influence of your organisation.

KARL MARX AND EDUCATION[1]

The Manchester School of Education has set me a particular problem in my subject for this lecture. Marx was very much an all-round man, something of a polymath. Not only did he make original contributions in many fields, especially philosophy, economics and politics, but he also had wide interests quite outside these, following modern developments in science and technology, for instance, extremely closely. He is therefore a difficult subject, the more so because it is impossible to docket him and place him in a specific category as we like to do nowadays, for instance, that of a sociologist.

In essence Marx's significance lies in the fact that he defined and elaborated a new way of looking at things, a new world outlook, one that has profoundly modified man's view of himself, of his relations both to nature and to his fellow men; and this, I think, is true whether Marx's interpretation is fully accepted or not. This outlook is not primarily a contemplative one, but if accepted compels to action, and as such Marx's ideas have profoundly influenced social development in large parts of the world. You will remember one of his famous theses: "The philosophers have only *interpreted* the world in different ways; the point however is to *change* it."

What, then, was Marx's outlook? It was essentially sociological. It represented a revolution in human thinking by providing a means of interpreting social institutions and ideas, indeed the evolution of human society as a whole, in terms of the changing characteristics of society itself. It therefore brought social evolution into the sphere of scientific investigation and held out the prospect of conscious human control over social development. With this, it provided a means of penetrating to the reality beneath the appearance, or of evaluating objectively human actions and ideas. Marx attempted, therefore, to enable man to arrive at a true picture of himself as man.

It was to this that Engels referred in 1883 at Marx's graveside—where, incidentally, among the small group present was Schorlemmer,

[1] This was the first of a series of lectures on leading sociologists, organised by the School of Education of the University of Manchester, delivered in January, 1963. Speakers were asked to discuss the significance of particular thinkers for the theory and practice of education, others covered including Durkheim, Karl Mannheim and Talcott Parsons.

Professor of Organic Chemistry at this university and Engels' closest friend in Manchester.

"Just as Darwin discovered the law of development of organic nature, so Marx discovered the law of development of human history: the simple fact, hitherto concealed by an overgrowth of ideology, that mankind must first of all eat, drink, have shelter and clothing, before it can pursue politics, science, art, religion, etc.; and that therefore the production of the immediate material means of subsistence and consequently the degree of development attained by a given people or during a given epoch form the foundation upon which the State institutions, the legal conceptions, the ideas on art, and even on religion, of the people concerned have been evolved, and in the light of which they must, therefore, be explained, instead of vice versa, as had hitherto been the case."[1]

In other words, human thought and actions can be explained sociologically—in terms of man's development in society; and the key to interpreting this development lies in the mode of production of a given form of society, the way in which social productive work is organised.

This key concept—or model—did not, of course, spring ready made into Marx's mind. In the early 1840s, when he first began to define this outlook, conditions were ripening for just such an intellectual synthesis. The French Revolution, a cataclysmic social upheaval, was a comparatively recent event; the '48 revolutions were preparing. In Britain the Industrial Revolution, based on new technological developments, was not only changing the face of the countryside but also the structure of society itself, giving rise to a new industrial bourgeoisie and to the factory proletariat. For the first time men became conscious, if often in a shadowy way, of history as a *process* of change and development; of inner struggles arising from contradictory, or conflicting, economic interests; and of the role of ideas and institutions in furthering—or hindering—social change. These ideas, refined and developed, were to form basic components of Marx's thinking.

Marx was brought up a Hegelian, and, as is well known, "sublated" (to use Engels' term) Hegel's dialectics in the service of materialism. It

[1] F. Engels, Speech at the Graveside of Karl Marx, *Marx-Engels Selected Works* (1950), Vol. II, 153.

was Hegel in particular who gave expression to the idea of movement, of change, of development as a *process* of coming into being and passing away. "What distinguished Hegel's mode of thought from that of all other philosophers," wrote Engels, "was the tremendous sense of the historical upon which it was based."[1] But for Hegel the real world was no more than the product of mind—as Marx put it, "the external, phenomenal form of 'the Idea' ". For Marx on the other hand, who took a materialist position, "the ideal is nothing else than the material world reflected by the human mind, and translated into forms of thought".[2]

There is not time to go into all the influences on Marx's thought which led him to this position. But the two essential components were acceptance of the classic materialist position—that, as Marx put it summarising Hobbes, "one cannot separate thought from matter which thinks"—and the fusion of this materialist approach with Hegelian dialectics. This was the crucial means of moving beyond the rigid, mechanistic materialism of the late eighteenth century which had already shown its inadequacy. It was this fusion of what had been until then two quite separate—even antagonistic—philosophical standpoints, that enabled Marx to advance a rational interpretation of social change—in terms of human activity in society, or in sociological terms.

There is, however, a third important element in Marx's thinking. When Marx first came to England in 1845 he travelled straight to Manchester with his friend Engels, and spent several weeks reading at the fine old library at Chetham's Hospital. Here he concentrated on the writings of the English political economists. It was Engels' articles in the *Rheinische Zeitung* in 1842–44 that first aroused Marx's interest in economic questions, through which he came to recognise the importance of economic and technological factors in the evolution of society. Here he found the key to what he regarded as the basic cause of social and ideological development—the changing modes of production of different social formations.

So, on the one hand we have the idea of constant change and development, the fluidity of movement, with internal contradiction as the motive force, on the other, the concept that man is a product of nature, that "nature exists independently of all philosophy", that consciousness is not given from outside, but is secondary and

[1] F. Engels, *Karl Marx, A Contribution to the Critique of Political Economy, Ibid.*, I, 337.
[2] K. Marx, *Capital*, ed. Dona Torr (1946), xxx.

derivative, to be interpreted in terms of man's activity. These are the foundations, established in a rigorous way, that underly all Marx's thinking and his interpretation of social and ideological change. And since men are forced of necessity to co-operate in societies to produce their means of subsistence, it is in the changing nature of that productive activity, and of the social relations arising from it, that is to be found the key to understanding changes in human consciousness. The pattern, then, is completed.

To turn to those aspects of Marx's thinking which have a special relevance to education, I must first make it clear that, unlike some of the other sociologists discussed in this series, Marx said very little directly about education as such—that is, about schools, universities, educational theories, and so on. What Marx was concerned with was the wider issue of social evolution as a whole, its laws and its future. He did, however, raise questions of profound importance to the theory and practice both of education and psychology, insofar as he was fundamentally concerned with the formation and re-formation of man. It will be necessary, then, to tease out the particular threads that concern us. I have arranged them, somewhat arbitrarily, under four heads:

(1) Marx's approach to human learning and psychology.
(2) His analysis of the effect of the division of labour on human development.
(3) Marx's conception of basis and superstructure, briefly referred to in the quotation from Engels; that is, of the nature of classes and class society and the role of institutions and ideas in that society, from which can be derived a sociology of education.
(4) His specific views on education.

(1) MARX'S APPROACH TO HUMAN LEARNING AND PSYCHOLOGY

The first area I have chosen has both a sociological and a psychological interest; Marx's views, I believe, cast very considerable light on the process of human learning, as contrasted, for instance, with animal learning. Here what is important is Marx's historical, or, if you like, developmental approach to man's social evolution, and so to human formation.

What is specific about man, said Marx, is that he produces his means of subsistence. By so doing, "men are indirectly producing their actual material life".[1] The specific form of activity of human beings is productive activity—necessarily a social, or communal, activity, and one which *creates* the social environment in which men have their being and develop.

"The first all-sided, scientific analysis of this activity was made by Karl Marx", writes the distinguished Soviet psychologist, Professor Leontiev, and I quote from part of his summary of Marx's standpoint:

"The human activity (both mental and material), which takes place in the process of production, is crystallised in the product of activity; that which at one pole is manifested in action, in movement, at the pole of the product is transmuted into a fixed property. This transmutation itself is a process in which there takes place an objectification of human abilities—the achievements of the social-historical development of the species. Every object created by man— from the simple tool to the contemporary electronic computing machine—embodies the historical experience of mankind and together with this the intellectual abilities formed in this experience. The same may be seen still more clearly in language, in science, in works of art."[2]

It is, then, in the process of social living that human abilities are created and new knowledge achieved; these are crystallised, externally to man, in the environment, or, to use Marx's term, are "objectified". In Leontiev's words, the achievements of man's historical development "are consolidated in the material objects, in the ideal phenomena (language, science), created by men". "Nature constructs no machines," wrote Marx, "no locomotives, no railways, electric telegraphs, self-acting mules, etc. They are the products of human industry, natural materials transformed into instruments of the human domination of Nature, or of its activity in Nature. They are instruments of the human brain created by the human hand; they are the materialised power of Knowledge."[3] "We presuppose labour in a form that stamps it as

[1] Marx and Engels, *The German Ideology* (1942 ed.), 7.

[2] A. N. Leontiev, "Principles of Child Mental Development and the Problem of Intellectual Backwardness" in B. and J. Simon (Ed.), *Educational Psychology in the U.S.S.R.* (1963), 72.

[3] From the *Grundisse der Kritik der Politischen Okonomie*, translated in T. B. Bottomore and Maximilien Rubel, *Karl Marx*, (selected writings) (1961 ed.), 91.

exclusively human", he wrote elsewhere, touching on the same conception. "A spider conducts operations that resemble those of a weaver, and a bee puts to shame many an architect in the construction of her cells. But what distinguishes the worst architect from the best of bees is this, that the architect raises his structure in imagination before he erects it in reality. At the end of every labour-process, we get a result that already existed in the imagination of the labourer at its commencement."[1] It embodies, we might add, his intellectual powers.

Since man can objectify—externalise—his knowledge and abilities in this way, the formation of man, human learning, takes place in entirely different circumstances from that of animals. Whereas the animal can only learn through adapting its behaviour to external circumstances, on the basis of its hereditary reflex mechanisms, and whereas animal experience must always be individual experience, with man the case is altogether different.

Human learning is a question of the mastery—or better, to use Marx's expression, the "appropriation"—of man's social-historical experience, embodied in the actual objects and phenomena created by previous generations of men. This process goes on in a specific, social situation. The child, from the moment of birth, is brought up in a humanised world, surrounded by objects created by human beings, and standing in a definite relationship to other human beings with whom he learns to communicate primarily by means of language. Language itself, said Marx:

> "is as old as consciousness, language is practical consciousness . . . for language, like consciousness, only arises from the need, the necessity, of intercourse with other men. Consciousness is therefore from the very beginning a social product, and remains so as long as men exist at all."[2]

It is through the use of language that the child is able to master, to "appropriate", the achievements of earlier generations of men. And this process of appropriation—itself a social process—involves the "reproduction in the individual of the historical formation of human qualities, abilities and characteristics of behaviour". As the child makes language his own, so there are formed in him "such specifically human abilities and functions as ability to understand speech, ability to speak,

---

[1] *Capital*, Vol. 1, 157.
[2] *The German Ideology*, 19.

such functions as the hearing of speech and articulation"[1] (each of which rests on the formation of complex functional systems in the brain).

As Marx wrote, it is "music alone (that) awakens in man the sense of music".[2] This concept is crucial to his thought, as expressed and elaborated particularly in *The German Ideology* and in the *Economic and Philosophical Manuscripts of 1844*. Thus he held that "the *forming* of the five senses is a labour of the entire history of the world down to the present".[3] The five senses, as well as what he called the "mental senses", are humanised through social living and labour, and man learns to govern his own behaviour. "By . . . acting on the external world and changing it", wrote Marx of man in a well-known passage, "he at the same time changes his own nature. He develops his slumbering powers and compels them to act in obedience to his sway".[4]

Insofar as the process is externalised it can be seen on the ground—in terms of what Marx called "humanised nature", or the objectification of human powers. "The history of industry—and the established objective existence of industry", wrote Marx, "are the open book of man's essential powers, the exposure to the sense of human psychology."[5]

Another way of illuminating this key aspect of Marx's thinking is to examine what he said of the relationship between consciousness and activity—or the crucial role of *practice*.

It will already be evident that what Marx held to be the key factor in human development is the individual's *activity* in specific circumstances.

It was from this standpoint that he criticised the old materialist outlook prevalent in his day, which held that man is, to all intents and purposes, the passive product of external circumstances. This conception—Owen's great slogan, for instance, "Circumstances make man"—was certainly a liberating one in its day. Change these circumstances, said Owen, and you change men, and this, as we know, he set out to do at New Lanark. But such an explanation of social and human change allows no scope for human activity or self-change. And, as Marx pointed out, it is logically defective, since it necessarily leads to dividing society into two parts, of which one is superior to society. Put simply, it implies that certain men (Robert Owen, for instance) are not themselves formed by circumstances, insofar as they are able, as it were, to

<hr />

[1] A. N. Leontiev, *loc. cit.*, 73.
[2] *Economic and Philosophical Manuscripts of 1844* (1959 ed.), 108.
[3] *Ibid.*, 108.   [4] *Capital*, Vol. 1, 157.   [5] *Ec. and Phil. MSS*, 109.

rise above them and form the circumstances of others. And this has a direct relation to education. "The materialist doctrine that men are products of circumstances and upbringing", wrote Marx in one of his theses on Feuerbach, "and that, therefore, changed men are products of other circumstances and changed upbringing, forgets that it is men that change circumstances and that the educator must himself be educated."[1]

The defect of this materialism, said Marx, was its failure to account for (or subsume) the *active* side of human development. This failure resulted from conceiving of reality only in the form of an object, for contemplation, "but not as human sensuous activity, practice, not subjectively" which is also a reality. This left the way open to idealist interpretations which could only be abstract, since idealism "does not know real, sensuous activity as such".

Marx expressed his synthesis, or seized the contradiction, thus: "the coincidence of the changing of circumstances and of human activity can be conceived and rationally understood only as revolutionising practice".[2] Man, through his own activity—*in the process of his activity*—both changes his external circumstances and changes himself. Man's consciousness and his activity are, then, one—a unity. And activity implies both changing consciousness and a changed external world. Engels makes very much the same point in *Dialectics of Nature*:

> "Natural science, like philosophy, has hitherto entirely neglected the influence of men's activity on their thought; both only know nature on the one hand and thought on the other. But it is precisely *the alteration of nature by men*, not solely nature as such, which is the most essential and immediate basis of human thought, and it is in the measure that man has learned to change nature that his intelligence has increased."[3]

This is to say that man literally makes himself. He has made himself through actively changing his circumstances—by means of social labour. This is what differentiates man from the animal world, and consequently it follows that laws other than the purely biological, apply to the formation of man. It is not possible to examine all the

[1] Engels, *Ludwig Feuerbach* (1947 ed.), 76.
[2] *Ibid.*, 75–76.
[3] Engels, *Dialectics of Nature* (1941 ed.), 172.

implications of this outlook for education and psychology but it may be noted that the widely accepted interpretation of human development in fundamentally biological terms—i.e. the interaction of heredity and environment—would clearly not have been acceptable to Marx. His approach calls into question received notions about the unchangeability of "human nature", fixed mental attributes, or "instincts", and the accompanying idea that development should be understood as a simple unfolding of innate qualities. Accordingly it opens up the prospect of new means of investigation of human mental development.

It points to the paramount role of activity in specific circumstances as the means of development of mental qualities—what we call variously abilities, mental operations, qualities of personality, attitudes, and so on—activity in a social setting which can be systematically ordered to achieve definite, or should I say, defined goals, and which, whether consciously ordered or not, plays the key role in mental development. This makes the function of the educator an extremely important one; he cannot evade his responsibility, whether in terms of actual teaching or the environment provided for the new generation. This general approach has been considerably developed by Soviet psychologists whose work is now beginning to be more widely known in the West. It is also beginning to be paralleled, to some extent, by experimental work here, particularly in relation to the role of language in child development.

(2) THE DIVISION OF LABOUR

We may turn now to the second area of discussion, that of the division of labour.

"For socialist man", wrote Marx in 1844, "the entire so-called history of the world is nothing but the begetting of man through human labour."[1] If man is created through his work then the nature and conditions of this work, together with the relations he enters into in the process of work, are decisive for human formation.

Since education is concerned with the development of human capacities, this question is clearly an important one for us. It formed, for Marx, one of the chief lines of analysis of the human condition, leading him to socialism.

[1] *Ec. and Phil. MSS*, 113.

Man is endowed with certain "natural and acquired powers" which require certain definite conditions for their development—"the *rich human being*", as Marx put it, "is simultaneously the human being *in need of* a totality of human life-activities"[1]—he requires, in effect, the widest possible scope to practise *varied* activities. Hegel, noted Marx approvingly, "held very heretical views on the division of labour, 'by well educated men', he said, 'we understand in the first instance, those who can do everything that others do'".[2] Correspondingly the great figures of the Renaissance, Leonardo, Albrecht Dürer, Machiavelli, were held up by Engels as models of the all-round man, "giants in power of thought, passion, and character, in universality and learning". They were such because of the *variety* of their activities, possible because, as Engels pointed out, "the heroes of that time had not yet come under the servitude of the division of labour, the restricting effects of which, with its production of one-sidedness, we so often note in their successors".[3]

The essence of the Marxist view is that the division of labour constricts human development. Marx was not alone in stressing this; but he was certainly alone in the emphasis he gave to it, and in the extraordinarily detailed study he made of the division of labour in its various forms.

The first and crucial division, he held, is that between mental and manual labour, the obverse side of which is the coming into existence of private property. These two terms—the division of labour and private property—are, said Marx, identical expressions; what the one affirms as regards *activity*, the other affirms as regards the product of activity.[4]

From this arises the conception of alienation. Labour becomes a commodity when it is sold to the owners of the means of production (later Marx spoke of "labour power"). In other words, the product of labour—"objectified labour"—is appropriated by another and this involves the estrangement, or alienation, of the labourer from this product. If the product of labour is alienated, the process of production becomes a process of active alienation.

In what, then, does the alienation of labour consist? "First," said Marx, considering a man set to work for another in order to live, rather than in a creative way, in "the fact that labour is *external* to the worker,

---

[1] *Ec. and Phil. MSS*, 111.
[2] *Capital*, Vol. 1, 358n.   [3] *Dialectics of Nature*, 2–3.
[4] *The German Ideology*, 22.

i.e. it does not belong to his essential being; that in his work therefore, he does not affirm himself, but denies himself, does not feel content but unhappy, does not develop freely his physical and mental energy but mortifies his body and ruins his mind." It consists in the fact that labour is "not voluntary, but coerced . . . not the satisfaction of a need (but) merely a *means* to satisfy needs external to it. Its alien character emerges clearly in the fact that as soon as no physical or other compulsion exists, labour is shunned like the plague. External labour, labour in which man alienates himself, is a labour of self-sacrifice, or mortification." Its external character "appears in the fact that it is not his own labour, but someone else's, that it does not belong to him, that in it he belongs not to himself, but to another . . . it is the loss of his self".[1] Thus in a society where there is private ownership of the means of production, and so a cleavage between the particular and the common interest, man's own working activity "becomes an alien power opposed to him, which enslaves him instead of being controlled by him". For each individual there is a "particular exclusive sphere of activity, which is forced upon him and from which he cannot escape".[2]

So man is estranged from the product of his activity, impoverished, alienated. More than this, according to Marx, there results also an estrangement of man from man.

As a further consequence of the primary division of labour in industrialised society, there occurs the concentration of intellectual activity at one pole in industry and in society, and of the purely practical activity of the worker at the other—a separation between theory and practice which finds its reflection in divisions in education in class society. It is tempting to develop this theme, since Marx placed so much emphasis on it; but in essence his position was that of the economist, William Thompson, whom he quotes in *Capital* as follows:

> "The man of knowledge and the productive labourer come to be widely divided from each other, and knowledge, instead of remaining the handmaid of labour in the hand of the labourer to increase his productive powers . . . has almost everywhere arrayed itself against labour . . . systematically deluding them and leading them (the labourers) astray in order to render their muscular powers entirely mechanical and obedient."[3]

[1] *Ec. and Phil. MSS*, 72–73.
[2] *The German Ideology*, 22.   [3] *Capital*, Vol. 1, 355n.

Marx analyses this position in detail in *Capital*, showing how the division of labour in the period of manufacture (lasting from the mid-sixteenth to the latter half of the eighteenth century) led to the splitting up of the process of production into innumerable detailed operations, so revolutionising the mode of production of the individual craftsman, and changing the nature of the individual himself. "It converts the labourer into a crippled monstrosity, by forcing his detail dexterity at the expense of a world of productive capabilities and instincts . . . the individual himself is made the automatic motor of a fractional operation."[1] Knowledge, judgment, will, previously needed by the handicraftsman, is now required only for the factory as a whole. Intelligence expands in one direction because it vanishes in many others. "In manufacture, in order to make the collective labourer, and through him capital, rich in social productive power, each labourer must be made poor in individual productive powers", wrote Marx, quoting the Scottish philosopher-historian, Adam Ferguson: "Manufactures . . . prosper most where the mind is least consulted"—the workshop "may be considered as an engine, the parts of which are men".[2] And, also, of course, citing Adam Smith's famous passage beginning "the understandings of the greater part of men are necessarily formed by their ordinary employments", and concluding that, as a result of the division of labour, the great mass of the labouring poor must necessarily become "stupid and ignorant"—unless educational counter-measures are taken.[3] But, in a class society, these are likely to underline social differences. So the division of labour affects man not only in the productive process itself, but also, said Marx, in "every other sphere of society, and everywhere lays the foundation of that all engrossing system of specialising and sorting men, that development in a man of one single faculty at the expense of all other faculties, which caused A. Ferguson . . . to exclaim: "We make a nation of Helots, and have no free citizens."[4]

The development of modern industry based on the introduction of machinery, Marx argued, had a twofold effect. First, by technical means, it swept away the manufacturing division of labour "under which each man is bound hand and foot to a single detail-operation", but reproduced it in a "still more monstrous shape", converting the workman into "a living appendage of the machine".[5] Such work

---

[1] *Capital*, Vol. 1, 354.
[2] *Ibid.*, 356.   [3] *Ibid.*, 356.
[4] *Ibid.*, 347.   [5] *Ibid.*, 489.

"does away with the many-sided play of the muscles, and confiscates every atom of freedom, both in bodily and in intellectual activity",[1] so that it is now "deprived of all interest"—the labourer "indifferent" to his work. This separation of the intellectual powers of production from manual labour is finally completed by modern industry on the foundation of machinery.

But modern industry, said Marx, also prepares the way for overcoming the division of labour, and therefore for overcoming its constricting effect on human development. The technological basis of this industry is revolutionary—new processes, new techniques, are constantly developed which impose new functions on the workers. In essence, modern technology imposes *variation of work*, consequently "fitness of the labourer for varied work", and so "the greatest possible development of his various aptitudes". "It becomes a matter of life and death for society", wrote Marx in a famous passage, "to adapt the mode of production to the normal functioning of this law. Modern industry, indeed, compels society, under penalty of death, to replace the detail-worker of today, crippled by life-long repetition of one and the same trivial operation, and thus reduced to a mere fragment of a man, by the fully developed individual, fit for a variety of labours, ready to face any change in production, and to whom the different social functions he performs, are but so many modes of giving free scope to his own natural and acquired powers."[2]

We must leave this analysis here. Marx went on to argue the need for social ownership of the means of production, and the effect this fundamental change could have on the nature of man is a point to which he frequently returns. Marx held that the socialist mode of production would bring to an end the basic division between mental and manual labour, that it would bring all men into a direct relation, not only with each other, but with the instruments of production—which embody man's intellectual powers—and therefore provide a basis for "the development of a totality of capacities in the individuals themselves". Once man's "self-activity"—by which Marx means activity which freely derives from and develops man's natural capacities and talents—coincides with material life, the conditions exist for "the development of individuals as complete individuals and the casting off of all natural limitations".[3]

[1] *Capital*, Vol. 1, 422.
[2] *Ibid.*, 494.
[3] *The German Ideology*, 66–68.

Marx's analysis of this topic has clear educational implications. It underlies his own proposals about education to which I shall return later. But it provides a key to understanding the educational system in a class society, for if intellectual activity is *not* required by the worker in his work—that is, in his primary social function—then the education provided for him, reflecting this situation, will lack intellectual content. Theory and practice will be separated from each other in the educational system just as in society as a whole—until, that is, contemporary developments force a change.

Marx's analysis is, therefore, relevant to problems raised in contemporary discussions. For instance, one of the key problems discussed in the Crowther Report is the need to educate for adaptability at a time of rapidly changing technique; again C. P. Snow raised related questions in his Rede lecture "The Two Cultures and the Scientific Revolution". Marx, in short, offers an explanation of that one-sidedness, that "all engrossing system of specialising and sorting men" that has been so clearly reflected in the educational world—and which, it is now very concerned about. Marx finds the cause deep in the heart of society, in its economic and social structure. If, for some, this is a depressing conclusion—since it implies that no palliatives can overcome the problem although they may, of course, modify it—Marx's answer would be that, in the interests of human and social development, it were better to face the implications squarely.

(3) BASIS AND SUPERSTRUCTURE: CLASSES AND CLASS STRUGGLE

We may now turn to those aspects of Marx's thought for which he is perhaps best known, and which may be summed up under the heading "Historical Materialism". It is here that Marxism bears directly on the sociology of education.

I referred earlier to Engels' speech in which he sums up, very simply, what he called Marx's great discovery. Marx himself, in describing how he formed his own outlook in the early 1840s, mentions his investigations into legal relationships which he undertook as a result of having to deal with concrete issues as editor of the *Rheinische Zeitung*. These led him to conclude—in opposition to prevailing ideas—that, "legal relations as well as forms of state are to be grasped neither from themselves nor from the so-called general development of the human mind, but rather have their roots in the material conditions of life . . . and that the anatomy of civil society is to be sought in political economy". He then briefly formulates a general conclusion which served as a "guiding thread" for his studies:

"In the social production of their life, men enter into definite relations that are indispensable and independent of their will, relations of production which correspond to a definite stage of development of their material productive forces. The sum total of these relations of production constitute the economic structure of society, the real foundation, on which rises a legal and political superstructure and to which correspond definite forms of social consciousness. The mode of production of material life conditions the social, political and intellectual life process in general. It is not the consciousness of men that determines their being, but, on the contrary, their social being that determines their consciousness."

In an epoch of social revolution, Marx continues, resulting from a contradiction between the state of the material productive forces and the existing relations of production, there is not only a change in the economic foundation of society but with this "the entire immense superstructure is more or less rapidly transformed"—as, for instance, at the time of the French Revolution. "In considering such transformations", Marx adds:

"a distinction should always be made between the material transformation of the economic conditions of production . . . and the legal, political, religious, aesthetic, or philosophic—in short, ideological forms in which men become conscious of this conflict and fight it out. Just as our opinion of an individual is not based on what he thinks of himself, so can we not judge of such a period of transformation by its own consciousness; on the contrary, this consciousness must be explained rather from the contradictions of material life, from the existing conflict between the social productive forces and the relations of production."[1]

Marx was seeking to discover, therefore, what were the real driving forces behind the conscious motives of men which impel them to

[1] Preface to *A Contribution to the Critique of Political Economy. Marx-Engels Selected Works*, I, 328–9.

action—in other words, he sought to discover the laws of social development which govern the complex interplay of seeming accident that appears to comprise history. He found the basic force in the mode of production—and the relationships between men resulting from the particular organisation of productive activity. Where there is private ownership of the means of production, these relationships are necessarily antagonistic—so that the bourgeoisie, for instance, as it developed with the expansion of commerce and manufacture, was brought into conflict with the feudal aristocracy, while in due course the proletariat (workers) is forced to form itself into a class in its conflict with the bourgeoisie. As Engels puts it, "all historical struggles, whether they proceed on the political, religious, philosophical, or some other ideological domain, are in fact only the more or less clear expression of struggles of social classes", the existence of which, and their collisions, "are in turn conditioned by the degree of development of their economic position, by the mode of their production and of their exchange determined by it".[1]

Here we come to the concept of "ideology" and its role in economic and social struggles. The English revolution of 1640–60, for instance, appeared to its participants to a large extent as a religious conflict, but Marx saw it as basically determined by economic and social factors, the need to replace feudal social relations and break existing economic restrictions—religion was only "the ideological form in which men become conscious of the struggle and fight it out". Historians who ignore the real basis of the political and religious struggles—who interpret matters in terms of the outward form of these struggles themselves, and so accord secondary factors the determining force, merely, according to Marx, "share the *illusion of that epoch*".[2] The illusion of an epoch is its ideology, which can take on a life of its own. As Engels puts it:

"Every ideology . . . once it has arisen, develops in connection with the given concept-material, and develops this material further; otherwise it would not be an ideology, that is, occupation with thoughts as independent entities, developing independently and subject only to their own laws. That the material life conditions of the persons inside whose heads this thought process goes on in the

[1] Preface to 3rd German edition of *The Eighteenth Brumaire*, *Marx-Engels Selected Works*, I, 223–4.
[2] *The German Ideology*, 30.

last resort determine the course of this process remains of necessity unknown to these persons, for otherwise there would be an end to all ideology."[1]

The dominant ideas in every epoch, said Marx, are necessarily the ideas of the ruling class, "the class, which is the ruling material force of society, is at the same time its ruling intellectual force".[2] The existence of revolutionary ideas—for instance those of the Encyclopaedists before the French revolution—presupposes the existence of a revolutionary class.

This, briefly enough, is the Marxist concept—or model—of the relations between basis and superstructure, between ideas and institutions on the one hand, and the material conditions of life on the other. In practice this concept has often been vulgarised or mechanically applied to support a straightforward economic determinism. Was it not Marx himself who said in relation to one such example, "All I know is that I am not a Marxist"?[3] Towards the end of his life Engels, in his letters, said that Marx and himself were partly to blame for this. "We had to emphasise this main principle in opposition to our adversaries, who denied it, and we had not always the time, the place or the opportunity to allow the other elements involved in the interaction to come into their rights."[4] In fact both Marx and Engels insisted that the superstructure itself reacts back on the basis—to have seen the relationship only as a one-way process would have been to fall back into the position of Helvetius, Priestley, and Robert Owen, which I have already discussed. There is not time to go into this very complex question further, except to point out, as Engels did, that each sphere of thought, and, for that matter, each institution has, as it were, its own logical (inner) development and it is this development that is *conditioned* by changing economic circumstances. Also that the connection becomes the more complex, the more remote the particular sphere of thought, or institution, is from production itself, from the state and legal forms, and from the class struggle. These qualifications do not detract from the great force and illumination of the concept which opens up an immense field for historical and sociological investigation.

Marx did not, as I have said, apply this "model" to the interpretation

---

[1] *Ludwig Feuerbach*, 65.
[2] *The German Ideology*, 39.
[3] *Marx-Engels Selected Correspondence* (1936 ed.), 472.
[4] *Ibid.*, 477 (letter to Bloch).

of education as such, except that in many places in *Capital*, but particularly in the section on the Factory Acts, he showed how the industrial bourgeoisie was indifferent, indeed antagonistic, to the education
of working-class children from the 1830s to 1860s. However he makes
it clear enough that there is no such thing for him as "pure" education,
uncontaminated by social factors. A passage in the *Communist Manifesto*, addressed to the bourgeosie, argues that contemporary education
is socially conditioned, "determined by the social conditions under
which you educate, by the intervention, direct or indirect, of society
by means of schools, etc. The Communists", he added, "have not
invented the intervention of society in education; they do but seek to
alter the character of that intervention, and to rescue education from
the influence of the ruling class."[1]

To elaborate a little on this general approach, I would say this.
Education, as a sphere of social activity, a social institution, has its
own inner development, both as regards its theory and its practice,
and any attempt to interpret educational development at different
historical epochs, as well as today, must penetrate this and grasp its
logic. But this can only be done by recognising that education is
profoundly influenced by the social circumstances of the time and
particularly by the relations between classes, both as regards the actual
institutions set up or modified at different periods, and as regards ideas
about the purpose of education, content and methods, which reflect
the interests and outlook, or if you like the ideology, of particular
classes.

The kind of education, for instance, given in the school attached to
the great Carpenters' Hall—a Chartist institution—in Manchester
in the 1840s, or, for that matter, in the day school attached to the
Owenite Hall of Science at the same time, differed markedly from that
given in the contemporary middle-class proprietary school, such as the
Hill's school at Hazlewood. This in turn differed in every way from
the education provided in the normal church and gentry dominated
grammar school—in the matter of content, of method, of pupil-
teacher relations, and of general ethos. To interpret these differences,
to understand the significance of the sharp conflicts in the sphere of
educational theory at that time, one has first to grasp the underlying
economic structure of society, the relations of production, and in
particular the complex and changing nature of the relations between
classes.

[1] *Marx–Engels Selected Works*, I, 48.

Thus, from the standpoint of Marxism, the history of education
ceases to be the history of great men who have benevolently conferred
education on the masses from above, or of great thinkers, educators,
whose thought, derived mysteriously from their own inner selves, has
persuaded men to act in a new way—or of the history of Acts of Parliament and other administrative measures, although all these, of course,
are significant. Great thinkers have certainly had an influence—but
the problem for the Marxist historian is to discover why a particular
set of ideas arises at a particular time, and what complex of social and
intellectual conditions allows them to become influential among
particular strata of society, to the extent of being taken up and brought
into practice.

In the Commonwealth period, to take one example, we find an
extraordinary variety of the most advanced ideas on education being
put forward, but, in general, it is 150 to 200 years later before such
ideas begin to be put into practice. What were the conditions providing
a fruitful soil for these ideas in the mid-seventeenth century? How and
why did they change so rapidly after 1660 that the ideas barely survived
in an attenuated form? And what were the changes in economic
structure, in class relations, and so in ideology which led to the formulation of similar ideas among certain circles in the late eighteenth and
early nineteenth century—in Manchester for instance—and to their
eventual application?

These are not academic questions—to find an answer is to illuminate
the crucial question of the relation between education and society;
one that cannot be answered by resort to abstract thought alone or
to naïve generalisation. And if this approach is valid in relation to past
history, so also, the Marxist would claim, it is valid for today. In recognising officially, in its recent statistical tables, that there is a significant
relationship between education and social class, and indeed in deliberately bringing out this relationship, the Ministry of Education would
seem to some extent to have caught up with Karl Marx.

There can be no doubt that if Marx were now alive and wished to
analyse the nature of the educational process, its present structure and
institutions, he would start with the mode of production in society
as a whole—the nature of productive relations, and therefore of classes
and class relations, and only against this background interpret the social
role of the different types of school and of the educational process
within each type. This is to make a Marxist approach, one which takes
integral account of the fact that education functions within the social

complex, with which it is connected in innumerable ways. Any analysis which elevates education into a kind of *primum mobile*—as *the* factor which can change society—would clearly be rejected by Marx. This, of course, is not to deny that education can operate in a progressive direction and can react back on the social structure, but to say that this can only be within the conditions determined by that structure.

(4) MARX ON EDUCATION

This brings me to my final point, what Marx said about school education as such. His views on this point were not elaborated—there are only scattered references in various of his works. Thus, in applauding the action of the Paris Commune in 1870, when for a few months the working class held power for the first time in history, he wrote that the church was disestablished and disendowed, the old army and police abolished, while:

"The whole of the educational institutions were opened to the people gratuitously, and at the same time cleared of all interference of Church and State. Thus not only was education made accessible to all, but science itself freed from the fetters which class prejudice and governmental force had imposed on it." Had the Commune persisted, it would have put "Enlightenment by the schoolmaster in the place of stultification by the priest".[1]

But what of establishing education as a means to developing human powers in an all-round way? Here Marx looked to Robert Owen as the pioneer. "From the factory system budded," he writes, "as Robert Owen has shown us in detail, the germ of the education of the future, an education that will, in the case of every child over a given age, combine productive labour with instruction and gymnastics, not only as one of the methods of adding to the efficiency of production, but as the only method of producing fully developed human beings."[2] Marx, as we have seen, saw man as the product of labour on the one hand, and of science, or knowledge, on the other. The concept has clearly far-reaching educational implications. Modern industry, he wrote, through revolutionising technology, requires for its operation "fully developed individuals fit for a variety of labours". It is this con-

[1] *The Civil War in France, Marx-Engels Selected Works*, I, 471, 476.
[2] *Capital*, Vol. I, 489.

ception that he develops, if briefly, elsewhere;[1] as well as intellectual and physical education, all pupils should receive a technical education which should familiarise them with the basic principles of the processes of production as well as with the utilisation of the most common tools of production—what he calls "polytechnical teaching". What Marx had in mind was not, of course, narrow vocational training, but the acquisition by the pupil of a wide understanding of science and its application in technology—that technology which embodies man's intellectual powers and enables him to control natural forces. What he looked for was a fusion of theory and practice in education, and so mastery by the new generation of a *variety* of activities, in the exercise of which they would become "fully developed human beings".

Marx placed great emphasis on the educative effect of combining productive labour and learning; presupposing a society in which labour had become a creative activity. The 1958 school reform in the Soviet Union on the relation of school to life, which provided that every child in school after 15 should, during the next three years, do the equivalent of one year's productive work under educative control and in relation to the school, and that this work should be related to the theoretical instruction in the school, is a proposal, like others discussed to develop polytechnical teaching, deriving from Marx.[2] "There can be no doubt", wrote Marx nearly 100 years ago, "that when the working class comes to power, as inevitably it must, technical instruction, both theoretical and practical, will take its proper place in the working-class schools."[3]

A few words in conclusion. Within two decades of Marx's death an extremely widespread discussion had begun to rage—more particularly on the Continent than in this country—about the validity of his ideas, in particular those concerning historical materialism, which has gone on ever since. In 1896 Antonio Labriola, a professor at Rome University, produced a systematic exposition, and defence, of historical materialism, emphasising the unifying nature of Marx's work, the way in which it transcended the normally isolated subject divisions: "The various analytical disciplines which illustrate historical facts",

[1] Marx and Engels, *Collected Works* (Russian ed.), Vol. XIII (1936), Part I, 198–9.
[2] As were earlier attempts to develop polytechnical education in the U.S.S.R. For a full discussion of the history and theoretical background of this approach, as well as a description of present methods, see the U.N.E.S.C.O. publication *Polytechnical Education in the U.S.S.R.* (ed. Shapovalenko, 1963).
[3] *Capital*, Vol. I, 494.

he wrote, "have ended by bringing forth the need for a general social science, which will unify the different historical processes. The materialist theory is the culminating point of this unification."[1] Such a theory necessarily proved a challenge to intellectuals, particularly those concerned with the now developing field of sociology. Durkheim, Croce, Gentile, Sorel, Masaryk, Weber, Sombart, Plekhanov, Kautsky, Mehring, and later Mannheim and Lukacs—these are only a few of those who, in the field of sociology, economics, philosophy and literature, sometimes agreeing, sometimes disagreeing, developed Marx's ideas in various directions, sometimes finishing far away from Marx himself. And there was, of course, Lenin, who in 1894 argued that with his "hypothesis"—which I quoted earlier from the Preface to the *Critique of Political Economy*—Marx "was the first to elevate sociology to the level of a science".[2] Lenin himself developed Marx's teaching in a rather different way from academic sociologists for whom sociology was primarily on analytical and interpretative activity. If there has been a considerable development of Marxist studies in this country, it has not been in the sociological field—until comparatively recently—but rather in allied fields; we might mention George Thomson's work on classical antiquity, Frederick Antal on the history of art, Arnold Kettle on literature, Eric Hobsbawm, Christopher Hill and Maurice Dobb on social and economic history.

I have tried to say something of the significance of Marx's outlook for the study of education, and of the psychology and sociology of education. I hope I have indicated that Marx can hardly be dismissed as an arid thinker, concerned only with economic categories to the exclusion of humanity, as he is occasionally presented; that on the contrary humanity, and the full development of human powers, which is fundamentally the subject matter of education, was from the first his main concern. "If man draws all his knowledge, sensation, etc., from the world of the senses", he wrote as a young man, summarising the outlook of the English and French materialists, "the empirical world must be arranged so that in it man experiences and gets used to what is really human and that he becomes aware of himself as man ... If man is shaped by his surroundings, his surroundings must be made human. If man is social by nature, he will develop his true nature only in society."[3] Whether or not we agree with the conclusions

---

[1] Antonio Labriola, *Essays on the Materialistic Conception of History* (1908).

[2] "*What the 'Friends of the People' are*", Lenin, *Selected Works* (1947), I, 82.

[3] *The Holy Family* (1957 ed.), 176.

to which Marx eventually came it must, I think, be conceded that he attempted to find the means whereby man could come to a full humanity, and in so doing evolved a theoretical approach which is both intellectually stimulating and very relevant to study of the theory and practice of education.

CLASSIFICATION AND STREAMING
A STUDY OF GROUPING IN ENGLISH SCHOOLS, 1860–1960[1]

The system of grouping children in schools, known as "streaming", is a phenomenon of considerable interest and importance. This method, as it developed in England after World War I, involved dividing children of a given age group into parallel classes on the basis of scholastic attainment supplemented by tests of "intelligence", which were taken to indicate educable capacity. Subsequently it became a general practice to divide pupils into A, B, and C classes in secondary schools according to their performance in the selection examination taken at the age of ten or eleven, which usually, at least from 1944, comprised objective tests in English, arithmetic, and intelligence; children in primary schools were correspondingly divided according to estimated performance in these tests, by which they would later be allocated to secondary schools. The objective was to form homogeneous teaching groups composed of children of the same age and roughly the same level of intelligence and attainment in the basic subjects so that teaching could proceed at varying rates in the parallel classes, in each case, at that rate and with that content appropriate to the level and capacity of the class as a whole.

This form of organisation, apparently unique to England as a "system" generally utilised in all schools, persisted more or less unchallenged for approximately three decades—from 1926 to 1956. In its classic form, this system determined the structure not only of primary schools large enough to admit of parallel forms but also of all types of post-primary or secondary schools, so that from the age of seven, and often earlier, each child was allocated to a particular stream that determined his place both within the individual school and in the school system as a whole throughout his school career, even if a small minority were transferred across the streams. Only in the mid-1950s was there serious questioning in some quarters, resulting in a tendency to break away

[1] Written in 1967 for the symposium *History and Education*, ed. Paul Nash, New York 1970.

from this pattern and find alternative methods of grouping based on new criteria.

The rise and decline of streaming is, therefore, an appropriate topic for an historical assessment, with the characteristics of a case study. Here is a particular, well-defined practice, which comes into being at a certain time, spreads and is consolidated, and later begins to die away. Behind it lie equally well-defined theories derived from psychology. To study this case, then, should throw light on the relation between theory and practice in education as well as on the relation between educational theory and changing social and economic conditions. Why, for instance, were the particular psychological theories that underpinned streaming—theories that postulated the fixed and determined nature of intelligence (and the possibility of measuring it accurately and reliably)—so unquestioningly accepted during these years? Why was the practice of streaming itself so widely welcomed by educationists? What conditions were necessary before the viability both of this theory and of this practice could be called into question? These are topics of interest not only to the history of ideas but to social history. For these ideas both arose from and were applied to the educational system with results that bore directly on the crucial question of human potentiality and its realisation. It was their wide practical application that gave these ideas social significance.

A study of this topic faces certain difficulties. So far as I am aware there are no monographs on the evolution of the internal organisation of the schools; and the necessary materials for a thorough investigation are widely scattered. But it is possible to sketch the structure of the schools at the outset of the period and trace the direction of development in response to various pressures, in an attempt to clarify the course of changes, their nature and outcome.

The pre-history of streaming

The first method of internal school organisation imposed nationally on the elementary schools by the central authority arose directly from the school grant system known as "payment by results", brought in by the Revised Code of Regulations of 1862. The imposition of this system was one aspect of the overall reconstruction of education in the period 1850 to 1870, when a series of royal commissions conducted detailed investigations of the universities, the "public" schools, the endowed grammar schools, and the elementary schools, and proposed changes, many of which were implemented by acts of Parliament.[1] This large-scale intervention by the state was directed to reforming the nation's educational institutions into an effective *system* of education. In accordance with the outlook of the Victorian age, and to meet specific social pressures, the public schools were remodelled to provide an appropriate education for the upper middle class in a semi-independent system, whereas the smaller endowed grammar schools were adapted to cater for three distinct sections of the middle and lower middle classes. Finally the state began to intervene more directly and decisively in the conduct of elementary schools designed for the working class.

In the stratified system that emerged, the elementary schools formed the broad base, though the model of a pyramid is unsuitable in that they were virtually isolated from the rest of the system. Most of the schools were, before 1870, provided and largely controlled by "voluntary" bodies—notably, however, by the Anglican Church—though the funds essential to their establishment and running were provided in considerable measure by grants of public money, available in increasing amounts from 1833. Because of the preponderating influence of the Anglican Church, and within this of High Church views, there was strong nonconformist opposition to the extension of state control on the pattern common in other European countries, since this implied consolidation of the influence of the established church. As a result, state intervention took the form of administrative measures—based on the power of the state as a source of finance—that gradually extended in scope; and here the introduction of the revised code can be seen as a decisive step.

Regular inspection of elementary schools together with control of the subjects examined (and so of the whole curriculum) now ensured that the schools functioned in accordance with a specific policy as laid down by the Education Department. If the religious (or social-disciplinary) function had been, and remained, of primary importance to the bodies managing schools, the government was also concerned to improve the inculcation of elementary skills. At this time there was no ladder linking the elementary schools to the endowed grammar schools providing secondary instruction and, therefore, no basis for introducing differentiation within the elementary schools to allow for promotion of some of their pupils. The prime purpose of these schools was mass instruction at an elementary level; the revised

[1] Brian Simon, *Studies in the History of Education, 1780–1870* (1960), pp. 277–336.

code spelled out the means by which this objective could be secured within the limits of the resources made available.

The main features of the code are well known. The level of attainment in the basic subjects to be reached at the end of each year was precisely defined and embodied in six (later seven) standards. No child could be presented a second time in the same grade, so each child had to work through the standards, being subjected to an annual examination. The amount of grant awarded to each school depended on the number of children who passed the examination in each of the subjects (reading, writing, and arithmetic). Originally two shillings and eight pence was awarded for each "pass".[1] The individual examination of every child in schools in receipt of grants involved a massive, nationwide operation by the inspectors (Her Majesty's Inspectors or the H.M.I.s) and their assistants in the course of which a definite form of organisation was imposed on the elementary schools. Inevitably, wherever it was possible, classes were organised according to the standards with the aim of promoting all children annually, so that classes became known as Standard 1, Standard 2, and so forth. This approach, appropriate to a system of mass education with severely limited objectives, brought into being what the Board of Education later described as a "rigid system of annual promotion" resting on a rigidly defined programme; the outcome was presentation of "one set 'quantum' as the exclusive possession of each 'standard' to be completed by all its members in the year—no more and no less".[2]

This remained the basic framework of school organisation, despite some modifications after the passing of the Elementary Education Act of 1870. Indeed the pattern continued long after "payment by results" had been formally brought to an end in the 1890s. A Manchester school in which the present writer taught in the late 1940s—an unreorganised all-age school for children aged five to fourteen—was still organised then on the "standard" system by age groups, with one class for each standard.

The passing of the 1870 Act and the advent of the school boards subject to local election and concerned to provide viable local systems of board schools did, however, materially change the climate in which elementary schools operated. The new schools provided were seen as

[1] The total grant awarded to each school depended also on the number of pupils making a given number of attendances each year.
[2] Board of Education, *Suggestions for the Consideration of Teachers and Others Concerned in the Work of Public Elementary Schools*, 1923 ed. (H.M.S.O., 1923), pp. 12–13.

a local possession; there was a new interest in their efficiency and a tendency to outgrow the elementary limits, particularly in the larger towns where higher grade schools were established.

In the 1870s and 1880s some teachers began to press for a degree of flexibility in the classification of pupils; and this trend was accelerated by a new factor that began to affect the elementary schools for the first time—the opportunity for promoting a few of the ablest pupils into a higher range of the system. In 1889 the Technical Instruction Act permitted school boards to establish a scholarship system from the elementary to what was known as "higher" or "technical" education—a category that then included grammar schools.

There naturally followed increased pressure from teachers, parents, and the school authorities to allow for more rapid promotion of the quicker pupils who wished to enter for the scholarship examination, usually taken between the ages of ten and twelve. This process of freeing the system from its original rigidity may be traced in successive issues of the code: "the objects of the alterations made in recent Codes", states a revised introduction to that of 1896, "have been . . . to give freedom of classification according to the attainments, abilities and opportunities of the scholars". There is evidence (in school log books) that by about 1900 advanced classes were being established in some schools specifically to cater for pupils preparing not only for the scholarship examination, but also for entry to pupil-teacher centres, which provided a secondary type of education for intending teachers in elementary schools.[1]

Moves in this direction were strongly reinforced by the Education Act of 1902. This, as is well known, abolished the school boards and cut back the development of an end-on system of secondary education, which was becoming established, if in embryo form, as a result of the foundation of the higher grade schools. Instead, the Act laid the basis for the establishment of a system of secondary schools separate from and (particularly as many had junior departments) parallel to the elementary schools; these schools charged fees and catered, as has already been noted, for a different social class, though a tenuous scholarship system allowing entry of a few pupils from elementary schools existed in most areas.

[1] For instance, the log book of Holycroft school, a large board school in Keighley, Yorks, records the establishment, at the instance of the school board, of an advanced class of this kind in January 1901, only three months after the school had been reorganized from the standard system to a class system involving the rearrangement of children every six months. (Information from Mr. G. F. Gibson.)

With this development the elementary schools were officially accorded a new function, first clearly defined in the prefatory note to the code of regulations issued in 1904—one of a series drafted by Robert Morant at this time, covering all aspects of education and defining the relations and objectives of different types of school in the new circumstances. Although the main function of the elementary school was to provide the entire day-school education for the mass of the children, an important subsidiary function was now "to discover individual children who show promise of exceptional capacity and to develop their special gifts . . . so that they may be qualified to pass at the proper age into secondary schools".[1]

To stress this latter function was to present the elementary school as a pool from which able pupils could be drawn in specific numbers, as determined by the scholarships available. More local authorities subsequently provided scholarships or "free places"; and in 1907, the Liberal government, encouraged by pressure from the newly formed Labour Party, which had won some fifty seats in Parliament, brought in the free-place regulations. Under these, any secondary school in receipt of grant (whether a former grammar school or a new local-authority school) must offer 25 per cent of its places free to pupils from public elementary schools. Although the free-place system was not officially intended to promote competitive entry, the scholarship bridge from the elementary to the secondary school was now firmly established.

There was to be strong pressure to broaden these opportunities after the war of 1914-1918, which, like other major conflicts, focused attention on education in a new way. Meanwhile, from 1905, some of the larger urban authorities, notably London and Manchester, made up for the lack of places in secondary schools by establishing central schools for a selective entry of pupils prepared to stay in school to fourteen or fifteen. These, in sharp contrast to the full secondary schools, which the board of education was firmly guiding into an academic course, had a bias towards industrial pursuits. Even more so had the junior technical (or trade) schools, also established from 1905, which provided a two-year course for ex-elementary pupils intending to take up apprenticeships and which recruited at thirteen.

With the development of opportunities to continue education in other schools (pupils could not stay in elementary schools beyond the age of fourteen) it seemed more than ever necessary to promote

[1] Brian Simon, *Education and the Labour Movement, 1870–1920* (1965), p. 240.

children of exceptional capacity rapidly so that they were prepared for the scholarship examination while they were still young enough to take it. To facilitate this, large schools containing ten or more classes now evolved a system of biannual and sometimes even triannual promotions; this sometimes involved establishing intermediate classes and arranging for some overlap in the curriculum to allow those who were rapidly promoted to catch up with their new class. Organisation on these lines was first officially proposed in the 1918 edition of the *Suggestions for Teachers and Others Concerned in the Work of Elementary Schools*. It was first issued in 1905, when there was a clear move from revised-code rigidity to more flexible patterns. Successive editions of this publication provide a useful index of adaptations of official policy; and it is noticeable that in 1918 a new section headed "Organisation and Classification" appeared for the first time.[1] After criticising "the rigid system of annual promotion which was the natural accompaniment of the old annual examination", it argued that children should be allowed "to progress through the school at varying rates, suited to their individual capacity".[2]

That this was already happening is clear, and the change of emphasis gradually became pronounced. The process is well summed up in a later edition of the *Handbook of Suggestions for Teachers* (1937), which notes that, with the disappearance of the old examination system, "teachers found it possible to take individual ability more and more into account in the promotion of children from one class to another. In consequence the custom spread throughout the country of pushing the brighter children ahead as they mastered their lessons, so that they might work with the highest classes while they were still eligible by age to enter for competitive examinations, e.g. those of the "junior scholarship' type". It should also be noted that, from 1918, emphasis was put on the need to establish a special class for backward children, so that these were not left permanently in one standard "condemned to repeat the same work year by year".[3]

---

[1] The 1905 edition contained only a very rudimentary section on organisation, stating that "The organisation of a school is good if scholars are properly distributed in accordance with their attainments and capacities" (pp. 17–18), a statement that was regarded as sufficient guidance until 1918. The handbook was issued by the Board of Education in various editions and with slightly modified titles until the 1927 edition, which appeared as the *Handbook of Suggestions for the Consideration of Teachers and Others Concerned in the Work of the Public Elementary Schools*.

[2] Board of Education, *Suggestions for the Consideration of Teachers and Others Concerned in the Work of Public Elementary Schools*, 1918 ed. (H.M.S.O., 1918), p. 12.

[3] *Ibid.*, 1923 ed., p. 14.

What the new flexible methods meant in practice was brought out in a survey undertaken in 1917 by Cyril Burt, educational psychologist to the London County Council. He found that in the schools of a London borough Standards 4 and 5 (theoretically for ten- and eleven-year-olds) "remain the most heterogeneous in age". In the schools surveyed, both these standards contained pupils ranging in age from eight to fourteen. "The oldest at this level", writes Burt, "are not backward enough for a special school; the youngest are too young for a [selective] central school."

To his report, Burt added an appendix entitled "Ideal classification of children according to educational ability at each age". He does not recommend the system later known as streaming (at this time it was still the general practice, where schools were large enough, to separate boys and girls and provide parallel classes for each sex); he does, however, propose that something should be done about Standards 4 and 5. "To avoid the difficulties of mixing children of eight with those of fourteen", he writes, "it would be desirable to duplicate one—preferably the lower—of these standards", if an extra class can be provided "and there is no need for it elsewhere, this seems the most advantageous point". The basic concept of homogeneity (in relation to ability as well as age) is already in evidence here. "In a well-organised school", writes Burt, "the various classes should be, and are, fairly homogeneous as regards general educational ability."[1]

This formulation reflects a new stage of generalisation. The conception of the elementary school as a pool from which exceptional children were to be drawn for the separate system of secondary education, advanced in 1904, had taken shape in practice and had had its effect. Superimposed on the former system of basic standards, it had resulted in a very wide age range in the middle classes of large schools, which at this time usually contained some fifty or sixty children; these now embodied a crude form of attainment classification across several age-groups. It was the need to find some solution to this new problem that prompted new proposals for class organisation. These proposals were made at a time when knowledge of the effect of social and family conditions in causing backwardness or maladjustment was limited and in the light of ideas then prevalent about the direct dependence of attainment and abilities on innate factors in children's minds. In sum, practical exigencies of mass education, the general development of a

[1] C. Burt, *The Distribution and Relations of Educational Abilities* (London County Council, 1917), Appendix 2.

selective secondary system with competitive entry, together with psychological theories about individual differences, all now pointed to the new concept of homogeneity according to ability and age as the basic principle of grouping children in classes. Such was the situation on the eve of World War I. This constitutes, as it were, the prehistory of streaming by ability in English schools.

Progressive differentiation—the Hadow report

The "Great War" of 1914–1918, together with the Education Act (1918), brought new factors into play. The question of access to secondary education became a political issue of considerable importance in the immediate postwar years. In 1922 the Labour Party published a policy statement, *Secondary Education for All*, drafted by R. H. Tawney—perhaps the most effective educational manifesto ever produced in Britain. This spelled out in detail the labour movement's traditional demand for wider educational opportunity for working-class children, while also broadening the conception of secondary education. Tawney was strongly opposed to the selective central school within the elementary system and advocated instead a variety of full secondary schools supplementing the academic grammar school type fostered by the board. The publication of this closely argued manifesto marked the culmination of years of agitation by the labour movement which, in 1902, had strongly opposed the establishment of a separate system of secondary schools lacking any organic connection with the elementary system.

There were also new expectations in wider fields in the postwar years. During the war the number of pupils at secondary schools had increased rapidly; by its close the demand for places far outran the supply. In 1913 there had been 54,141 entrants; in 1919 there were 81,357. New buildings were not available, so that schools were overcrowded and classes increased in size; but, in spite of the increase in numbers, in most places demand was unsatisfied. At this time most authorities ran a qualifying examination for secondary education, so that all pupils who reached a certain standard passed—a logical enough procedure but one shortly to be superseded. In 1919, some 18,000 children who had qualified and wished to attend secondary schools were excluded—9,271 because of lack of accommodation, a further 8,780 because there were no free places available.[1] The issue was

[1] Board of Education, *Report of the Department Committee on Scholarships and Free Places* (H.M.S.O., 1920), Appendix I, Table D.

sharpened by the fact that some 66 per cent of the places available at secondary schools were taken up by fee payers for whom, at this stage, there was normally no effective entrance test.

In 1919 a departmental committee was set up by the board of education, including members of all political parties, to examine the whole position in regard to scholarships and free places—a step taken with some trepidation.[1] In its report the following year this committee proposed that, ideally, 75 per cent. of the nation's children should have some form of secondary education. The key clause of the Act of 1918, which the committee took as defining its task, stated that "adequate provision shall be made in order to secure that children and young persons shall not be debarred from receiving the benefits of any form of education by which they are capable of profiting through inability to pay fees" (Section 4 [4]). This clause, the committee noted, would effect a revolution and bring "a new order", because it introduced a new principle. It followed from this that provision for secondary education "can no longer be based on a limited percentage of free places, but should be based on the number of children 'capable of profiting' ". In view of postwar economic stringencies, however, the committee held that the immediate target should be to increase the proportion of free places in secondary schools from 25 per cent to 40 per cent. Some kind of formal test was necessary to determine transfer, one that would test "capacity and promise rather than attainments".[2]

Clearly there was a danger that the floodgates would be opened and it is not surprising to find the Board of Education concentrating attention, from this moment, on the development of tests to determine

[1] "Of course," minuted Selby-Bigge (permanent secretary to the Board of Education) agreeing to the proposal, "there is a danger that the Labour Party may take the opportunity to renew their demand for Secondary Education and for wholesale maintenance, involving the state in an expenditure to which it would be hard to put any limit." There should be a "pretty strong" committee. (June 18th, 1919.) Board of Education private office papers in the Public Record Office, Ed. 24/1187.

[2] *Report of the Departmental Committee on Scholarship and Free Places, op. cit.*, p. 8. It is interesting to note that four members of the committee registered a profound objection to the proposal that all children should take the proposed transfer examination, characterizing it as "a blunder of the first magnitude"; they agreed there was a need for a competitive test, due to the "very inadequate provision of various types of schools", but proposed that this should be done by an internal assessment. They stressed the cramping, distorting effect of an external examination, and argued that, having recently got rid of this system, it should not now be reintroduced in this form. The signatories were E. R. Conway, F. W. Goldstone, R. F. Cholmeley, and R. Richardson; the first three represented teachers; Richardson was a member of the Durham Education Committee and of the Labour Party.

the capacity of eleven-year-olds—a system of examination that could consolidate the widely varying scholarship examinations run by local authorities. The relevant files of departmental papers make it clear that this was seen by the board's officials as an essential element in the new equilibrium it was hoped would be established in the 1920s. Selby-Bigge, the chief official, commenting on his embarrassment at finding how many secondary-school pupils were under eleven (middle-class fee payers), minuted in January 1922: "Broadly speaking we have got to work on the principle that as there are not enough places to go round, selection to fill them must be on merit and by competition." The local authority examinations, he added, are unsatisfactory, the inspectors (H.M.I.'s) "have got a very big piece of work in front of them to get them on better lines . . . I certainly think that unless the school authorities make a conscientious effort to prefer for admission those children who are likely to profit most by a secondary school education, they and we will be in a position difficult to defend." Tests for fee payers were also necessary.[1]

In the outcome, the Board of Education and inspectors devoted a great deal of attention to methods of selection, advising local authorities by circular and pamphlet, reviewing their examinations, and proposing improvements, while also carrying out their own enquiries.[2] In 1920 the Consultative Committee to the Board of Education was asked to advise on the use of psychological tests of "educable capacity", which the Departmental Committee on Scholarships and Free Places had suggested "would constitute the best method if they could be applied easily and give trustworthy results".[3] It is clear enough that, given the structure of the school system and the pressures to which it was now subject, the development of eleven-plus selection along the lines it eventually took (comprising objective tests in English, arithmetic, and intelligence) was inevitable, even if it was many years before this pattern became general. Meanwhile, the establishment of a more streamlined scholarship examination was bound to affect profoundly the elementary schools, promoting further differentiation within these to prepare pupils for what inevitably became a highly

---

[1] Public Record Office, Ed. 12/348.

[2] For instance, Pamphlet No. 63, entitled *Examinations for Scholarships and Free Places in Secondary Schools* (1928), contained a review of seventy-five local authority examinations.

[3] *Report of the Departmental Committee on Scholarships and Free Places, op. cit.*, p. 21. Such tests were first used in the Junior Scholarship examination at Bradford (in 1919) and Northumberland (from 1921).

competitive system of entry. It was, it may be noted, on the selection of under 4 per cent of elementary school pupils for free places that attention was concentrated, because there was little material expansion of secondary schools. Consequently the answer to increased parental, or political, pressure was an attempt to perfect selection procedure and defend it as equitable.

It is interesting to note that, besides the four dissentients to the departmental committee's recommendation about this examination (see 2, p. 209), there were others who objected to the course taken. An article in *The Times* in November 1919 declared that the scholarship system was a "a mere lottery", an educational sieve leaving behind a helot class. It was impossible with justice to attempt to differentiate children before the age of eleven. The article condemned earlier preliminary selection within the elementary school by forming scholar-ship classes or grades for the purpose of competition at eleven and argued strongly that "a secondary school for all up to the age of fifteen is an easier suggestion than that a handful should be chosen for the coveted prizes". The draft circular on admission to secondary schools was also critically received by some of the heads of schools and administrators to whom it was sent for comment. "I hope, for my part", wrote the head of Colston Girls School, Bristol, "that I shall never be head of a school consisting only of clever or even of promising children, for it takes all sorts to make a happy school, and the apparent failures so often leaven the lump while they are there and so greatly reward us after they have left"; the circular "leaves human sentiment out of account by treating it exclusively from the point of view of intellectual efficiency". A similar point of view was expressed by Salter Davies, the distinguished Director of Education for Kent.[1]

All this prepared the way for streaming by ability as between and within schools. But this form of grouping did not appear as inevitable until other administrative changes had been introduced in the school system. These, however, were also under way in the early 1920s.

The Education Act of 1918, which brought all children up to the age of fourteen into school full time, included a clause placing on local authorities the duty of providing "adequate and suitable provision by means of central schools, central or special classes, or otherwise" for courses of advanced instruction "for the older and more intelligent children" attending elementary schools, including those staying on beyond the age of fourteen. It must be remembered that the typical

[1] Public Record Office, Ed. 12/348.

elementary school at this time was an all-age school (five to fourteen), often with only one class in each of the top standards. In the larger cities, however, schools were organised in three departments, an infant school for those up to seven (or sometimes nine) and two senior departments, one for boys and one for girls, for the older children. The number of pupils in each class appears originally to have been the decisive factor in determining the overall size of the school or department. Senior departments normally had about 350 pupils (with entry at seven this gave seven classes of fifty pupils each, one for each standard). In this situation there was no possibility of specialist teaching, nor, given the large classes, of meeting the needs and interests of individual children. In their development plan of 1920, for instance, the London County Council proposed building new secondary schools and extending their selective central schools (from 50 to 100), but state clearly that it is the 80 per cent of children who do not go at eleven to secondary or central schools "who present the greatest difficulties"; nevertheless for these the plan makes no important suggestions. "In regard to the ordinary elementary schools", runs the report, "the problem confronting the Council is to introduce new methods for teaching the great mass of children of eleven to fourteen and over, who are not considered suitable for transfer to secondary and central schools, and who remain behind in the ordinary elementary schools."[1]

The adaptation of methods of teaching was hardly a solution of a long-recognised social problem. The alienation of the older children in elementary schools, the need to make their education more purposive in relation to future employment, had often been emphasised before the war.[2] New approaches might do something to overcome this but a new organisational form would give greater scope. "It is now generally recognised", stated the London County Council in its 1920 scheme, "that in elementary education there are three distinct phases, the first covering the period of a child's life from five to seven, the second from seven to eleven, and the third from eleven to fourteen plus, or even fifteen plus where the parents desire to retain their

---

[1] London County Council, *Education Act*, 1918. *Draft Scheme of the Local Authority* (London County Council, 1920), p. 64.

[2] Many official committees before and during the war had commented on the "individual demoralisation and social wastage", as the Hadow Committee later put it, following on the completion of elementary school life. These included the Report of the Consultative Committee on Continuation Schools (1909), the Majority and Minority Reports of the Poor Law Commission (1909), and others. Report of the Consultative Committee to the Board of Education, *The Education of the Adolescent* (H.M.S.O., 1926), pp. 41–42.

children to this later age".[1] If London did not yet see its way to an overall reorganisation, having already concentrated a minority of children in selective central schools, a few other urban authorities were finding a solution involving a shift to a new school for all the pupils at eleven—to nonselective as well as to selective central schools.

One of the most advanced urban authorities at this time was the city of Leicester, which, under an energetic director, had by 1923 reorganised most of its elementary schools into separate primary and post-primary schools on this basis, provoking, in the course, a considerable outcry from parents.[2] The city was divided into five districts, in each of which was established a central (in this case called intermediate) school with selective entry and two or more senior schools. All these, in parallel with the city's secondary schools, recruited at eleven and separated boys from girls, though in the senior schools the two sexes often shared a building—even in some cases, the same floor of one of the large board schools erected in the 1890s. This reorganisation was achieved simply by shifting the children around, utilising existing buildings. Variants of this scheme were introduced in a number of city and county areas—for instance, Carnarvonshire, Rutland, Bradford—most of which involved a break at eleven, even if, as at Leeds, the "advanced instruction planned was to take place in senior departments of elementary schools, rather than in a separate school". By 1925 some 5 per cent of the pupils over eleven in elementary schools were in reorganised senior departments.[3]

To the Board of Education, concerned with containing the demand for secondary education for all, reorganisation of elementary schools along these lines seemed a desirable development. Already in 1923, in discussing the new brief to the Consultative Committee, which resulted in the Hadow Report, Selby-Bigge had made it clear to a deputation of its leading members that proposals to introduce secondary education for all would be out of the question. "If, however," he added, "the deputation felt that the path of salvation for the majority of children lay through advanced elementary rather than secondary education (properly so called) he was at one with them." To this an influential member of the committee, Alderman Jackson, added that an enquiry by the Consultative Committee into advanced elementary education "would be useful in dispelling the Socialist and

---

[1] *Education Act*, 1918. *Draft Scheme of the Local Authority, loc. cit.*
[2] M. Seaborne, *Recent Education from Local Sources* (1967), p. 76.
[3] *The Education of the Adolescent, op. cit.*, Table III, p. 283.

Labour war-cry of 'Secondary Education for All' ", and that it was "important to dispel that notion if possible before the Labour Party came into power".[1]

In January, 1925, the board issued Circular 1350, presenting this pattern as official policy to which all new building must henceforward conform. The age of eleven was described as "the most suitable dividing line between what may be called 'junior' and 'senior' education", and, it was stated, the board would in future find it difficult to approve school planning that "fails to make provision for advanced instruction of children over the age of eleven, by giving opportunities for suitable classification and organisation".[2]

This last proviso is noteworthy. By "suitable classification" at this stage the board almost certainly meant some form of streaming within the individual departments. In Leicester, the senior schools, both boys' and girls', were already organised on the basis of three parallel forms with differentiated curricula.[3] Indeed there is evidence that streaming was also developing in the embryo junior departments in areas where reorganisation had already taken place. As we have seen, the conditions had been maturing for this development since 1907, and reorganisation provided a new spur.

The report of the Consultative Committee in 1926 (the Hadow Report) marks the crucial turning point in this development. This committee was asked to report on "the organisation, objectives and curriculum of courses of study" for children remaining at school "other than secondary schools" up to the age of fifteen. The express exclusion of the secondary schools, it may be noted, reflected the long-standing official policy of maintaining the division between secondary and elementary education.[4]

The committee's main proposal, that elementary education should be divided into two stages, primary and postprimary, with a break at

---

[1] The records of this discussion are to be found in the Public Record Office, Ed. 24/1224.

[2] Board of Education, "The Organisation of Public Elementary Schools", Circular 1350 (January 1925).

[3] Seaborne, op. cit., pp. 74–79.

[4] The terms of reference were worked out by the Board of Education under the Conservative administration of 1923–1924. They were accepted by Charles Trevelyan, the incoming president of the Board of Education in the Labour government of 1924–1925 and transmitted with his approval to the Consultative Committee. (Public Record Office, Ed. 24/1224.) The Hadow Committee in fact recommended that all postprimary education should be regarded as secondary, but did not outline the administrative and legislative measures necessary to bring this about.

eleven (on the lines already adopted by some authorities and approved by the board), was accepted by successive governments; this set the seal of official approval on the essential step necessary for the more precise classification of children of all ages. The Hadow Report, wrote Selby-Bigge after his retirement, "has been hailed as heralding a new era and a revolution in English education. For purposes of practical reform it endorsed the Board's policy of transferring all the senior children in elementary schools at the age of eleven plus to schools or departments organised specifically as senior schools".[1]

Selby-Bigge spoke as an administrator; and this recommendation, it is now clear, was virtually inescapable on administrative grounds. The age of eleven had already become the main age of transfer not only to secondary schools but also to senior schools, whose pupils rarely remained in school after fourteen; only in this way could a viable three-year course be provided (in fact for many pupils the course lasted under three years). Nevertheless the committee grounded its proposal in large part on evidence received from psychologists, whose advice is summarised as follows:

> Educational organisation is likely to be effective in proportion as it is based on the actual facts of the development of children and young persons. By the time that the age of eleven or twelve has been reached children have given some indication of differences in interest and abilities sufficient to make it possible and desirable to cater for them by means of schools of varying types, but which have, nevertheless, a broad common foundation.[2]

This evidence provided the necessary bridge to presenting the age of eleven as an educationally vital turning point. If all children were to be adequately provided for, postprimary schools must be differentiated in type—parallel to the full secondary school (excluded from examination or reconsideration), there should be three or four different types of postprimary school; indeed the whole educational process must be seen as one of progressive differentiation whereby each child receives that kind of education fitted to his individual needs and abilities. As schools should be differentiated, so also should classes within schools. From the standpoint of internal organisation the key aspect of Hadow

[1] L. A. Selby-Bigge, "Raising the School Leaving Age", *The Nineteenth Century* (November 1929), p. 614.
[2] *The Education of the Adolescent, op. cit.*, p. 74.

"reorganisation"—as it came to be called—was that both primary and postprimary schools could now be established large enough to allow for two, three, or four parallel classes in each year; as we shall see, this became the key factor in determining the size and design of schools.

Intelligence testing and classification

We may now turn to the theoretical aspect, in the first place to the psychological ideas that lay behind the expert advice given to the Hadow Committee. This is no place to outline the development of the psychology of individual differences in general and psychometry in particular; but it may be noted that the vast testing programme under-taken in the United States Army in 1918 gave currency to a new confidence in testing intelligence on a mass scale—the kind of testing that was to become a directive feature of the English educational system.

In the early years of the century it was generally held that intelligence, as measured by tests of widely varying kinds, was innate; and nowhere was there a more favourable climate for acceptance of this view than in England, with its particular social structure still incorporating a considerable hereditary element. More specifically, the work of Francis Galton had had considerable influence in shaping the outlook of psychologists. In the educational field, moves towards a more scientific methodology and approach in the 1890s, together with the popularity of Froebelian ideas about the need to provide for the natural, spontaneous development of the child's inner powers, favoured the acceptance of what appeared to be the most scientific psychological findings about the child mind. Leading educationists such as John Adams and Percy Nunn popularised the whole subject, while P. B. Ballard was an effective propagandist for scientific mental measurement and a corresponding organisation as opposed to subjective judgments and muddling through.[1] Within the school system, as has been seen, the need to select children at eleven for free places in secondary schools —preferably according to promise rather than present performance— stimulated the search for objective tests of capacity. It was within this

[1] T. Percy Nunn, *Education: Its Data and First Principles* (1920), Chap. 9; John Adams, *Modern Developments in Educational Practice* (1922), Chap. 3; P. B. Ballard, *Mental Tests* (1920) and *Group Tests of Intelligence* (1922). These books were reprinted many times. For the background of this movement see R. J. W. Selleck, "The Scientific Educationist, 1870–1914", *British Journal of Educational Studies*, XV, 2 (June 1967), and the same author's *The New Education* (1968).

general framework that testing was increasingly used in schools, closely influenced by, as well as influencing, the actual structure and development of the school system.

The idea that capacity, rather than attainment, could be measured by tests was first clearly canvassed in the report of the Consultative Committee entitled *Tests of Educable Capacity* (1924). This report, in fact drawn up by a subcommittee including leading psychologists,[1] followed that of the Departmental Committee of 1920, which had advocated tests on these lines to select for secondary education. At this stage psychologists were reasonably chary of making claims. But the belief that ability was inborn and capable of accurate measurement lay at the heart of the Hadow proposals for progressive differentiation. It was apparently Percy Nunn, himself imbued with this belief, who— though not a member of the committee—played the major part in drafting the relevant sections of the report.[2]

The Hadow Committee, it may be recalled, advocated four different grades of postprimary school for those over eleven, on the grounds that such increasing differentiation met children's needs: the full secondary school, the selective central school, the nonselective central or senior school, and senior classes in elementary schools for the children "somewhat slower and more backward than their fellows". This was to provide the conditions for the general introduction of streaming throughout the school system; but it should be stressed that the committee did not itself recommend this course. The long sections of the report on the content of education in senior schools do not propose any differentiation *within* the school. In fact there are only three references to streaming in the whole report, and these are incidental or oblique. At one point it is pointed out, incidentally, that the separate junior schools resulting from reorganisation will be considerably larger than former departments, allowing "better grading" as well as larger classes—"with proper grading, it is possible to arrange that larger classes are taken by fewer teachers";[3] this, despite the emphasis on meeting individual needs, was evidently seen as one of the chief administrative (and practical) advantages of homogeneous teaching groups. At another point the committee refers to experience in Carnarvon where, by concentrating the two top standards from

---

[1] C. E. Spearman, C. S. Myers, and P. B. Ballard.

[2] C. Burt, "The Examination at Eleven Plus", *British Journal of Educational Studies*, VII, 2 (May 1959), 100. Nunn was co-opted as a member of the drafting committee.

[3] *The Education of the Adolescent, op. cit.*, p. 56.

various schools together "it is not only possible to provide a teacher for each standard, but to subdivide each standard according to the ability and attainments of groups of individual pupils". Finally, it is noted, in areas where only one type of postprimary school (in addition to secondary schools) can be established, "the necessary discrimination between pupils of different degrees of ability will require to be made . . . by a system of parallel forms".[1]

It is all the more interesting to find, only two years later, the board of education throwing its whole weight behind the system of streaming. In pamphlet number 60 (1928), which is specifically concerned with problems of organisation, the need for differentiation *within* the new senior schools is heavily stressed. "The success of the nonselective senior school . . . is, of course, dependent on our ability first to concentrate and then to classify the children." The organisational issue "is that of the adaptation of the existing elementary school system so that the older children, and not a selected few, may receive an education suited to their age and special needs, practical in the broadest sense, and so organised as to allow for classification and differentiation between pupils of different types of capacity and of different aptitudes".[2] This pamphlet, in short, places a much stronger emphasis on differentiation than does the Hadow Report itself, though in terms of the Hadow recommendation that *all* children must now be provided with a suitable postprimary education.

It is noteworthy how far the system of streaming is taken for granted in this pamphlet—no alternative forms of organisation are suggested or even discussed though the Dalton Plan was a live issue at this time.[3] Thus the selective central school, it is underlined, must have at least two streams—only so will it be large enough "to make possible a really good classification—and some differentiation in curriculum". The fundamental principle of the nonselective senior school is that it must be large enough "to provide for some degree of internal classification". There should be "at least two parallel classes", there-

[1] *The Education of the Adolescent*, pp. 58, 89.
[2] Board of Education, *The New Prospect in Education*, Board of Education Pamphlet No. 60 (H.M.S.O., 1928), pp. 2, 6.
[3] From the early 1930s the Dalton Plan, supported by progressive educationists, had been introduced in many English elementary schools as an appropriate technique allowing for individualisation and the use of initiative by the pupils and for differences in the level of pupils in the top standards. This movement as it developed in England would make an interesting study; it appears to have died away with the spread of streaming and classification in the 1930s. See especially, A. J. Lynch, *Individual Work and the Dalton Plan* (1924) and C. W. Kimmins and Belle Rennie, *The Triumph of the Dalton Plan* (1932).

fore a total of six classes, preferably seven—eventually eight. Consequently with classes of forty, schools should be planned for 240 to 280 children, or eventually 320 (if the leaving age is raised to fifteen); 200 is the minimum number. In larger towns there should be three parallel classes, with schools for at least 400 pupils.[1] It is interesting to find precisely similar methods of calculation, in the light of similar ideas about individual capacity, in the Ministry of Education's circulars twenty years later in relation to comprehensive schools.

The attitudes to learning concomitant with ideas about innate intelligence are more clearly indicated in the detailed examples from current practice referred to in the pamphlet. For instance, in an industrial area, backward children in the junior schools are put in "special classes with a simpler curriculum and a modified scheme of work", whereas schools with many very bright children group these together in a special class or section "to cover the last year before transfer". In senior schools children are divided into A, B, and C classes on entry, based on the transfer examination. Different curricula are arranged for the parallel courses, French being confined to the A class, which also takes algebra and geometry, whereas "an easier course in mathematics is planned for the B forms, and the C forms take only simple Practical Arithmetic"; another boys' school "has arranged for an extensive course in gardening as part of the training for the C scholars".

Clearly, at about this time, streaming was becoming the key feature of reorganisation. In 1927 a new edition of the *Handbook of Suggestions for Teachers* included a rewritten section on backward children, proposing the organisation of special classes for these children —a proposal later abandoned in favour of streaming. Appendix A, however, reprints a *Report to the L.C.C.* by Cyril Burt, published in 1925. Here is to be found the first clear statement presaging the classical form of streaming. "The ideal plan", Burt writes, "would perhaps comprise a 'treble track' system—a series of backward classes for slow children, a series of advanced classes for quick children, both parallel to the ordinary series of standards for children of ordinary average ability". He restressed the need for variation: "To these different types of children different teaching methods are appropriate", but added that cross transference should be provided for, as "often a child's rate of mental development will profoundly change"—a point that seems to have been forgotten later. It is worth noting that at this point

[1] *The New Prospect in Education*, pp. 23–24.

point Burt's argument is based largely on the needs to provide for the backward child; the need to isolate the more advanced had already been sufficiently stressed in relation to more rapid promotion.[1]

Such was the position in the late 1920s. Schools large enough to permit streaming, both at the primary and postprimary level, were being brought into being. Official directives emphasised the need for effective classification of children according to both age and ability. Group verbal intelligence tests were beginning to be developed on a large scale for use in selection at eleven plus, and the technique of constructing these tests was being refined. Finally, the theory behind intelligence testing, concerning the preponderance of the hereditary component in measured intelligence, was being firmed up in the psychological journals. The conditions soon existed for the development of streaming as a system as closed and rigid as the old discredited system associated with payment by results.

The iron laws of psychometry

In 1933 Burt wrote:

> By intelligence, the psychologist understands *inborn, all-round intellectual ability*. It is inherited, or at least innate, not due to teaching or training; it is intellectual, not emotional or moral, and remains uninfluenced by industry or zeal; it is general, not specific, i.e. it is not limited to any particular kind of work, but enters into all we do or say or think. Of all our mental qualities, it is the most far-reaching; fortunately it can be measured with accuracy and ease.[2]

This carefully formulated paragraph, in a book for popular consumption (originally a series of broadcast talks) admirably summarises the ideas underlying the whole process of streaming and selection that came to dominate the educational scene from the early 1930s. The theory tended to be propagated and accepted in this dogmatic form, in spite of the fact that some psychologists, Godfrey Thomson for instance, held that environmental factors accounted for as much as 50 per cent of the variance in test scores. A theory of this kind was necessary, of course, if the validity of early selection was to be upheld. As intelligence tests became more generally used in selection, so they provided both the practical means of dividing children up for dispatch

[1] Board of Education, *Handbook of Suggestions for Teachers and Others Concerned in the Work of the Public Elementary Schools*, 1927 ed. (H.M.S.O., 1927), p. 422.
[2] C. Burt (ed.), *How the Mind Works* (1933), pp. 28–29.

to different types of postprimary school and the theoretical justification for this division.

If intelligence was innate and subject to accurate measurement by the tests in use, then the results obtained should have shown that a child's I.Q. (Intelligence Quotient) remained constant over time. It is an interesting fact that this was not normally the case, though in theoretical terms this constancy of the I.Q. was consistently propagated. "This Intelligence Quotient", wrote R. B. Cattell, educational psychologist at Leicester, in a well known textbook *A Guide to Mental Testing* (1936), "remains constant for any given individual both during childhood and in adult life".[1] Many similar quotations could be taken from similar books; and, as P. E. Vernon was to show later, this is the assurance with which teachers were armed in training college and university.[2] For instance, in *Learning and Teaching*, a textbook that has sold some 250,000 copies since its publication in 1937, the authors affirm that "it has been found, that a child's mental ratio or intelligence quotient is generally consistent. This means that if children are dull or bright in early years, they will in normal circumstances be equally dull or bright as they grow up". Not until the edition of 1959 was any modification introduced.[3]

In these circumstances, streaming appeared the obvious method of school organisation. In 1931 the Consultative Committee produced a report entitled *The Primary School*. By this time reorganisation was well under way, but there was still pressure for extended secondary facilities, and the examination at eleven plus was becoming acutely competitive. At this formative stage in the evolution of the junior school, it was recommended, once more relying on the evidence of psychologists, that streaming be generally introduced, the case being put, yet again, as if no alternative existed. "The break at the age of eleven", the committee concluded, in a now famous passage, "has

[1] R. B. Cattell, *A Guide to Mental Testing* (1936), p. 7. The statement was repeated in the 1948 edition.

[2] P. E. Vernon, "The Assessment of Children," in *The Bearings of Recent Advances in Psychology on Educational Problems*, University of London Institute of Education, Studies in Education, No. 7 (1955).

[3] A. G. Hughes and E. H. Hughes, *Learning and Teaching: An Introduction to Psychology and Education* (1937), p. 59. The formulation quoted remained much the same in the new edition of 1946. In the third edition, published in 1959, however, the quoted passage is preceded by the words "It is often said that a child's mental ratio", and so forth. "This statement", the authors continue, "should not be taken as a precise statement of fact." A child's I.Q. would "only by chance" remain the same; yet it is sufficiently constant to act as a provisional prognosis of academic progress. Both the first and the second editions of this handy textbook were reprinted nine times.

rendered possible a more thorough classification of children. *It is important that this opportunity should be turned to the fullest account.* One great advantage of the self-contained primary school is that the teachers have special opportunities for making a suitable classification of children according to their natural gifts and abilities." The committee goes on to recommend the three stream or "tripletrack" system, in almost precisely the same words as in Burt's 1925 report.

> In general we agree with our psychological witnesses that in very large primary schools there might be, wherever possible, a triple-track system of organisation, viz: a series of "A" classes for the bright children, and a series of smaller "C" classes or groups to include retarded children, both series being parallel to the ordinary series of "B" classes or groups for the average child.[1]

There is abundant evidence that this proposal was acted on in junior schools, wherever these were large enough—that is, particularly in the cities. It is now that streaming becomes *de rigueur* and the limitation of abilities an article of faith laid down in a dogmatic form by many distinguished educators. A child's intellectual powers, wrote Susan Isaacs in a book concerned specifically with seven to eleven-year-olds, are "fixed by his original mental endowment"; although there is some confusion in the argument about the relative effect of "ignorant homes" and lack of innate intelligence, the conclusion, driven home with considerable force, is that, for teaching purposes, the need is "to lessen the differences found in any one group. It is with this in mind", Susan Isaacs goes on, "that many head teachers are now beginning to use the native intellectual ability of the children as expressed in mental age as the chief basis for grading classes. Of all the differences between one child and another, inborn intelligence turns out to be the most stable and permanent. It is the most significant for success in school and career. The best teaching in the world may prove barren if it falls on the stony ground of an inherently dull and lifeless mind. And we cannot cater properly for the brightest and the stupidest children together in one class . . . such a classification makes it so much more possible to give to each according to his needs."[2]

[1] Board of Education, *Report of the Consultative Committee on the Primary School* (H.M.S.O., 1931), pp. 77–78.

[2] Susan Isaacs, *The Children We Teach: Seven to Eleven Years* (1932), pp. 25, 28–29. In *The Psychological Aspect of Child Development*, a scholarly paper first published in 1935 and since reprinted as a pamphlet (1963), Susan Isaacs puts the view that streaming is the organisation best suited to individual and group methods and so for "free activity", pp. 41–42.

By this time the whole purpose of Hadow reorganisation was being presented officially by the board of education not as an opportunity to provide secondary education for all, but as the means to precise classification and streaming. In 1937 the new system was, as it were, codified in a new edition of the *Handbook*, in which the relevant section, on school organisation, has been completely rewritten. Though it is "not yet ten years since the last edition was published", it is stated in the introduction, "the development in educational thought and practice has in the meantime been so rapid as to make the issue of a substantial revision desirable". Stressing the increased importance now attached to "individual differences among children", a new section on classification "By Streams" claims that "It was recognition of the difficulties of classification in schools organised on traditional lines that led to the Hadow principle of reorganisation, the adoption of which would make it possible to have in junior and senior schools both promotion by age and classification by ability at the same time". To get the full benefit of Hadow reorganisation, the passage continues, "relatively large numbers and annual promotions are essential. These conditions alone make it possible to meet the needs of different types of child by providing continuous and complete courses of work of a differentiated kind which can be followed uninterruptedly by each type of child for the whole period of his attendance at school."[1]

The chief proposal of the 1926 Hadow report, that all post-primary education be regarded as *secondary* in character, is here thrust altogether aside. We are now in the realm of official solution of problems of school organisation—problems, which, as we have seen, developed in the period after the ending of payment by results. The solution now found—that of making appropriate groupings according to age and ability—itself bears a close resemblance at a new stage to the earlier system of control and containment.

The 1930s, then, saw the triumph of the idea of homogeneous grouping based on age but modified by intelligence; wherever feasible, children of similar chronological age were now grouped according to mental age, which allowed reversion to the system of annual promotions. Certainly this brought order and system into the schools as compared with the situation in the early 1920s and before. But to look back on this practical situation is to see that the large classes (which

---

[1] Board of Education, *Handbook of Suggestions for the Consideration of Teachers and Others Concerned in the Work of the Public Elementary Schools*, 1937 ed. (H.M.S.O., 1937), pp. 6–7, 33–34.

increased in numbers rather than being reduced following the Geddes cuts in the early 1920s)[1] encouraged the imposition of the kind of structure whereby large groups of children could be taught as a single unit; and this remained the administrative objective to which talk of providing for individual differences was little but an obligato. That group verbal intelligence tests provided reliable measures of inborn intelligence was widely accepted as the basis for selection and classification, whereas little or no attention was paid to cultural influence on test results, and so on individual needs in this respect; the emphasis was necessarily on teaching *at* the level of the homogeneous groups created rather than on compensating for poverty of experience or stimulating learning.

Certainly psychologists were often genuinely concerned about providing better for the backward as well as opportunities for the bright child from a very poor home whose intelligence might be masked. But in general at this period a class outlook appears as endemic and unrecognised—it stands out in the writings of Nunn, Isaacs, and others, as well as in the test items selected by psychologists as appropriate measures of intelligence.[2] It was only considerably later that the class limitations of tests and the attitudes they embodied were brought to light by sociologists.

The emphasis on selection and classification by intellectual criteria alone was itself a reflection of the narrowly academic purposes and limited educational objectives of the full secondary school. In the prevailing conditions there was little room for a conception of education as a broad process of human development covering social, aesthetic, moral, and physical as well as intellectual development; rather secondary education came to be seen in terms of the passing on of certain academic knowledge and skills and the application of these in certain specific fields—in accordance with the social function of the secondary school and traditional educational ideas of long standing. The concept of learning implicit in such an outlook is the old one of cultural assimilation, the quicker ones being able to absorb more rapidly the given bodies of knowledge presented, whereas the slower require a watered-down version administered at an easier pace. That education should so easily be regarded as a race in which the fittest survived, reflected the realities of a selective and competitive system.

[1] The coalition government of 1922 had accepted the Geddes Committee's recommendation that the size of classes should be increased to not less than fifty children per teacher.
[2] B. Simon, *Intelligence Testing and the Comprehensive School*, p. 63.

It must be recalled, in an attempt to understand the extent of closed mindedness and complacency—the lack of corroboration for the key claims of intelligence testing is the most outstanding example—that his was a period of industrial stagnation, slump, and mass unemployment. In conditions in which the abilities of the population could not be effectively used (opportunities in the white collar and professional fields were also restricted) there was unlikely to be concern about the development of abilities among the new generation. In this climate the fatalistic theories adumbrated by psychologists, which in essence claimed that education could do nothing to *develop* abilities, tied in appropriately with the existing situation. Once incorporated in the educational system, at the vital points of selection and classification, they operated to justify that system and to stratify it even more effectively—so providing additional proof of the static nature of social forms. Here was a closed circle from which it was to prove all too difficult to break out.

Even modest proposals for the extension of educational opportunity came up, at this period, against the iron pressure of psychometric "laws" and corresponding forms of educational organisation. There was still pressure to extend secondary education to all, at this time in the proposition that all post-primary schools be brought squarely into the secondary system; and this had its effect, but only within strict limits, as is illustrated by the final report of the Consultative Committee before World War II, the Spens Report of 1938.

The Consultative Committee was, on this occasion, permitted to take the secondary schools into consideration and asked particularly to report on a possible alternative to the academic school in the form of technical high schools (the former junior technical schools upgraded). But in the event its report merely advocated the transference of the existing divided post-primary system into the secondary field—as a triple-track system of schools. Once more psychological advice played a decisive role in the justification. Though there are minor modifications in formulation of the doctrine, it remains fundamentally as before. What is added is a new emphasis on the predictive power of intelligence tests, together with a firm statement of the doctrine of limits.

Intellectual development during childhood appears to progress as if it were governed by a single central factor, usually known as "general intelligence", which may be broadly described as innate all-round intellectual ability. It appears to enter into everything which the child attempts to think, to say, or do, and seems on the whole to be the most important factor in determining his work in the class-room. Our psychological witnesses assured us that it can be measured approximately by means of intelligence tests. . . . We were informed that, with few exceptions, it is possible at a very early age to predict with some degree of accuracy the ultimate level of a child's intellectual powers.[1]

From this psychological evidence the committee drew the conclusion that "different children from the age of eleven, if justice is to be done to their varying capacities, require types of education varying in certain important respects". Justice to the child could be assured by the use of intelligence tests in selection for different types of school in a tripartite secondary system—the grammar, the technical, and the modern school.

The perfected system and its demise

During World War II there was a ferment of educational thinking, an enhancement of educational aspirations, greater than in the years 1914–1918. Once again there were concessions to the pressure of public opinion, but the official recommendations preceding the Education Act of 1944 and subsequent regulations made under it were based essentially on the thinking of the 1920s and 1930s. Thus the Act laid down that all post-primary education should come under a single code of regulations; but secondary education was to be provided according to the "age, ability, and aptitude" of pupils, a proviso that lay behind subsequent imposition of a secondary system rigidly divided into grades and gave enhanced importance to the doctrine of intelligence.

This was the more the case in that a new factor now came into play with the abolition of fees in the old secondary (now called "grammar") schools as well as the abolition of their contributory junior departments. Grammar schools now provided 100 per cent free places in common with other types of school. Postwar aspirations and long-standing demand for "secondary education for all" ensured the

[1] Board of Education, *Report of the Consultative Committee on Secondary Education with Special Reference to Grammar Schools and Technical High Schools* (H.M.S.O., 1938), pp. 123–125. The whole passage is printed in italics.

maximum pressure for entry to these schools, the only secondary schools hitherto and clearly still the chief ones.

The effect was to increase the rigidity of the whole process of streaming, which now became (with eleven plus selection at the midpoint) the means whereby the selective function of the educational system was maintained and consolidated. Indeed with access to the grammar school and higher education still restricted in face of rising demand, the whole schoool system now began to appear primarily as a vast selective process.

The tripartite system, proposed by the Spens Committee and advocated after 1944 by the new (and much more powerful) Ministry of Education, did not come into being as planned, for few technical schools were established. Instead a rigid bipartite system developed of selective grammar schools for the few (about 20 per cent) and modern schools for the rest. Only the former opened the way to the universities, colleges, and professions—in 1952 only one pupil in 22,000 proceeded directly from a secondary modern school to the university. Hence pressure to enter the grammar schools greatly increased, especially because these were now free. Middle-class parents, who had earlier entered their children as fee payers, now wished them to pass the eleven-plus examination; surveys show that by and large these hopes were realised, because the proportion of children from the working class in grammar schools hardly increased after the war. Under fresh pressure, junior schools streamed rigorously, as a matter of course, wherever they were large enough, preparing their A streams specifically in the skills of English, arithmetic, and intelligence.[1] Streaming penetrated down into the infant school. Necessarily, a great deal of effort was put into perfecting the mechanism of selection, so that it could stand up to public examination and criticism as a scientific procedure; the National Foundation for Educational Research, established after the war and financially supported by local authorities, spent most of its resources in producing tests required for selection to the virtual exclusion of other forms of educational research.

The characteristics of streamed schools have been described in Brian Jackson's *Streaming, an Education System in Miniature* (1964), and more recently by David Hargreaves' *Social Relations in a Secondary*

---

[1] Brian Jackson has pointed out that, as the Hadow reorganisation was speeded up after the war, resulting in larger primary school units, "primary school streaming appears to have spread with barely credible rapidity all over the country". *Streaming: An Education System in Miniature* (1964), p. 150.

School (1967), based on a single secondary modern school. No full analysis has yet been completed of streaming in grammar schools, although these also seem increasingly to have utilised this system—here the objective was, of course, to segregate the most advanced pupils in preparation for university and college entrance, which also became increasingly competitive in the postwar period.[1] Research has shown that, in spite of Burt's proviso in 1925, the amount of transfer between streams was very small (though consistently overrated by teachers) so that placement in the *A* stream of a junior school at the age of seven became an important condition for gaining a place at a grammar school. As Hadow reorganisation was completed in the 1950s— extending to cover hitherto backward towns and all rural areas—the school system acquired a complex structure in which a continuous selective role was played by the internal streamed organisation of individual schools. This may be represented schematically:

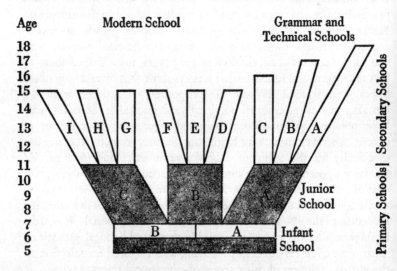

Fig. 1. *The Streamed System of Education*

In short, the system of streaming provided the educational machine with a number of conveyor belts, distributing pupils leaving school

---

[1] But see C. Lacey, "Some Sociological Concomitants of Academic Streaming in a Grammar School", *British Journal of Sociology*, XVII, 3 (September 1966) for a penetrating study of some aspects of this process. See also Lacey's *Hightown Grammar* (1970) (ed.).

at a variety of different levels, each offering different employment prospects.[1] The years from 1945–1955 saw the apotheosis of this classical form of streaming, as the justification of eleven-plus selection continued and moves to provide a single (comprehensive) secondary school were blocked by the Ministry of Education (except in the case of a few influential and determined local authorities). By the early 1950s the system was so much taken for granted, together with the psychological doctrine underlying it, that it was barely questioned. Yet, a decade later, questioning, both by psychologists and educationists, was widespread. In 1967 an official report (the Plowden Report) welcomed the movement to unstream junior schools; and evidence was beginning to come to hand of experiments in unstreaming secondary, including comprehensive, schools. Why had the apparently impregnable closed circle of theory and practice—the product of years of directed development—been broken open?

It is only possible at this stage to enumerate factors in the situation. Among the most fundamental were the changing economic and social conditions of the postwar years by comparison with whose between the wars. The maintenance of a relatively high level of employment, technological change, a slow but consistent rate of economic growth, measures of social reform, and a relative increase in affluence by comparison with the hungry 1930s provided a new background of society in some sort of movement. In time this gave rise to new demands on the educational system in the form of slow but insistent pressure for higher educational qualifications at many levels—a pressure corresponding to that of parents for greater educational opportunities.

Within the educational system itself, despite official doctrines designed to maintain and consolidate divisions, teachers in a few secondary modern schools found and took opportunities in the early 1950s to break out of the rigidly defined functions that they had been allotted and to enter their pupils for the same examinations as those for the grammar schools (rather than continuing to minister to them at the level of their supposedly innate intelligence). Their success in this brought both the dicta of psychologists and the administrative fetters

[1] That, to some, this represented an acceptable situation was made clear in a broadcast talk by Cyril Burt at this time: "Obviously, in an ideal community, our aim should be to discover what ration of intelligence nature has given to each individual child at birth, then to provide him with the appropriate education, and finally to guide him into the career for which he seems to have been marked out." C. Burt, "Testing Intelligence", *The Listener*, November 16th, 1950.

imposed by the Ministry of Education increasingly into question.[1] It was in the junior schools, however, where the pressure of the eleven-plus examination was most acutely felt to negate positive educational endeavour, that the first moves were made at this time to supersede streaming and new criteria sought for grouping pupils.

The head teachers who initiated these moves derived support for their new, and almost revolutionary, initiative from various sources, but in particular from those tendencies in psychological research that laid stress on learning as a *process*. Formerly, in the 1930s, little or no attention had been paid to this aspect nor, indeed, to relevant research in grouping, which had been carried on on a considerable scale in the United States in the 1920s and 1930s. In 1934, for instance, Charlotte Fleming had published a short book that questioned the prevailing tendency toward "prismatic" streaming and reported relevant research in the United States on ability grouping; but such publications had been rare and almost totally ignored by officials, theoreticians, and teachers.[2] Similarly, the rejection of streaming in the U.S.S.R. as far back as 1936, based on a critique of test psychology, which had excited little interest at the time, was now recalled; and to this was added, perhaps particularly in the late 1950s, knowledge of the work and outlook of D. O. Hebb on the growth of intelligence and of Soviet psychologists such as A. R. Luria. The latter stressed the formative power of education and explicitly denied the rationale underlying streaming.

The development of sociology, which began to accelerate at this time in England,[3] also introduced a new approach and research findings undermined old contentions. It was found that social-class influences greatly affected measured intelligence, that middle-class children preponderated in *A* streams and working-class children in *C* streams (as had been found in the U.S.S.R. twenty years earlier), and even that a child's initial (and therefore vital) stream placement was to some extent a function of the month in which he was born, older children being placed more frequently in *A* streams than those born later in the academic year. Finally, in 1964, J. W. B. Douglas's longitudinal

---

[1] It was commonly held at this time that only children with I.Q.s of 115 and over could benefit from a grammar school education, but some children with I.Q.s between 80 and 100 gained up to five passes in the general certificate of education examinations specifically designed for grammar school pupils. Brian Simon, *The Common Secondary School* (1955), 66.

[2] C. M. Fleming, *Individual Work in Primary Schools* (1934), 15 ff.

[3] In 1962 there were only three chairs of sociology in British universities; in the next two years a "sudden proliferation" led to the establishment of some twenty new chairs in the subject. I. Neustadt, *Teaching Sociology* (University of Leicester Press, 1965), 4.

researches pointed to the conclusion—long suspected—that the process of streaming was in fact a self-verifying procedure; children of equal measured intelligence, if placed in A streams, improved their performance, if placed in lower streams, deteriorated. Intellectual functioning was, therefore, to some extent a function of stream placement.[1]

As these developments gained momentum, psychologists were bound to pay attention, and criticism from the professional field of what may be called the classic doctrine of intelligence gathered way. New stress was now laid both on environmental influences on the growth of intelligence and on the deficiencies of group verbal tests used as a measure. Here a landmark was the publication, in 1957, of the report of a working party set up by the British Psychological Society, comprising most of the leading educational psychologists in the country. This specifically rejected the formulation referred to earlier from the Spens report, stressed environmental influences on the growth of intelligence, and underlined the dangers of streaming in junior schools, which was held artificially to exacerbate differences.[2]

The replacement of streaming as an educational strategy can best be seen in the grouping procedures of comprehensive schools since 1950. Although one of the main objectives of comprehensive schools was to overcome selection at eleven plus, the earliest comprehensive schools took over the system of streaming intact, dividing their intake along the lines shown in the diagram earlier—though overcoming the broader divisions in the educational system. Thus Holyhead School in Anglesey, one of the first, was based avowedly on the principle of progressive differentiation, the children streamed into seven or eight parallel classes on the basis of tests given shortly after entry.[3] Similarly at Kidbrooke, the first of the London purpose-built comprehensive schools, opened in 1954, the children were arranged in fifteen streams on the basis of the eleven-plus results, which all had taken. Experiments with mixed ability groups (for nonacademic subjects) were, however, being made in the mid-1950s, while today, as the country moves over to comprehensive secondary education, the whole quest-

---

[1] J. W. B. Douglas, *The Home and the School* (1964), 118.

[2] P. E. Vernon (ed.), *Secondary School Selection: A British Psychological Society Inquiry* (1957). See p. 152. It is worth noting that in the same year (1957) the Ministry of Education reprinted (for the last time) the 1937 edition of the *Handbook of Suggestions for the Consideration of Teachers and Others Concerned in the Work of the Public Elementary Schools* which stressed the need for classification and streaming in all types of school based on Hadow reorganisation.

[3] T. Lovett, "Comprehensive Years—Progressive Differentiation", *Times Educational Supplement*, January 27th, 1956.

ion of criteria for grouping in these schools is being discussed anew. This trend has recently been reinforced by the publication of the UNESCO symposium *Grouping in Schools*, edited by A. Yates, formerly a research officer of the National Foundation for Educational Research. A few comprehensive schools are now experimenting with complete nonstreaming, particularly in the early years.[1]

It seems likely that this movement will continue, though the doctrine of intelligence still retains a strong hold among sections of the teaching profession and others. The spread of comprehensive education will provide a different set of conditions in the schools; and, at the time of writing in 1967, attention is increasingly turning to new forms of curriculum planning that incorporate use of new technological aids and, in some areas, a radical revision of teaching methods leading to more flexible organisational forms within the schools. Pressure in the lower forms of secondary schools has also been somewhat lightened by the expansion of higher education following the Robbins report of 1964. It seems, therefore, that the stage is set for a period of continuous, and possibly considerable, educational change.

Nevertheless, if this is the perspective, streaming still remains the prevalent form of organisation in English schools. Moreover it is probable that, as the upward thrust of the secondary school continues and the expansion of higher education fails to keep pace, the bottleneck at eleven—with all its attendant social and ideological blocks—will be replaced by another at the stage of sixteen or eighteen. With financial support from the Department of Education and Science (as the Ministry of Education was renamed in 1965) psychologists are developing a new British Intelligence Scale designed for sixteen-year-olds. There are, therefore, signs that the breakout from the particular set of views described here is only a stage in a continuing process.

Theory and practice in education

It is impossible, within the scope of an article concerned with one particular aspect of the educational system, to analyse and assess all

[1] D. Thompson, "Towards an Unstreamed Comprehensive School", *Forum*, VII, 3 (Summer 1965); A. W. Rowe, "I Abolished Streaming", *New Education*, III, 4 (April 1967). The theoretical issues involved in grouping in comprehensive schools today are outlined in D. A. Pidgeon, "Intelligence Testing and Comprehensive Education", in J. F. Meade and A. S. Parkes (eds.), *Genetic and Environmental Factors in Human Ability* (1966). Reports of conferences on nonstreaming and articles on teaching in nonstreamed comprehensive schools have frequently been published in the educational journal *Forum*.

the forces at work and their relative strength in determining the course of development. But one point does seem to emerge: during the period in educational history here covered, educational and psychological theory tended to be determined by current practice and to revolve within its limits, to an extraordinary extent. One of the reasons for this may be the insular isolation of England between the wars, which precluded comparative studies of a kind that have since played a notable part in opening English eyes to English social limitations; though there has been no response so spectacular as the American reaction to the first Russian sputnik (1957). Another may be the deeply rooted empiricism, not only in the academic sense but also on the political plane, a factor that precluded from the continuous pressure of the labour movement for increased educational opportunity the kind of criticism that extended to the theoretical plane. This aided the consolidation of a closed system, which was perfected to such a point that the ideology of the 1920s and 1930s could be carried over to shape the school system of the 1940s and 1950s, at a price in failure to develop human capacities, which the country may well be paying for another generation.

It has been seen that, at least from the outset of this century, when new methods of state control replaced the overt stringencies of the revised code, a clear official policy was inexorably translated into practice, leaving little scope for local initiative in the development of alternative patterns. The key feature of this policy was the restriction of grammar school places to a specific proportion of the child population. Parallel with this went a determination to preserve the grammar school as an academic enclave, stressing an abstract and highly verbalised approach to learning on traditional lines; this implied, it may be noted, the predominance of literary over scientific studies still prevalent in the 1960s, despite attempts to correct it. The checks and balances necessary to maintain this equilibrium and reorganise the mass elementary school on a new level by comparison with that of the period 1870–1900 resulted in the system that has been described—a system stratified not only in terms of grades of school but also of streams within each grade.

This structure of the school system was so at odds with democratic aspirations, and indeed with democratic principles, that it demanded a rationale or set of justificatory principles. As Elie Halévy drily observed, referring to the vulgarisation of classical political economy by such men as James Mill and McCulloch, the Industrial Revolution was "demanding its principles";[1] so the hierarchical structure of the public educational system during the first half of the twentieth century also required a rationale—in the form of appropriate psychological theories.

One of the morals has been pointed out by a psychologist, Ben Morris, who was for many years secretary of the National Foundation for Educational Research, a body at one time almost exclusively concerned with producing objective tests. Morris stresses as a necessary task for educational psychology "a constant scrutiny of its presuppositions". Failure to do this "necessarily involves its offering itself purely as a technology, afraid or unconcerned to avow the presuppositions necessarily built into it through its intrinsic relations with educational thought"—and, it might be added, practice. Morris's argument is so closely relevant to this discussion that it deserves quoting in full:

> "An example of such failure, which is at the same time a grave warning, is close at hand. The psychology of mental measurement, through failure to scrutinise adequately its presuppositions, developed into a technology concerned with establishing and measuring the more or less fixed intellectual abilities with which it supposed children to be endowed at birth, irrespective of the cultural and educational milieu in which they developed. In this country the growth of this technology was nourished by convictions, having deep ideological roots, that education required rigid systems of classifying children in terms of such abilities. Because it appeared to achieve practical success in carrying out such classification, educational psychology tended to become identified with the technology of mental measurement. We are now witnessing the slow crumbling of this technology, and of its supporting ideology, as the presuppositions of both become exposed to radical criticism.[2]

Another psychologist, still actively concerned with testing, has conceded that "psychologists themselves were not wholly free from blame" in propagating, as scientific findings, unproven hypotheses (such as that of the general constancy of the I.Q.). Indeed "they were

[1] E. Halévy, *The Growth of Philosophic Radicalism*, Mary Morris (tr.) (1928), 370.
[2] B. Morris, "The Contribution of Psychology to Education", in J. W. Tibble (ed.), *The Study of Education* (1966), 106. The fact that ideological factors have entered into the theory of "intelligence" is recognized by S. Wiseman in *Intelligence and Ability: Selected Readings* (1967), 13–14.

often guilty of oversimplifications when they addressed themselves to teachers"[1] or, more materially it might be added, to official advisory committees and administrators. Insistence that such advice was scientifically grounded effectively rebutted political and social criticism. In the event a whole conjunction of circumstances mostly arising from social practice in the schools and outside was necessary before these theories, and the system of education which they underpinned, began to crumble. It is worth noting that it was a decision on the political plane—to introduce comprehensive education at the secondary stage—that was ultimately necessary to alter the direction of educational development.

There remains a new and vital stage of reorientation to be negotiated in such a way as to build in possibilities for continuous educational change; change, that is, concomitant with the revolutionary nature of contemporary scientific and technological advance but directed to increasing the potentialities of humanity and of life itself for each individual. Although educational practice must necessarily be founded on psychological findings, there seems little likelihood that a particular psychological theory can again exercise so exclusive an influence. Other disciplines have increasingly moved into the educational field, notably sociology and, in England, a particular form of analytical philosophy, both of which are making their own contributions to educational theory and practice. Disparate approaches may, in future, be the greater danger, or source of confusion, to educationists. In the circumstances, the historian of education may see it as a chief task to disentangle the background of current controversies in order the better to understand their nature, so making way for the relevant and coherent development of education in theory and in practice.

As has been remarked by one concerned to find the reasons for the decline of science in ancient Greece, it is a difficult task to discover how the science of one age becomes transformed into the superstition of the next—as, in a sense, was the case with intelligence testing. But this task is assigned to history:

"History is the most fundamental science, for there is no human knowledge which cannot lose its scientific character when men forget the conditions under which it originated, the questions which it answered, and the function it was created to serve. A great

[1] Wiseman, *op. cit.*, 12.

part of the mysticism and superstition of educated men consists of knowledge which has broken loose from its historical moorings."[1]

To no field is this comment more relevant than to education.

[1] Benjamin Farrington, *Greek Science: Its Meaning for Us* (1949), Vol. II, 173.

INTELLIGENCE, RACE, CLASS AND EDUCATION[1]

In the summer of this year, Arthur Jensen, Professor of Psychology at the University of California, visited this country. He addressed two meetings at Cambridge, one organised by the Brain Research Association, the other by the Cambridge Society for Social Responsibility in Science—both, incidentally, of recent foundation.[2] He was invited specifically to explain and discuss his very controversial views as to the nature and distribution of human intelligence, views which had aroused a furore in the United States and had immediate repercussions here. Briefly, Jensen appeared to argue that, owing to genetical endowment, blacks in the United States are innately less intelligent than whites, and also that working-class whites are less intelligent than upper and middle-class whites. Jensen claimed that his evidence— derived from psychometry (mental measurement, or intelligence testing)—indicated overwhelmingly that both racial and class differences are inherited, and so impervious to change by way of social or educational policies.

We may note first, that this is a revival, and extension, of old arguments derived from psychometry which have been exposed in practice and discredited in this country. We may then go on to examine the circumstances in which an old contention has been refurbished, what have been the reactions of scientists in related fields, and how the controversy affects us all.

It is now twenty years or more since Marxists in this country were forced to make a detailed, critical, analysis of this specific branch of psychology and the uses to which it is put. Conclusions derived from intelligence testing, carried out on a mass scale, provided an apparently scientific foundation for social, and in particular, educational policies of an extremely reactionary nature which militated against the working class. The rationale—or justification—for the rigid divisions in education, which have only recently begun to be broken down, rested fundamentally on assumed "laws" about the distribution of intelligence derived from psychometry.

[1] Reprinted from *Marxism Today*, November 1970.
[2] The latter is a branch of the British Society for Social Responsibility in Science, formed at a meeting at the Royal Society in April 1969.

In the period immediately following World War II, despite the existence of a government, committed by a series of Labour Party Conference resolutions, to comprehensive secondary education, a divided (or bipartite) system was firmly established, with the eleven plus examination as the means of selection for the restricted number of grammar schools which monopolised the road to higher education. An essential ingredient of this were mental tests. At the same time rigid streaming in primary schools became widespread, so that a child's whole future could be, and in most cases was, determined by his stream placement (into A, B or C stream) at the age of seven or even earlier.

This procedure was justified on the grounds that children differ markedly in intelligence and that education must take account of the fact. It was held that intelligence is an innate quality of mind, genetically determined—i.e. not open to modification by education—and that it can be accurately measured by a specially constructed test. It was also held that, as I have put it elsewhere, "in every population—whatever the differences in social and educational background and the changes in social living that may take place—there is always a given (small) proportion of highly intelligent people at one end of the scale and an equivalent proportion of very dull people at the other; the majority of the population is strung out between these two extremes, tailing off through the moderately clever at one end and the moderately stupid at the other to the two end points of genius and idiocy". (This pattern follows what statisticians call "the normal curve of distribution".) Finally, it was held, and widely believed, that intelligence test results prove conclusively that working-class children are, on average, born less intelligent than middle and upper-class children.

Intelligence testing not only provided the rationale for streaming and selection but also the practical means whereby children were allocated to different types of school (grammar-modern) and to different streams within the school. Theory and practice reinforced each other, therefore, in maintaining a divided and segregated system of education; one which, like the society it served, offered opportunities and rewards to an élitist minority while relegating the vast majority to an inferior form of education. This last was "appropriate" to the mass of working-class children, assumed to lack the "intelligence" required for abstract (conceptual) thought and so to be incapable of significant intellectual achievement.

For a considerable time this "system"—in fact a self-justificatory one—appeared impregnable. The theoretical framework had been developed and firmed up in the 1920s and 1930s, particularly under the influence of Cyril Burt who advised successive official committees on the psychological considerations which should underly the development of the state system of education (the Hadow Reports of 1926 and 1931, the Spens Report of 1938). These ideas still informed official thinking when the 1944 Act was drafted and were in due course put into practice when it was implemented, playing the key ideological role in preventing the general introduction of comprehensive schooling. Once the divided system was established, with intelligence testing as an integral part, it became possible to assert that this was the only right and proper system.

To make a fundamental critical analysis of the theory and practice of intelligence testing was indispensable. It is not easy now to recall the atmosphere of those days—how unquestioningly these ideas were accepted by the vast majority of educationists as well as psychologists, whatever their social outlook or political standpoint. Teachers had been brought up in these beliefs, embodied almost as a dogma in text-books—though some, finding through their own experience that children's intellectual powers could be stimulated and developed, remained sceptical. The critique of intelligence testing, its theory, technology and educational outcome, could at that time only be undertaken from an independent standpoint, geared to seek out and challenge the basic, unstated assumptions of intelligence testing embedded in its technology.

Marxism is such a standpoint. And it was in Marxist journals that criticism of the fundamentals of intelligence testing—criticism now very widely accepted—first began in 1949.[1] As early as 1950 the Communist Party organised an open conference on intelligence testing and its effect on the schools, and in 1952, at a public conference on the secondary modern school, the problems of eleven plus and streaming in junior schools were sharply raised, particularly by parents. This implied straightforward rejection of the view that the public must passively accept expert guidance, in favour of a challenge to the experts in a socially responsible way. The collective discussion on teaching and selection during this period was summed up, and presented in popular form, in my *Intelligence Testing and the Comprehensive School* (1953).

[1] B. Simon, "The Theory and Practice of Intelligence Testing", *Communist Review*, October 1949; and "Science and Pseudo-Science in Psychology", *Education Bulletin*, October 1949; Joan Simon, "Mental Testing", *Modern Quarterly*, Vol. 5, No. 1, winter 1949–50; Max Morris, "Intelligence Testing and the Class System of Education", *Modern Quarterly*, Vol. VI, No. 2, Spring 1951.

Since that time there have been many developments, in both the practice and theory of education. The eleven plus has been discredited, comprehensive schooling is becoming established, streaming has been abandoned in many primary schools and is beginning to be superseded in some secondary schools. Although the old ideas still persist and have their defenders, as we shall see, in general both educationists and psychologists now have a positive attitude to the promotion of human learning and the "educability" of children.

In 1957 a working party of the British Psychological Society, comprising most of the leading educational psychologists in the country, produced a report acknowledging a growing revolt against what were beginning to appear as sweeping and doctrinaire theories, as well as mounting public objection to the whole business of selection.[1] This specifically referred to criticisms by Marxists (labelled as "left-wing" critics) and stated "we accept some of their arguments, and will attempt to supply reasoned answers to others". In the outcome the report specifically condemned streaming in the primary school and early selection. For, in the light of research results which undermined the former position, it had to be conceded that tests could *not* now be said to measure an innate quality of mind—and this, in effect, removed the justification for the segregated school system.[2] Teachers also helped materially to force this change of front, insofar as many were proving beyond dispute that children classified on test results as of low intelligence could, with effective teaching and high expectations on the part of their teachers, reach a level of achievement well beyond the limits of their potentialities as predicted by intelligence test theory.

There has, then, been a substantial revision of earlier theories and the view that intelligence is largely fixed at birth (or better, perhaps, conception) finds relatively little support today. The more widely accepted standpoint is summarised in the Newsom report, an official document published in 1963:

"Intellectual talent is not a fixed quantity with which we have to work but a variable that can be modified by social policy and edu-

---

[1] P. E. Vernon (ed.), *Secondary School Selection: A British Psychological Society Enquiry* (1957).

[2] This report, which made important concessions but also contained a number of theoretical confusions, was assessed in some detail in "Secondary School Selection: A reply to the intelligence-testers", *Marxism Today*, January 1958. See p. 152.

cational approaches . . . the kind of intelligence that is measured by the tests so far applied is largely an acquired characteristic."

In other words, how a child develops intellectually depends on his life experiences, both at school and at home—in a given neighbourhood with given conditions of housing, health and so on. The corollary is to be found in a recommendation of the Plowden Report on junior schooling (1967), that there should be a policy of "positive discrimination", i.e. one which directs additional funds and aid to sub-standard schools in sub-standard areas. All this amounts to a recognition in practice of the decisive role of education in development, and a consequent recognition that more education should be provided for those at a disadvantage rather than less education on the grounds that they are backward—which was, effectively, the advice of the "intelligence-testers".

It is always mistaken to suppose that victories are absolute in conditions of continuing class conflict, particularly in ideological matters. Given the basic economic and social conditions of class society, there will always be a recrudescence of conflicting ideas in changing forms. That "intelligence" testing was so effectively exposed was largely owing to the fact that, by the 1960s, it was becoming increasingly clear that economic and technological needs dictate a move away from the wastage of ability inherent in a selective school system. The urgent need to raise the educational level was pressed by several official reports, notably the Crowther Report (1958) and the Robbins Report (1963). In most European countries, not merely England, secondary education is being opened up on non-selective lines.

Nonetheless, to provide a full education for the majority inevitably implies encroachment on what has for centuries been regarded as a minority privilege and this provokes reaction. Parallel with the Tory policy to maintain at all costs the private sector of education, and so far as possible selective grammar schools within the state system, there has been an ideological counter-offensive (accorded immense publicity) in the two Black Papers on education (1968, 1969). These were directed to criticising current trends in educational advance—not only comprehensive schools and non-streaming, but new methods of teaching. It is relevant to note that no scientists figure among the academics contributing to these very non-academic documents, but two psychometrists, both deeply committed to intelligence testing, figure prominently—Professors Burt and H. J. Eysenck.

Meanwhile there have been developments in the United States where class oppression takes its most vicious form in racial suppression of the blacks, extending to gross educational deprivation. Here there has not been an élitist school system on the English model but a much more open one. But there has been a growing tendency for black children to become segregated in separate schools in downtown areas in the North, to parallel open segregation in the deep South. With the development of the civil rights movement and the black power movement, it has been on the desegregation of schools that official policy has concentrated. In conjunction with this policy, only gradually being enforced, the Federal government has invested large sums of money on "compensatory" educational programmes in the cities, of which "Operation Headstart" is perhaps the best known here. These are geared to provide special, concentrated, teaching for children from sub-standard areas, intended to enable them to start school on more equal terms with others. Leading psychologists and educationists have also been working out new methods of teaching which are beginning to produce results and open up a whole new field of educational and psychological research, particularly in relation to stimulus in early childhood.[1]

It is in opposition to this development that the backlash in America has come. The relative lack of success of some rehabilitation programmes, hastily mounted on sketchy lines without adequate prior preparation, was an obvious point to be exploited. It was exploited by Arthur Jensen who, presenting an appropriately depressing picture of new programmes, went on to argue that the whole policy is mistaken; that failure is inevitable given the inferior intellectual equipment of blacks by comparison with whites. In the process he revives all the arguments that have ceased to carry weight in this country, capped by the hypothesis that "intelligence" tests indicate basic ethnic differences in the level of intelligence. Here it should be noted that to apply the theory and practice of testing in a racially diverse society such as the United States—where various ethnic groups which maintain an identity such as Puerto Ricans and Mexicans as well as blacks have been particularly exploited—is inevitably to add to a "class" interpretation of the distribution of measured intelligence, a "racial" interpretation. That is, if there is insistence that "intelligence" as measured by tests, can, and must, be seen as an inherited characteristic.

[1] A good account of this movement, for the general reader is Maya Pines, *Revolution in Learning* (1969).

Early in 1969, Arthur Jensen's now celebrated paper—of 120 pages, the length of a small book—appeared in a relatively obscure academic journal, the *Harvard Educational Review*. It opens with the claim that the great majority of schemes for compensatory education, launched in different areas, have failed to achieve any improvement of significance. There is a simple reason for this. Social scientists who claim that, by changing the environment, people can be changed, have misled the government. As a consequence resources have been wasted and a great deal of effort expended in a fruitless endeavour. A new approach is called for.

Jensen's "new" approach is to reiterate old and discredited views deriving from mass "intelligence" testing, notably the view that heredity determines the level of intelligence. At least 80 per cent of the variance in intelligence is due to heredity, he argues (in common with Cyril Burt), only 20 per cent to environmental factors. The probability is that, just as lower class whites are inferior (in terms of measured intelligence) to middle and upper class whites, so blacks are innately inferior to whites, by reason of an inferior genetic make up.

There are, Jensen suggested (and here his theory is similar to that propagated in practice in our bipartite educational system until quite recently), two types or "levels" of intelligence. Level I corresponds to the ability for "associative learning", i.e. simple rote learning, power of recall, etc. Level II corresponds to the ability to grasp concepts, solve problems, in short, to *think* (or actively manipulate the materials of thought). He postulates that these two levels are, as a result of genetic factors, distributed differentially among the population "as a function of social class". Education should be differentiated accordingly. For the working class (as a *class*, individual variation is allowed for as is customary) the appropriate education is one based on rote, or associative learning (where input=ouput). This, of course, covers the vast majority of blacks. For the middle and upper classes, alone capable of conceptual thinking, education should be designed to build on and develop this capacity.

This is the essence of an immensely long article, in which Jensen specifically sets out to rehabilitate the hereditarian theory of intelligence in terms not only of class but "race". To do this involves him in a detailed defence of the techniques of mental measurement developed over the last three or four decades, as well as in a survey and reinterpretation of the vast amount of data collected over this period, primarily in the U.S. and Britain. Jensen, not himself a geneticist, also uses arguments from genetics (especially population genetics) where these seem to support his general approach.

The article is serious, closely reasoned, and in parts highly technical and abstruse. It can, therefore, easily be mistaken for the disinterested scientific enquiry it purports to be. But the entire argument depends on the techniques, the closed world, of psychometry—a specialised off-shoot of psychology resting on some very definite assumptions. And these techniques, as has long since been demonstrated, specifically exclude the concept of *development* of human abilities, and so inevitably lead to the writing off of those who start at a disadvantage. Hence the rationale—or apparent scientific basis—Jensen's arguments provide for discriminatory educational practice, in a country which has not lived through the operation, decline and supersession of the eleven plus.

Inevitably Jensen's main conclusions were widely reported—as if they were scientific findings, rather than hypotheses which he was advancing for examination and discussion, as he had insisted. Their practical (or political) significance immediately became clear when his standpoint was quoted in the South in lawsuits against integration in the schools. In the light of this, it could now be argued that it would be right and proper to have all-black "remedial" schools (for "backward" children) and admit blacks to white schools only if they passed standardised tests; i.e. segregation, far from being abolished, should be streamlined on "scientific" grounds.

The article was publicly discussed all over the States, by politicians as well as scientists and those professionally engaged in education. The two subsequent numbers of the *Harvard Educational Review* were filled with articles and correspondence, primarily in protest but also in support, and Jensen replied to some of the criticisms raised. To this we may turn later, after considering reactions here and Jensen's meetings with scientists in Britain.

The Jensen thesis almost immediately made the front pages in Britain, though usually as controversial rather than as an exposition of the latest scientific knowledge. Thus following up the question in February 1970, the *Sunday Times* ran two full-page articles, in successive issues, on "Race, Class and Brains", sub-headed "Brian Silcock investigates an explosive scientific controversy".

But the first serious discussion of the thesis took place in the May 1969 issues of the *New Scientist*, a popular but informed weekly journal. Introducing the discussion, the editorial referred to the "storm of protests and invective" which greeted Jensen's thesis in the States, noting the implication that "he has struck political dynamite". It went on to link the matter with current social and educational issues in this country:

"Dr. Arthur Jensen's claim that U.S. Negroes are less intelligent than their white countrymen. Haringey Education Committee's decision to distribute immigrant children on the supposition that they are less intelligent than British pupils, and recent pronouncements by Lord Snow and others, have all focused attention on the emotive subject of intelligence and 'race'."

To the *New Scientist* it was clear that, in the resultant controversy, "science, politics and prejudice have become inextricably mixed".[1]

In the discussion in the journal, Professors Burt and Eysenck, inevitably, made contributions. Both are well known for their support of the outright hereditarian thesis, now a minority view. Both, though critical on minor aspects, supported Jensen's standpoint, though Burt drew the line at the question of race, as has long been customary here, saying that he does not believe there are important ethnic differences. By contrast, Eysenck, in two emotionally charged contributions, underlined ethnic differences, asserting that Jensen, and others, who have brought this matter "from under the carpet where it had been swept" have done "a great service to humanity". Eysenck also stressed the *educational* implications of Jensen's theory, in terms of the necessity for streaming and selection. Subsequently, in Black Paper Two (October 1969) he and Burt both figured—in what turned out to be a more strident and irrational publication than the first—joined by another psychologist, Richard Lynn, who expressed even more openly reactionary views with less cogency.

The underlying assumption of the hereditarians outlined in this Black Paper is a simple one, echoing one of Jensen's key contentions. In the course of history, the mass of the people have lost all their "intelligent" individuals to the upper classes as a consequence of social mobility, leaving a muddy sediment at the base amidst which only the occasional pearl is still to be found by careful probing. Thus Burt observes the "obvious" fact that:

[1] *New Scientist*, May 1, 1969. C. P. Snow is referred to in relation to certain statements he made on Jewish intellectual and artistic achievement, which he attributed to genetic endowment, when on a visit to the States early in 1969. These seemed to lend support to Jensen's thesis, though Snow added that he wished Jensen had been "a little more careful".

"Bright children from the poorer classes forge their way upward, and duller children from the higher class drift downward. Class differences thus become inevitable in any civilised society. The use of intelligence tests was intended, not to pick out the dull or defectives, but to reveal ability in cases where it would otherwise have remained unnoticed."

Richard Lynn elaborates on the point. One of the most serious suppressions of truth by "progressives" is their assertion:

"That it is the fault of society that slum dwellers are impoverished and their children do badly in school. To the young red guards, it follows that society is unjust and must be overthrown. They do not realise that slum dwellers are caused principally by low innate intelligence and poor family upbringing, and that the real social challenge is posed by this."

H. J. Eysenck caps the conclusion with the argument that compensatory policies for the deprived can do no good (here he draws on Jensen), but only harm insofar as *"with limited resources available for all of education, special help to some means less education for others"*, notably those selected by I.Q. tests as the innately superior in intellect.[1] This is the unspoken assumption underlying what has been a far greater expenditure on grammar schools than on modern schools, the kind of policy the Newsom Report directly challenged.

The Jensen article has also been discussed, more seriously and moderately, in educational and psychological journals, as well as the popular press. It may be noted that all this coincided with a revival of what might be called "biologism"—or moves to interpret the activity of human beings in society in terms of animal behaviour or biological urges. Such were Desmond Morris's *The Naked Ape*, and C. D. Darlington's, *The Evolution of Man in Society* which attempts to rewrite history in terms of the key role of genetics. The latter—given the full treatment not only in the daily and weekly press but in a serious historical journal, *Past and Present*—was critically scrutinised in the *New Statesman* by Robert Young, who found it a "trap for the unwary". Darlington claims to have made major corrections to the historical record on the basis of scientific evidence which leads him to conclude

[1] *Black Paper Two*, pp. 20, 30, 37–38.

that "the processes by which human societies evolve are . . . in principle the same as those working at a pre-human stage of evolution."[1]

The theory of intelligence fits into this general picture as an attempt to ascribe human development largely to biological factors, if not primarily to the inheritance of key mental powers.

The climax came in July this year when Jensen visited England to address meetings at Cambridge. These were widely reported, in particular an open meeting arranged by the C.S.S.R.S. which has since published the proceedings. These cover Jensen's address and the ensuing critique by experts from various related disciplines.[2]

The meeting was specifically arranged because of the social and political implications of Jensen's thesis, loudly canvassed by reactionaries, and the failure to report scientific objections to his arguments. As the C.S.S.R.S. put it:

> "The segregationalists of the southern United States, the Powellite element of the Tory party, and the more-means-worse authors of the Black Paper on Education have all used the scientific evidence of Professor Jensen's article to bolster their political aims. In contrast to their uncritical acceptance and that of the popular press, Professor Jensen's views have not received much support among his fellow scientists. Many eminent psychologists, geneticists and educationalists have been provoked to produce rebuttals and protests, but, as is usual, these have been accorded far less publicity than the original article."

All the contributions to the discussion—from essentially allied disciplines—were highly critical. For genetics, Professor Hirsch (a behaviour geneticist from Indiana, U.S.A.) spoke of the extraordinary complexity of genetical differences and their assessment, since each individual is now estimated to possess 100,000 genes. His conclusions are: (i) that there is no evidence to suggest "a linear hierarchy of inferior and superior races", (ii) that heritability estimates in the study of man "turns out to be a piece of 'knowledge' that is both deceptive and trivial", and (iii) that no general statement can be made about "the assignment of fixed proportions to the contributions of heredity and environment either to the development of a single individual . . . or to the differences . . . among members of a population".

[1] *New Statesman*, September 26th, 1969.
[2] C.S.S.R.S. Bulletin, available from Union Society, Bridge Street, Cambridge.

This line of argument (a direct refutation of the position taken by Burt and Eysenck) ties in with the criticism made by two distinguished geneticists in the earlier discussion in the *New Scientist*, Professors Auerbach and Beale, both Fellows of the Royal Society.[1] In their view the whole argument about racial differences in intelligence is scientifically meaningless—since this is a question it is altogether impossible to submit to scientific proof. Much of the evidence in fact brought forward is derived from work with identical twins, but this has no relevance whatsoever to a comparison of whites and blacks in the United States. A fully effective experiment to determine the degree to which genetically determined racial differences in "intelligence" exist would require "randomising" the environment, in order to exclude its effect. But "for human populations", they write, "even this way out of the dilemma is barred, or at least will be barred until all individuals from all races will be found in all schools, all professions, all of society: in fact until that state of desegregation has been reached that persons like Eysenck believe impossible because of the presumed genetic inferiority of the black race".

Returning to the point in a later contribution—which supports Hirsch as "excellently qualified for presenting the geneticist's point of view", Auerbach and Beale develop their criticism of Jensen at greater length, and underline again that twin studies in white populations (heavily depended upon by Jensen) "have been used freely, incorrectly and mischievously as evidence for the innate intellectual superiority of the white race over its coloured compatriots".[2] As mischievous, it may be added, are psychometrists' frequent claims to have "eliminated" environmental influences in their investigations— merely by statistical manipulation.[3]

Hirsch made another very relevant point at Cambridge. "High or low hereditability", he says, "tells us absolutely nothing about how a given individual might have developed under conditions different from those in which he actually did develop". The various possibilities

---

[1] *New Scientist*, May 29th, 1969.

[2] *Times Educational Supplement*, July 31st, 1970.

[3] Thus, P. E. Vernon, lending qualified support to Jensen, allows the influence of the environment but states that some ability differences still persist "even when environment is effectively eliminated" (*Times Educational Supplement*, September 11th, 1970). Since there has been no question of "randomising" the environment, nor indeed any form of experiment over and above applying tests, this simply means that psychometrists *believe* they have allowed for the factor "environment" through their statistical techniques. This is the only possible basis for highly questionable calculations of the relative influence of heredity and environment in determining "measured intelligence".

open to any specific individual, due to variations in his life experiences, are "effectively unlimited". It is for this reason that the search for general laws of behaviour has been unfruitful—"the heritability of intelligence or of any other trait must be recognised as still another of those will-o'-the-wisp general laws". In the light of this Jensen's claims are inacceptable.

Liam Hudson, Professor of Educational Sciences at Edinburgh University, summarised the defects of Jensen's position. His ideological commitment has led him to make unjustified assumptions about the validity of Intelligence Tests (which "favour the obedient, conforming middle-class child"); he "systematically misrepresents published evidence", particularly in the field of genetics; and, despite constant appeals to the authority of science and "other human virtues like democracy", his research "shows every sign of springing from, and contributing towards, a rising tide of racial and social tension in the society in which he works".

Hudson does not deny that the I.Q. can be a useful technical device. But "the belief that it can serve, by some magic, to define the limits of our intellectual capability is a myth; one that it has taken psychologists fifty years to sell to the general public, and to themselves—and will take them a further fifty years to buy back".

The importance, and social danger, of work of the nature of Jensen's, like "the importance of 'Powellism' in British politics", arises "from its appeal to more primitive aspects of human involvement: Us and Them, Black and White", etc. Hudson underlines that the insidiousness of the appeal matches the deviousness of an argument which ends by destroying what it professes to uphold:

> "It plays on the human impulses of loyalty and snobbery; our need to think well of ourselves and poorly of our neighbours. Pursued naïvely, scientistically, it leads to the misuse of evidence, to heightened social tension and polarisation, and—rapidly—to the abdication of precisely that quality, intelligence, that it originally sought to illuminate."

As in the case of genetics, so also in neurophysiology, recent research puts the statistical speculations of psychometrists out of court. S. P. R. Rose, a neurobiologist, concentrated specifically on the environmental determinants of brain function. While certain basic brain mechanisms are clearly genetically specified, genetic differences within specific strains (e.g. rats, mice, human beings) "are much harder to demon-strate". On the other hand "environmental effects on the brain struc-ture of individuals are profound and well documented". In particular, malnutrition, occurring at the period of maximum brain growth "can result in permanent deficits in brain structure and the interrelation of cells". These can create gross differences between individuals. Less extreme forms of deprivation may also result in deficits in the func-tioning of the brain. In relevant experiments with cats and rats certain forms of stimulation (or enriched experience) improve the structure and functioning of the brain cortex (and vice versa). Even quite brief exposure to novel or "learning" situations leads to "changes in the rates of production of certain key biochemical substances within the brain (e.g.RNA and proteins)", while concurrent changes take place in the degree of connectivity of the brain cells. All these studies lead to the conclusion that environmental effects "result in a series of well defined changes in brain structure and performance", i.e. it is not so much "the brain" a child inherits that matters but the processes it undergoes during his life as a result of experience and education.

Similar views have often been expressed by the distinguished Soviet psychologist A. R. Luria and his colleagues. They lead Rose—who points out that the claim as to the dominance of genetic factors "is not supported even by the statistics adduced by Jensen himself"—to conclude that what is crucial to any individual child's development is the provision of "adequate food, continuous love, affection and intellectual stimulation in its environments during the critical periods of development".

There is, then, a considerable difference between the situation in 1949—when Marxists first challenged the "intelligence" testers—and today. Not only has the battle for increased and improved educational opportunity for the majority begun to be won on the ground, with the transition to comprehensive schooling—which a Tory government may delay but cannot halt. There have also been important develop-ments, in the biological sciences, in psychology (that is experimental psychology, as opposed to the statistical methods of psychometry), in sociology. From the new vantage points, scientists now often react strongly against a move to revive, and make large claims for, a methodology which cuts directly across current developments in allied fields.

It has always been a weakness of "intelligence" testing that it has no firm roots. The founding father of the whole method, it might be said, was Francis Galton, initiator of eugenics—that mode of thought which contributed much to fascist ideology. Psychometrists are not far wrong when they conclude—as does one in a recent textbook—that they "have done little more than validate and systematise the flashes of insight" that Galton "that hereditary genius" (he was a nephew of Darwin) produced in the 1890s.[1] By the same token, they have remained isolated from advances in other scientific fields, continually reproducing the ideas which they originally set out to justify.

Meanwhile there have been advances in neurophysiology (as some of the arguments quoted indicate). It has moved on from locating different centres in the brain (a form of research to which the "intelligence" testers could attempt to latch on) to investigating complex biochemical reactions which put such clumsy methods as "intelligence" testing—taken as a guide to fixed qualities of the brain transmitted by heredity—out of court. Similarly genetics has moved into new fields and geneticists also revolt against the rule of thumb interpretations whereby psychometrists attempt to uphold arguments about intelligence as transmitted by heredity and its distribution in whole populations.

But one of the penalties of rapid scientific advance is that specialisms tend to become highly technical, and sometimes to get out of touch, and this allows for the continuance of older branches of study which altogether fail to subsume new developments in knowledge. Deeply embedded in psychometry, for instance, are theoretical assumptions which could not now stand the light of day. Whereas in the physical and life sciences the road of advance is relatively clearly delineated, and to take it is also to overhaul former findings, this is not the case with less developed disciplines, least of all those whose key relations are with the social structure.

What has kept "intelligence" testing going is not that it is the best and only way of discovering more about the make up of the human mind, and continually comes up with new information—far from it. But it is a convenient and instrumental method of detecting the kind of people who may be most useful to industrial management (one of the main fields of application nowadays is in selection for such jobs in industry), and is also a convenient tool for controlling access to the higher ranges of the educational system. That it also has its uses, on a restricted scale, in clinical research and practice is not to be denied; indeed this is its proper place. By breaking out from this role into

[1] Stephen Wiseman (ed.), *Intelligence and Ability: Selected Readings* (1967).

activities for which it is unsuited, it has exercised a decisive (and damaging) influence on social life. But that breakout resulted from immediate social and political pressures, e.g. in the educational field the need to find some unassailable means to select children given an intention to continue restricting secondary education anyway. Similarly in America today, the pressing need to find some unassailable rationale for maintaining segregation, or more generally for white supremacy, has given a new and dangerous lease of life to an ideology which had all the appearance of being on the way out here.

Even in the exact sciences there is a danger that specialists, after a lifetime investigating their subject and some important advances, come to feel that they have all the right answers to the most general questions. Thus, in relation to C. D. Darlington's genetic interpretation of history, Robert Young cited the moral:

> "A specialised scientist stares down his microscope for forty years and does very good work. Towards the end of his career he asks himself about the wider meaning of it all. He racks back the focus knob on the microscope, tilts the instrument back, and looks about him through its eyepieces. He stares hard for a time, a marvellous gleam comes into his eyes, and he exclaims, 'I understand all!'"

Once the conviction has taken root, nothing will shake it, however much the resulting views cut across the findings of social scientists, and, in effect, represent a departure from rules he has normally followed in his own work. In place of the humility which is the mark of the scientist, always ready to make a new advance upsetting the old standpoint, there then appears arrogance and dogmatism and insistence on the absolute rightness of a standpoint and the blindness or ignorance of all who question it. By these marks the layman can recognise when something is wrong with supposedly scientific claims.

It has been said that psychometry introduces basic assumptions which cannot now stand the light of day. In fact, the whole edifice of theory and practice rests on a single basic assumption—that human mental development, like the development of animals, can be explained in terms of the interaction of heredity and environment.

Why is this a false assumption? Because there is a key qualitative difference between the mode of life—and so the mode of experience or development—of human beings and animals, a point that hardly needs explaining to Marxists. But it has been usefully outlined by

Soviet psychologists, when indicating how different is their approach to investigating children's mental development—and the problem of backwardness—from the approach associated with "intelligence" testing which has, until recently, dominated in the west. As A. N. Leontiev has written:[1]

> "What, then, is this experience that is exclusive to man alone? In the course of history, men, governed by the action of social laws, have developed higher characteristics of mind. Thousands of years of social history have produced more, in this connection, than millions of years of biological evolution. The achievements of mental development have been accumulated gradually, transmitted from generation to generation. This is the way they have been consolidated. Could they have been consolidated in the form of biological, hereditarily transmitted, changes? No; because the historical process is extremely rapid, always accelerating, and consequently the demands upon man's abilities made by the conditions of his life in society change rapidly, quite out of relation to the much slower tempo of biological fixation of experience."

How are human achievements consolidated and transmitted?

> "In a particular form, namely, an exoteric, external form. This new form of accumulating phylogenetic (or, more precisely, social-historical) experience has arisen because man's specific form of activity is productive activity. This is the basic activity of people, their work."

Thus, by contrast with the development of animal species "whose achievements are consolidated in the form of changes in their biological organisation, in the development of their brains, the achievements of men's historical development are consolidated in the material objects, in the ideal phenomena (language, science) created by men. The point hardly needs to be argued."

This approach leads to an understanding that what requires investigation is the process "of mastery, of appropriation" by the human child of the achievements of development of preceding human generations,

---

[1] "Principles of Child Mental Development and the Problem of Intellectual Backwardness", trs. in *Educational Psychology in the U.S.S.R.*, ed. B. and J. Simon (1963). A. N. Leontiev is head of the department of psychology, Moscow University.

which are "embodied in the actual objects and phenomena they have created". In short, children learn in a social world surrounded by humanised objects, primarily with the aid of language. Moreover the child does not merely *adapt* to the social environment, "but takes it to himself, i.e. appropriates it" by learning to speak and other specifically human activities. This is the process "whereby there takes place in the child that which is achieved in animals by the action of heredity; the transmission to the *individual* of the achievements of the development of the *species*".

It is clear, then, that the key to human development is not heredity but *education*. The primary task becomes to discover what forms of education best further acquisition by the child of the human heritage. From this task "intelligence" testing inevitably deflects attention insofar as it specifically rules out the role of education as described. Instead it recognises only "heredity" and the vague generalised category "environment" (subsuming a whole variety of active and passive influences) as determining factors. If two children in similar "environmental" conditions (crudely distinguished) show different mental attributes, then an attempt is made to measure *internal* differences—i.e. the supposed quality of "intelligence"—and there is virtually no other course than to attribute this to heredity, because of the initial assumption. This is a false assumption and to remove it brings the whole structure of "intelligence" testing—and the foreseeable arguments derived from it—to the ground.

The same mode of circular argument can be traced at every level of psychometry. When there is recourse to measuring mental differences by tests, labels are attached to the "factors" isolated statistically which reflect not experimental findings but the presuppositions with which the constructor of the test set out. Thus when a psychometrist constructs an "intelligence" test, he makes up questions which he *thinks* test what he *thinks* is intelligence. There is no other way of defining the factor labelled "intelligence" than in terms of the actual questions of which tests are made up. Professional psychologists operating in a given social and educational situation, necessarily produce tests which equate "intelligence" with—say—the kind of teaching provided in academically-oriented grammar schools for which their tests will serve as a selective instrument. Obviously such a concept of "intelligence" is socially-conditioned, and application of the criterion can only perpetuate existing educational practice, besides dividing up groups of children in relation to it.

Nor is this all. The whole process of constructing and validating tests reinforces the concepts built in at the outset. There is no space to go into the details here.[1] It must be enough to say that any new test must conform to the findings of previous tests to be "valid". If anyone constructed a test based on the culture of the blacks in the United States, a test which, when applied, enabled black children to score more highly than white, it would not be accepted as a "valid" test of intelligence on the grounds that the results fail to correlate highly with the results of a whole backlog of other intelligence tests applied over the years. So the whole process becomes self-perpetuating. Under the circumstances, the finding that working class children are more stupid than middle class children, blacks intellectually inferior by comparison with whites, is less a reflection on those measured than an illustration of the essential limitations of those who construct the instruments of measurement.

The point was made by M. P. M. Richard, a social psychologist, at the C.S.S.R.S. discussion. "Far from being 'objectively scientific' ", he says, "psychological testing involves making social and political judgements in the very process of test construction and validation." Test constructors "are middle class white academics, and, not surprisingly, the test items represent their values" and their motivation. "Why should a black slum child be interested in the white lady's questions about poets and presidents?"

What is of interest and importance is to find a means of breaking out from the situation in which the majority—of whatever colour—are penalised as a direct result of the adverse conditions under which their children develop by comparison with the minority. That they lack good homes and food, and are denied education or a wide range of experience, necessarily leads to low scores in tests geared to the outlook of those who live well and have a wide range of experience. There could be no cruder means of perpetuating the situation than to claim that the tests measure genetic differences—and then to argue that it is innate inferiority that produces the bad conditions of life in the first place. It is a very old argument—and, as John Stuart Mill once remarked, a very vulgar one.[2]

That it can persist, on the basis of research *grounded on* "intelligence"

---

[1] I have discussed them at some length in *Intelligence Testing and the Comprehensive School* (1953), pp. 59–82 (this edition).

[2] The statement, from Mill's *Principles of Political Economy* is recalled in an examination of the whole issue by a French Marxist, Lucien Sève, *L'Ecole et la Nation*, May/June 1967.

testing—which in turn is grounded on the false idea that the interaction of heredity and environment determines human development—is the result both of underlying social divisions, with their ideological accompaniment, and the high level of technicality at which the argument is conducted which veils the slenderness of the basic assumptions.

It needs, then, to be said—and understood all round—that an "intelligence" test tells us *nothing of any significance* about the actual development of the mental processes, or powers of thought and analysis, of any individual child. All it can do is to set out in order, or classify, a group of children according to their answers to a given set of questions administered at a particular point in time. The test gives no indication why a particular child achieved a particular result and no other—the very question to which the educationist requires an answer—but merely the flat fact, that he comes above or below other children. In short, testing is incapable of throwing light on how mental abilities operate and develop—and so spreads the idea that they are given and do not develop. Consideration of the crucial questions are thus *excluded* by the whole apparatus of mental testing, in particular by what might be called its technology.

It is at this point that educationists and psychologists, faced with successful developments in school practice which severely dented the assumptions of mental testing, and desiring to further them, have stepped in.

In the U.S.S.R., where testing was abolished in 1936, A. R. Luria has well outlined the link up between new methods of investigating the learning process in children and new developments in neurophysiology:

"It is now generally accepted that in the process of mental development there takes place a profound qualitative reorganisation of human mental activity, and that the basic characteristic of this reorganisation is that elementary, direct activity is replaced by complex functional systems, formed on the basis of the child's communication with adults in the process of learning. These functional systems are of complex construction, and are developed with the close participation of language, which as the basic means of communication with people is simultaneously one of the basic tools in the formation of human mental activity and in the regulation of behaviour. It is through these complex forms of mental activity

... that new features are acquired and begin to develop according to new laws which displace many of the laws which govern the formation of elementary conditioned reflexes in animals."[1]

Elsewhere this link is only beginning to be made now—the present controversy will further it. But psychologists and educationists in Britain and America have been progressively breaking free from the trammels of psychometric theory and practice.

In America, the work of J. McV. Hunt, Jerome Bruner, and others, has led to an entirely new appraisal of human potentialities and their realisation. Hunt's *Intelligence and Experience* (New York 1961) makes a devastating historical and critical analysis of the whole theory and approach of psychometry and has played an important part in enforcing revision or retraction. Milton Schwebel's *Who Can be Educated?* (New York 1968) also made an all-round analysis of the determinants of educability, leading to the complete rejection of the claims of psychometry. Both these authors were attacked by Jensen, both have replied.[2] In Britain the work of many educational psychologists has taken a similar direction, an important paper being that by D. A. Pidgeon, "Intelligence testing and comprehensive education".[3] This whole movement implies a fundamental challenge to the techniques, and assumptions, of psychometry on which Jensen bases his entire case.

The issues are well summarised by Professor Morris, a psychologist much concerned with the production of intelligence tests when secretary of the National Foundation for Educational Research. Psychometry, he claims, failed to scrutinise adequately its presuppositions, and so "developed into a technology concerned with establishing and measuring the more or less fixed intellectual abilities with which it supposed children to be endowed at birth, irrespective of the cultural and educational milieu in which they developed". In this it appeared to achieve practical success, but, he adds, "we are now witnessing the slow crumbling of this technology, and of its supporting ideology, as the presuppositions of both become exposed to radical criticism".

[1] Luria's standpoint is easily available in a fascinating twin study—differing markedly from those designed to uphold psychometric theories—*Speech and the Development of Mental Processes in the Child* (trs. and ed. J. Simon, 1959). This book has had a profound influence both in the U.S.A. and Britain, figuring in most relevant bibliographies.

[2] *Harvard Educational Review*, Nos. 2 and 3, 1969.

[3] In *Genetic and Environmental Factors in Human Ability*, ed. J. F. Meade and A. S. Parkes (1966).

Such failure is, at the same time, "a grave warning" which educational psychologists should take to heart.[1]

This was written in 1966. It is an argument to which Arthur Jensen would do well to pay attention, as has been heavily underlined by his critics in the States.

This brings us back to the criticisms of Jensen's article in the *Harvard Educational Review* where it appeared. Although he finds some support, the majority of articles and correspondence in the succeeding two numbers of the journal are critical. This is particularly evident in the 50 pages of correspondence printed—there is no indication how much was received.

First place may be given to contributions from blacks and, not surprisingly, some were forcefully expressed. The Black Students Union of Harvard Graduate School, stating that "the question is, of course, far more political than scientific", protest strongly at the failure to consult black students or teachers before publication. The union "seriously doubts that the question of Jewish inferiority, Irish inferiority or any other racist-inspired argument would have been thrust so arrogantly into prominence by the current Editorial Board". Demanding the right to respond to the article "at an appropriate time of our own choosing", the union also calls for safeguards against "the future printing of racist literature that is directed at maligning Black people in this country and/or abroad under the aegis of the Harvard Graduate School of Education".[2]

Roy Brown, from Chicago, quotes Jensen: "Heredity . . . plays some role in the heavy representation of Negroes in America's lower socio-economic groups." This "is unbelievable when one considers the fact that absolutely nothing is said about the extreme deprivation that blacks have endured—300 years of the cruellest slavery known to mankind: 100 years of barbaric servitude, murder, lynching, burning, and intimidation, superimposed with an arrogant, savage con game. There was literally no intention of treating blacks as human beings; but, rather, they were to be exploited and kept in servitude by any and all means, legal and illegal."

---

[1] See p. 234 for a fuller quotation from Ben Morris, "The contribution of psychology to the study of education", in *The Study of Education*, ed. J. W. Tibble (1966).

[2] The *Harvard Educational Review*, which apparently commissioned Jensen's article, is edited by a group of graduate students at Harvard, that is students working for higher degrees. "Editorial policy", it is stated, "does not reflect an official position of the Faculty of Education or any other Harvard faculty"—a disclaimer only published *since* the furore about Jensen's article.

What blacks need, Brown concludes, "is not the white man's genes, but more and more of the spirit of rebellion against racism and injustice".

A black neuropsychiatrist says Jensen's main argument, is simple: "Negroes are born stupid; its genetic; there's nothing you can do about it." But the article is confusing as an "elaborate assortment of truths, half-truths, falsehoods, exaggerations, faulty deductions and speculations". Pointing to the ideological presuppositions, he notes that the author "is hired by the University of California at Berkeley where rebellious, disorderly and disruptive black militants have incurred the wrath of Dr. Jensen's boss, the governor" (Reagan). But this is a carefully reasoned contribution, the only one (to my surprise) which analyses the nature of the most widely used intelligence test (the Wechsler Test) and its specific components, to illustrate how far questions are weighted against deprived (and primarily black) children. Among other telling points, it is noted that Jensen equates intelligence with vocational achievement—each finds his proper place—an underlying assumption of hereditarians as we have seen. "So we see that the prestige hierarchy of occupation is a reliable objective reality in our society." Would Jensen, then, explain how "the Russian serfs of 100 years ago are the rulers of Russia today?"

Then there are reactions from two organisations concerned with the social implications of science. The New York Scientists' Committee for Public Information (SPCI) notes that mischievous misuse of such an article "is inevitable in a society that rationalises the pervasive racism of its major institutions". Though scientifically the paper is "perplexing", the hypothesis may well be accepted as proven fact "and guide educational policy accordingly". Leave aside many questionable arguments, the whole approach ignores the elementary rule of genetics, formulated by the distinguished (American) geneticist Dobzhansky: "Equal or unequal potentialities cannot be judged unless similar environments are provided. Hence, it is quite unreasonable to argue that we must first find that potentialities are equal and then provide similar environments. We must do the reverse."

This is precisely the point made by British geneticists cited earlier, and by educationists.

An organisation to which leading psychologists belong, the Society for the Psychological Study of Social Issues (SPSSI) declares:

"As behavioural scientists, we believe that statements specifying the hereditary components of intelligence are unwarranted by the present state of scientific knowledge."

Noting that such statements "may be seriously misinterpreted, particularly in their applications to social policy", the society stress the "immeasurable burden" that racism and discrimination imposes on the blacks, as an obvious determinant of level of achievement. Tests in use, which are biased against blacks "to an unknown degree", cannot be taken as accurate measurements of innate endowment. Jensen is charged, by implication, of insufficient care, failing to guard against over-generalisation of his conclusions and misunderstanding of the social relations of his work.

Many emphasise the latter point—the actual use to which the article has been put in current struggles on the racial issue. After the wide publicity, the main point of the thesis, itself half-digested, was widely canvassed by racists and reactionaries. Even in Britain, National Front leaders frequently quoted Jensen at meetings in Haringey on the "banding" issue.[1]

These arguments, writes Martin Deutsch, a leading American psychologist who formerly worked with Jensen and is thoroughly familiar with all the data he used, point inescapably to the conclusion "that the central theme of the Jensen piece is a wholly anti-democratic eugenic position". As one who has known Jensen many years, and collaborated with him on an SPSSI sponsored volume—*Social Class, Race and Psychological Development*, of which the orientation "was diametrically opposed to his current stated position"—Deutsch points out the destructive nature of this position and its "negative implications". Jensen's conclusions, unwarranted by the existing data, "reflect a consistent bias towards a racist hypothesis". Finally, there is a direct challenge to Jensen to "summon the social courage necessary to repudiate the positions that have been taken in his name". With this, he should re-examine his data and argument in the light of factors "with which apparently he was not familiar at the time he wrote the article", in short, reconsider his entire thesis.[2]

There is no indication, in Jensen's reply to the discussion, that he is considering any such course of action.

This, then, is the present stage of the controversy. It has been discussed here mainly from the angle of education, the vital angle, with which I am most familiar, but by no means the only one. There remains much more to be said about the reactions of scientists in allied fields,

[1] *Times Educational Supplement*, July 24th, 1970.
[2] *Harvard Educational Review*, Summer 1969, pp. 523–557.

raising anew the whole question of the social function of science, the social responsibilities of scientists, the extent to which ideas extrinsic to the particular scientific matter in hand penetrate thinking, and so on. These questions have often been discussed but need fresh thought in relation to this particular manifestation of the problem.

For there can be no doubt about it, the questions now brought into the arena are matters about which the layman—working in the labour movement and concerned with educational advance no less than racial propaganda and the whole range of social and political life—needs to be clear.

There can, therefore, be no acceptance of the argument that this is a scientific controversy into which it is illegitimate to "import" social or political considerations. There is no question anyway of importation when the implications are clear to the average newspaper reporter who has helped precipitate them into the general arena. Moreover the way the "keep out" notice has been posted, by psychometrists, alone rules out respect for it. Thus Eysenck likened those who deny Jensen's thesis to the Aristotelian philosophers "who refused to look through Galileo's telescope". And then—claiming that a clear-cut demonstration had been given that individual differences in intelligence "are largely due to hereditary causes"—dismissed those who challenged this interpretation as characterised by "an ignorance alike of psychometric techniques of intelligence testing and biometric techniques of genetic analysis". It seems unreasonable "to discuss the problem or write about it, when one cannot tell the difference between epistasis and meiotosis, reduce a Hessenberg matrix, or determine an Eigen-value".[1]

There is an arrogance about this attempt to "blind with expertise" (mounted before the Cambridge meeting relegated the argument) which is altogether out of tune with the scientist's approach, up to and including the mention of Jensen in the same breath as Galileo—though, as has been indicated, the theories he espouses have a good deal more in common with blind Aristotelianism, or ideas left over from an earlier epoch. It was in the heyday of British imperialism that Galton launched eugenics, from which "intelligence" testing directly derives.

Moreover, if psychometrists are so keen to keep the matter in expert hands, why did Eysenck—and Burt—lend open support to the Black Papers? Were these not directly political acts, openly intended to influence legislation, in that they were prefaced by a letter to M.P's and freely distributed to every one? In the light of this, Burt's appeal in

[1] *Times Educational Supplement*, December 12th, 1969.

Black Paper Two for education to be kept out of politics is—at best—an example of basically confused thinking. Or, to look at it another way, this is the only route whereby hereditarian psychometrists, outflanked in their own field and in education, can look to regain lost support—a return to the old structure and methods of education in which their techniques were perpetually justified and indispensable.

In the present controversy, an old one relaunched in the light of Jensen's initiative in the particular current circumstances in the United States, psychometrists have been careful to avoid mention of their defeats in the recent past, and the resulting rejection of their approach in the educational system. Yet this provides an answer to the plea that "science" must be allowed to proceed under its own steam without interference. It was the public revolt against 11 plus, the developments in the schools which led directly to rejection of selection techniques by administrators no longer able to defend them, that actively undermined psychometric doctrine and practice. And it was this, in turn, that forced psychometrists to modify a theory which was only beginning to be questioned internally. So much for independence from social conditions, never a mark of this particular branch of psychological investigation.

The next stage, in which the influence of scientists in allied fields will be of key importance, is likely to be a questioning of the very foundations of psychometry in order finally to eliminate wide-ranging speculations disguised as scientific evidence or findings.

Two aphorisms of Francis Bacon—that outright enemy of blind Aristotelianism in his own day—seem to fit the situation well.

"The axioms now in use, having been suggested by a scanty and manipular experience and a few particulars of most general occurrence, are made for the most part just large enough to fit and take these in; and therefore it is no wonder if they do not lead to new particulars. And if some opposite instance, not observed or not known before, chance to come in the way, the axiom is rescued and preserved by some frivolous distinction; whereas the truer course would be to correct the axiom itself."

And

"The idols and false notions which are now in possession of the human understanding, and have taken deep root therein, not only so beset men's minds that truth can hardly find entrance, but even after entrance obtained, they will again in the very instauration of the sciences meet and trouble us, unless men being forewarned of the danger fortify themselves as far as may be against their assaults."

CONTEMPORARY PROBLEMS IN
EDUCATIONAL THEORY[1]

While it is certainly the case that Marx himself wrote little more than a few short passages directly bearing on education—its structure, processes and general character—there is no question that the Marxist approach is very relevant to analysis of a wide range of educational issues; indeed there are no important educational problems that cannot be tackled from the standpoint of Marxism.

There are today very many controversial issues in the area of educational theory and practice that urgently require attention, but have, unfortunately, been neglected by Marxists. The result is a tendency to confusion and disarray among left/progressive forces. This is inevitable, given that no clear lead has been forthcoming, grounded in a rational analysis of current theoretical issues based on Marxism. Partly for this reason the Black Papers, for instance, and like phenomena can make a considerable impact.

Challenges of this kind must be more effectively met in the future, and it is not as if there is not an arsenal of weapons on which Marxists can draw in making a critical assessment of contemporary trends and developments. The objective must be to define more precisely both short-term and long-term objectives; to clarify the issues at stake, and to define a theoretical standpoint which can act as a guide to practice. It is to assist in this process, and, hopefully, to stimulate a wide-ranging discussion, that this paper is offered.

Education is best seen, in my view, as an area of class struggle where opposing objectives meet. Though established through the medium of (or by) the state, the educational system cannot be equated with the armed forces, police, judicature, as an oppressive weapon of the state, even though it certainly contains such an element. But the organised labour movement fought for universal compulsory education, and, once established, has sought consistently to transform it—to render it more democratic, more open, more appropriate to the aspirations of working people. This is the sense in which education embodies opposing objectives.

Hence, in a capitalist society, conflicts necessarily arise within

[1] Reprinted from *Marxism Today*, June 1976.

education itself. For instance, the organised labour movement, expressing the interests of the working class, sees education (and has done so historically) as one means, if auxiliary, of economic and political emancipation; while the bourgeoisie see it now and have seen it in the past primarily as a means of social control—as a means by which the masses are brought to assimilate the ideology of capitalism, and of "appropriate" norms of behaviour. These attitudes clearly reflect quite opposite intentions.

Again, the labour movement and its allies see education as formative—as the means by which the younger generation may develop their personality, abilities, skills—their potential. In practice, however, the system operates as a selective, winnowing device, distributing life chances, allowing a strictly controlled degree of social mobility, fitting the new generation into the existing occupational structure, or ensuring the reproduction of social relations.

Most of the important contemporary issues in education arise from contradictions of this fundamental kind, involving different conceptions as to the nature and purpose of education. It is not surprising, in view of the basic conflict of interest embodied in the system, that very many controversial questions emerge, both as regards the theory and the practice of education, at all levels, since this fundamental conflict expresses itself in many different forms.

In the existing crisis of capitalism all such contradictions are sharpened, become more specific, since education is closely linked with economic and political conditions generally. For instance, inflation leads inevitably to a fiscal crisis relating to the financing of education. Local authorities claim that they have not got the necessary means to carry on the system now developed, while worse times are threatened. Local initiative and democratic controls are today being weakened partly by local government reorganisation—resulting, in many areas, in a direct threat to the maintenance of local educational systems (through increased bureaucracy together with imposition of the resources management approach), and partly by the rapid growth of the centralised state bureaucracy now clearly bidding for direct control over education. This has recently been brutally indicated in the Department of Education and Science's policy concerning colleges of education and higher education generally.

Contemporary financial pressures coincide with a certain disillusion as regards education's potential for solving some of the sharpest, and most sensitive, problems of capitalist society. This is the case in the

United States in particular, where great hopes were placed on education as a palliative for social discontent. Today it is more common there to speak now of the crisis in education, resulting from urbanisation, racial conflict and poverty. Widely publicised enquiries like the Coleman Report and the Jencks survey entitled *Inequality* feed this disillusion. On the basis of massive correlation studies, these conclude that "Schools make no difference"—a very convenient conclusion for those wishing both to cut public expenditure and to put a brake on educational advance.

Here, incidentally, we see another effect of positivist social science, which reaches conclusions about the nature and role of education and its potentialities by looking only at data derived from the existing situation, ignoring its historical development, the nature of monopoly capitalism, and any assessment of the role education can and does play in different socio-economic formations and at moments of fundamental social change.

The leading ideological or theoretical issues today are all related to the great perennial questions in education, which can be put quite briefly. What should be taught? To whom? How?

These questions pose themselves afresh in each generation, and are now posed in a new situation in this country—that is, in the light of the partially successful move to comprehensive secondary education. In spite of all the difficulties and problems with which the schools are faced, we should not underestimate the significance of this development. It is a move to an organisational form which *potentially* (or theoretically) allows the *whole population*, without distinction of class, caste, stratum or grade, to be educated together, and experience a common basic education which (again *potentially*) can impart a general, humanistic, formative culture, embracing also the fundamentals of science and technology. To turn this potentiality into actuality must surely be the socialist perspective.

The achievement of comprehensive secondary education throughout the country (involving the absorption, or demise, of the independent schools) would not only mark a victory in itself for the labour and left-progressive forces in general, but is also the necessary organisational form for the further transformation of education. In particular, it would mark the demise of the functionally organised school system, whereby each individual is docketed almost from birth and programmed (or processed) to be turned out again at a given occupational level through the system of streaming and selection. This system was paramount until quite recently, and still persists in some forms.

But here a note or warning. It would be quite wrong to exaggerate the extent of success and quite utopian and illusory to think that the new organisational form automatically brings with it a new and transformed content of education, and new procedures, in line with the aspirations of the working class. The transition to comprehensive education has taken place, of course, in a capitalist society, marked by sharp class antagonisms which are certainly reflected in the schools in all sorts of ways. But the history of this movement shows that the new system itself is in process of evolution, that it is not fixed and static but has undergone important changes.

The first comprehensive schools simply took over the old inner content, in the form of differentiation of pupils through streaming and other divisive measures inside the school. But the tendency towards the unification of the school, and away from the docketing and labelling of pupils, has been slow but continuous. Today a common undifferentiated education (or common core of studies) up to 14 or even 16 is on the order of the day as a practical objective in very many comprehensive schools in the country. Let's be clear that this has been achieved through the struggle of advanced forces—particularly teachers, but with the support of the labour movement and of progressive local authorities, advisers, etc., who have been clear as to their objectives, and that it has been a very considerable achievement, one which can, and must, be taken further.

The development of comprehensive education along these lines, partly because of the perspective this opens up for further development, represents a success by the labour movement and left-progressive forces. There can be no doubt of that. But we begin to understand some of the complexities of the situation when we realise that, in some senses, comprehensive education was a necessity for the survival of capitalism. This was understood by the more far-sighted members of the establishment impressed by evidence produced by sociologists relating to the so-called "wastage" of human ability under the old, divisive system, which weakened Britain in the inter-imperialist struggle (a standpoint reflected, for instance, in the Crowther report, 1958, and the Robbins report, 1963).

While in this sense a necessity for the survival of capitalism, comprehensive education at the same time represents a threat, and potentially a very considerable one, to long-established procedures, vested interests, privileges of the ruling class and their dependants. Hence the resistance to its further development, which becomes sharper the more firmly it is established, and the more its potentialities are realised. This opposition is expressed in all sorts of ways—in the Black Papers, in books like Wilson's *Education, Equality and Society* (1975), in Lord James's speeches in the House of Lords, in the Tory Party's campaign led by St. John Stevas, in the moves to cut educational expenditure and slow the rate of change, in the campaign against comprehensive education waged by the mass media, and so on. At the same time the public education system itself is experiencing the effects of the sharpening economic crisis which expresses itself in the so-called urban crisis, in increasing alienation of the youth from traditional procedures and established (and establishment) values, in the reflection in the schools of racial antagonisms, and so on. Add to this a certain confusion in the schools, understandable enough in the present situation, as to educational objectives and means (sharply focused in the Tyndale enquiry), and it is clear that all is not plain sailing, and that there is an urgent need for clarity and broad agreement among the left-progressive forces as to the way ahead.

It may be worth giving here a general, no doubt crude and over-simplified, answer from the standpoint of Marxism to the three questions raised earlier. What shall be taught, to whom, and how? Briefly we would say that primary and secondary education should impart a general, formative, humanistic culture to be followed by professional (or specialised) preparation—and that this should be imparted to *all*; that is, that all children in an advanced society should experience such an education. *How* should this be done? By grasping and utilising all the resources of modern pedagogy, and I would claim, with Comenius in the seventeenth century and Jerome Bruner and A. R. Luria today, that we know how to do it.

I will come back to these points later. But it is in relation to these general objectives that ideological (or theoretical) issues arise that Marxists see as important. In general, these are those standpoints which oppose these objectives *either* on the grounds that they are undesirable in themselves, *or* that they are impossible of achievement (so reducing confidence in the task).

We have had experience of one crucially important ideological standpoint that had to be smashed (or, rather, subjected to a sharply critical evaluation) if advance was to be made, and we can learn from that. This was the battle, fought some 20 years ago, about the practice of selection and its ideological justification in the theory and practice of intelligence testing. It was essential to examine this critically both because the practice of intelligence testing was the instrumental means on which the divided, functional system of education was based, and because, at the same time, the theories derived from intelligence testing provided the rationale—or justification—of the selective system, in that it held (and claimed to have proved) that only a small proportion of the population was capable of benefiting from a systematic secondary education. In other words, that the perspective outlined above is simply impossible of achievement.

The vicious thing about this practice, which claimed a scientific basis, lay not only in its practical utilisation in the school system as the means of streaming and selection, but, even more important, in the way it affected (and determined) the whole approach to the educational enterprise. Teachers (with some exceptions) were convinced that the mass of the children could achieve little, and lowered their sights accordingly. Children themselves assimilated a negative self-image, and this affected their level of aspiration and so their achievement; the theory was used to convince parents of the innate failings of their own children. A whole ethos of failure developed which profoundly affected attitudes to education, and therefore the nature of the process itself. The fight against this theory—or more accurately ideology— was both an ideological and a practical matter, and one that had to be carried through in the schools and classrooms as well as in the study. But it was essential to win it in order to transform the atmosphere, or climate, in which the practice of teaching and educating was carried on—and in order to transform the school system in parallel with establishing a *positive* view as to the potentialities of schooling and education.

This issue is, of course, still with us; it has raised its head in a different context, that of racialism, in the United States in particular. But the old arguments are being revived in this country also in relation to the schools (as in the Black Papers, by Burt, Eysenck, Lynn) so that a struggle against them is still necessary. Marxists have played their part in this along with others and must continue to do so. But in the meantime a number of other issues have come into prominence— having (objectively) similar aims: to prevent, or hold back, the implementation of genuine secondary education for all.

First, we may refer briefly to those ideas which can be categorised as the direct expression of bourgeois ideology. These include a set of a priori arguments against extending secondary education to all.

The most recent expression of this standpoint, on a high or abstract level, is Bryan Wilson's *Education, Equality and Society* (1975), a symposium. In his introduction, Wilson (a sociologist and fellow of All Souls College, Oxford) bewails the rejection of "categories" which, he says, "is itself an important element in the contemporary campaign for equality". Streaming, which "was an attempt to teach pupils in accordance with their actual differences in ability", is now under attack; "setting", he adds, "now suffers the same ideological assault". Such categorisation, he claims, is offensive to "egalitarians" who—he now makes a considerable leap, "wish to destroy the whole social apparatus of order, gradation, status, distinction and categorisation". There is space here only to give a taste of this kind of conservative philosophising which finishes by attributing to comprehensive education most of the responsibility for what the author refers to as "the breakdown in discipline", "the growing problem of truancy", "the alarming reports of inability to spell . . . ignorance of basic geography, general knowledge", and so on.

This book, incidentally, contains a long exposition from G. H. Bantock as to the necessity for minority culture in a mass society, and hence for an élitist education for the few and a popular ("affective") education for what Bantock calls "the folk"; and another by the late Cyril Burt representing his well-known views as to social class differentiation of intelligence—remarkable chiefly for the historical rationalisation he produces to explain how it has come about that the middle classes are genetically superior to the working class, as "proved" by Intelligence Testing. "Ever since the days of the legendary Dick Whittington," Burt writes, "and indeed long before his time, bright and energetic youngsters from the poorest homes have steadily worked their way up to the merchant or professional classes, while the duller and lazier children of the middle or upper classes have tended to drift downward."

No historian, I believe, would accept this kind of analysis of the historical process required to "substantiate" the conclusions drawn from Intelligence Testing; this argument is symptomatic of the blind alleys people get themselves into in defending the doctrines of this pseudo-science. However, enough has been said to indicate the type of arguments—philosophical, sociological, psychometric—brought together in the assault on the kind of educational developments now being brought about in the schools. These cover a wide range and deserve stringent criticism from a Marxist standpoint.

Burt, Jensen, Eysenck, etc., present a set of ideas to the effect that the mass of the children are not capable of benefiting from a systematic secondary education due to hereditary disadvantage. Marxists reject this thesis, and have made their opposition to it absolutely clear. But I would like to make equally clear that Marxism also rejects the parallel but seemingly opposite argument that it is not heredity, but *environmental disadvantage*, which also has this effect. This standpoint claims, in effect, that the mass of working-class children are so disadvantaged by the nature of their family life as to be incapable of abstract, conceptual thought, and therefore of systematic education.

The argument here is based on the theory of linguistic deprivation, and derives initially (paradoxically) from A. R. Luria's pioneering work on the relation between language and cognitive (or intellectual) development generally—though Luria would certainly not go along with the development of his ideas in this direction. The theory, as so developed, is, of course, highly speculative. Linguistic deprivation is advanced as the reason why working-class children "fail" when confronted with the demands and rigours of an academic curriculum. Thus this argument also, and this is typical of all such standpoints, finds the cause of failure within the children themselves, or their families, rather than in the circumstances of a class-divided society with its attendant housing, health and innumerable other problems, all of which can only be solved by social action on a massive scale.

Environmental determinism (for such is the position) can be as vicious as hereditarian determinism, and is equally unacceptable on rational grounds, perhaps in particular to Marxists. The conception, basic to Intelligence Testing theory, that the child's development is the simple product of the interaction of two "factors", *heredity* on the one hand, and a supposed unchanging *environment* on the other, is essentially metaphysical. In this theory, the category "environment" is seen as comprising the total environment of the child as a kind of global entity, including family, conditions of life, schooling, and so on, which is seen as external to the child and which operates on him—to which he is passively subject. When Burt/Jensen, etc., futilely claim that the variation in children's intelligence is determined 80 per cent by heredity and 20 per cent by "environment", this is the sense in which they are using the term.

Marxism utterly rejects this metaphysical approach. The matter is far more complex than this, as I shall hope (briefly) to show towards the end of this paper. But it is relevant here to remind ourselves that the Marxist approach to child development places the main emphasis on the child's active relationship with adults, other children, the school, and with the other phenomena, both natural and artificial, surrounding him, through which process of activity the child's specific abilities, skills, habits, speech and behaviour generally are formed. Burt used to claim that the theory of the primacy of "intelligence" as a factor of the mind lent support to the idealist philosophical outlook, and he is right. The environmentalist approach, which reaches its apotheosis in Skinnerian behaviourism, is a modern expression of our old friend mechanical materialism. The two, as Marx showed, are opposite sides to the same coin. What both ignore, or fail to grasp, is *dialectics*—the very possibility of movement and change; the interconnection, or inter-penetration, of subject and object which lies at the heart of education.

How does the argument proceed, and why is it important? Children, it is claimed, who are linguistically—or educationally—deprived require (in their own best interests, of course) a special, *differentiated* educational content, or forms of educational activity. It is here that we meet with a wide variety of ideological standpoints which deny the desirability—or even the possibility—of providing common, basic educational experiences for all children, and which lead, objectively, to differentiation and back to divisiveness in education.

All sorts of ingenious theories are utilised to support this position—some of them dressed up as "radical", even revolutionary nostrums. The spectrum ranges from the arguments for special "community based" curricula for EPA (Education Priority Area) children, advanced on the grounds that the specific features characterising EPAs—poverty, overcrowding, congestion, lack of cultural or other amenities—are with us for ever, so that children must be enured to cope with the situation, to the overtly sophisticated relativism of what is defined as "new direction" sociology. This latter advances an unbelievably a-historical (and entirely speculative) theory as to how "high status" curriculum and subject matter becomes so defined, and enshrined in the school curriculum (as a result of battles for status and "legitimacy" between competing groups), and "legitimises" (to use their term) the conclusion that any curriculum is "as good as" another; that the knowledge man has accumulated over the last two to three thousand years and more is "bourgeois knowledge" and therefore by definition alienating to the working class—more particularly if conveyed by teachers who are themselves, again by definition, middle class.

The "radical" nature of this relativist ideological position, and the danger of taking it seriously, is shown in practice by those young teachers who, accepting this view of knowledge, and in their sentimental generosity identifying with their working-class pupils, begin to see their role as one of shielding them from the demands of formal schooling, and acting more the role of social worker (imbued sometimes with a smattering of "dynamic psychology") rather than as teacher, with the specific function of inducting their pupils into the knowledge, skills and abilities that derive from the objectives of an all-round, humanist education appropriate to the mid-late twentieth century. The dangers of this approach are evident; its relativist position in relation to knowledge (in the last resort a solipsist standpoint) provides a new ideological means of denying to the working class access to knowledge, culture and science.

Linked with these approaches, in some senses, are a whole set of what might be called libertarian/anarchist ideas or ideological positions which deny the need for structure, purpose, direction, or any kind of authority in education; usually basing themselves theoretically on an idealist position (in the philosophic sense) as to the nature of the child and the potentiality of his inner, spontaneous, "natural" development. Unfortunately there is not space here to enter into a critique of this position—though it should certainly be undertaken from a Marxist standpoint. The importance of such theories in the context of this paper is, of course, that they deny the desirability of a common educational experience, stressing what is unique and so what differentiates every individual rather than what human beings have in common. These ideas tie in with the de-schooling movement associated with the names of Ivan Illich and Everett Reimer, which derives its main ideological basis and its general ideas from the American anarchist/ educationist Paul Goodman.[1] Proponents of these views naturally find it difficult to work within the state system of education and form the spearhead of the so-called "alternative" school movement both in the United States and in Britain—a largely middle class inspired movement; or, with Illich, devote their energies to the attempt to destroy the system of education holding that, if achieved, a joyous and convivial Utopia will supersede the technocratic, monopoly dominated, consumer society.

This is not the place to enter into a critique of the kind of historical and social analysis put forward by Illich, Reimer and others to support

[1] Ivan Illich, *De-Schooling Society* (1971), *Celebration of Awareness* (1971); Everett Reimer, *School is Dead* (1971); Paul Goodman, *Compulsory Miseducation* (1962).

and justify their standpoint. Everett Reimer's position seems to stand in the tradition of American petty bourgeois radicalism. Far from presenting any kind of threat to the established order, in terms of the dominance of monopoly capital, the objective function of these ideas is rather, through the use of "radical" and even "revolutionary" formulations, to divert attention from the main issues and points of attack, and, in the social analysis offered, to confuse and obscure.

It is to be hoped that these writings will be subjected to a Marxist critique, as they have had a certain influence in Britain; even if Reimer himself modestly disclaims the value of his analysis. "Even Illich may disagree with parts of it", he writes, towards the end of his well-known book *School is Dead*. "By the time it is published it is quite likely that I will too." He adds that since writing these words in his first draft, four chapters have been jettisoned and eight new ones added, but even so "the sentence stands". This hardly gives confidence in the whole enterprise—and indeed a lot of the book appears as the product of "instant thought".

In so far as this whole movement, which may be characterised as anarchist/libertarian, represents a reaction (if an exaggerated one) from the hierarchical and rigid educational structures of the past (and present) and from the passive approach to learning symptomatic of the old type grammar school, it can be said to have positive elements which Marxists, with its stress on human activity as formative, should recognise. But objectively this standpoint, particularly that of de-schooling, undermines confidence in the school system, and particularly in the value of attempts to transform this system through, for instance, the development of comprehensive education, the abolition of streaming, and the evolution of humane and educationally justifiable pedagogic means. Such efforts to transform the school are written off as mere attempts to preserve the existing system which ought to be destroyed.

It is perhaps worth noting that the de-schooling/anarchist literature, which burst on the British scene in a co-ordinated and massively popular form a few years ago, was largely produced by Penguin Education, a subsidiary of Pearson/IPC, with an ex-Tory Minister of Education (Boyle) as a member of the Editorial Board.

This prompts the thought that whereas universal compulsory education was finally accepted as being in the interests of the ruling class in the late nineteenth century, we may now be entering a phase where it is no longer so evidently so, so that attempts to destroy, or, better, perhaps, to emasculate the system may now have high-level support. True, the school-leaving age has been raised, but there have been many signs of lack of enthusiasm. This is particularly the case in the United States at present where, in many areas, no serious attempt is made to maintain existing laws relating to compulsory education.

While some of the criticisms of existing school practice by this movement are certainly worth taking into account, the solution of destroying the schools in favour of learning "networks", and similar schemes, plays directly into the hands of the modern Geddeses—only too ready to wield the axe—and is clearly in no sense in the interests of the working class. In this situation, I suggest, it must be our function to defend and extend the school system while working for its transformation; and we ought to be quite clear about this.

I have outlined some only of the contemporary ideological issues and given some indication of what I conceive to be a Marxist approach to them. Clearly each and every one of them is worth a detailed analysis and critique, but this cannot be done here. But it may be appropriate to sketch in what I conceive to be a Marxist approach to education and learning (or to some aspects of these), in the hope that this can provide a standpoint, or set of criteria, from which an evaluation can be made of these and other ideological issues in education.

How do we approach the crucial question of the content of education—what shall be taught? In the first place, I suggest, Marxists reject pluralistic notions—the provision, as a basic principle, of different sorts of curricula for different groups or classes, or for that matter sexes, either when based on some conception of differential needs, or on a functional basis. And certainly Marxists reject the notion that education for the working class must be based on, or be derived from, some kind of specifically working-class or proletarian culture—and the concomitant view, quite widely held, that the knowledge now taught in schools and colleges is necessarily some kind of bourgeois knowledge that must be rejected.

It is worth recalling that Lenin was faced with exactly this problem in relation to the Proletcult movement in the early 1920s—a movement which also rejected science and culture as bourgeois, and nailed its flag to a conception of an independent proletarian culture. This view also rejected entirely the content as well as the methodology of the "old" school—the pre-revolutionary schools of Tsarist Russia. How did Lenin deal with this question?

In his speech on *The Task of the Youth Leagues*, delivered to the YCL Congress in October 1920, Lenin discussed the nature of education in the new Soviet Republic.[1] He stressed two things. First, that it was absolutely right to reject the methods and ethos of the old school—the stress on rote learning, the aridity, the way the school was cut off, isolated, from life. But secondly he stresses again and again in that speech what he sees as the crucial issue—that to be a Communist (and the schools must aim to educate Communists) the student must acquire human knowledge as it has been accumulated in man's long advance from savagery to civilisation. Marx himself, he points out, took his stand on the firm foundation of human knowledge gained under capitalism.

So today young people must assimilate this knowledge, and assimilate it *critically*. "One can become a Communist", he said, "only when one enriches one's mind with a knowledge of all the wealth created by mankind" and (he added) when one knows how to apply it. Certainly we must abolish the old school, "but we must take from it all that mankind has accumulated for the benefit of man". In place of the old drill methods—which led to hatred of the old school—we must put the ability "to take for ourselves the sum total of human knowledge".

In the draft resolution he submitted shortly after this speech to the Central Committee for approval at the Proletcult Congress he carried on the battle:

"Marxism won for itself its world-historical significance as the ideology of the revolutionary proletariat by the fact that it did not cast aside the valuable gains of the bourgeois epoch, but on the contrary assimilated and digested all that was valuable in the more than 2,000 years of development of human thought and culture. Further work on this basis and in this direction, inspired by the practical experience of the dictatorship of the proletariat in its last struggle against all exploitation, can alone be regarded as the development of really proletarian culture."

The draft resolution goes on to reject "as theoretically wrong and practically harmful all attempts to invent a special culture"—and to use it as the basis of development and education.

I have cited Lenin at some length because he expresses with his usual incisiveness and clarity what I take to be the Marxist viewpoint, and because it is closely relevant to contemporary issues and arguments.

[1] *Selected Works*, Vol. 9, pp. 467–483.

Lenin was concerned with the kind of education required to build a socialist society having communism as its aim. That is not, of course, our position in Britain at the moment; we are still engaged in the struggle to bring about the transition to socialism. All the more necessary, then, to fight to make available to the working class—even under capitalism—the sum total of human knowledge in Lenin's sense, since this must necessarily be the foundation for all effective social and political action.

Of course, this kind of statement does not finally solve the problem of the content of education—at primary or secondary level; it provides the guidelines within which the solution may be found. There is still the difficult problem of selecting its basic content, of establishing the interrelations between different aspects, and of arranging its structure in terms of levels or stages in the development of the child. There is also the crucially important question of identifying and separating the specifically *ideological* components of knowledge from what, for brevity, may be called knowledge itself. Such components play a key role from the standpoint of assimilating the new generations to capitalist ideology, of gaining, through the process of education, the consent of the governed—of habituating people to the status quo.

Such ideological components (in the sense of distortion through bourgeois ideology) are particularly prevalent in the social sciences as we have seen, for instance, in the case of Intelligence Testing. This is precisely what Lenin meant when he stressed the need to assimilate this knowledge *critically*, and there is a lot of work to be done in this field. What is necessary is an analysis of the way bourgeois ideology penetrates the various subjects with the aim of winning acceptance of the existing social framework, of the power relations between classes in production, and in capitalist society as a whole. But it is worth repeating that the principle on which the content of education should be established, as enunciated by Lenin, is clear—and it is one that is very relevant to contemporary controversies on this topic in Britain today.

Another leading Marxist who was deeply concerned with the nature of education and its role was the Italian leader, Antonio Gramsci, whose notes "On Education" in *Prison Notebooks* are well worth studying.[1] The common school, he says, has the entire function of educating and forming new generations; the aim of the primary

[1] Q. Hoare and G. Nowell Smith (eds), *Selections from the Prison Notebooks of Antonio Gramsci* (1971), pp. 26–43.

school is to develop what he calls a "dynamic conformism" (assimilation of co-operative forms of social behaviour (?))—and of the school system generally to prepare the student as an autonomous, creative, responsible person. His objective is what he calls the "creative school"—organised as a collective, and developing the "capacity for intellectual and practical creativity, and of autonomy of orientation and initiative". (It may be supposed, incidentally, that Gramsci is speculating here on the nature of education and schooling in a socialist society.)

Gramsci saw education as a collective, participatory process—in some senses as a transaction between teacher and taught; he refers to the need for "the truly active participation" of the pupil in school. The relation between teacher and pupil is seen as active and reciprocal so that every teacher is also a pupil and every pupil a teacher. This difficult but, in my view, stimulating and rewarding concept of the nature of the educational process is derived by Gramsci from that central kernel of Marx's thinking, the *Theses on Feuerbach*, and particularly that where Marx is concerned with the dialectics of human change—"the educator must be educated".

Gramsci stressed the importance of activity in education; nevertheless, quite correctly, in my view, though sympathetic to their endeavours he took issue with some aspects of the "progressive" theorists of his day. Thus, criticising one of the exponents of the theory that teachers cannot predetermine "from outside" the development of the "spiritual activity" of the child, Gramsci wrote:[1]

"It is believed that a child's mind is like a ball of string which the teacher helps to unwind. In reality each generation educates the new generation, i.e. forms it, and education is a struggle against instincts linked to the elementary biological functions, a struggle against nature, to dominate it and create the 'contemporary' man of the epoch."

Again, stressing the active nature of the common school, Gramsci wrote: "The entire common school is an active school, though it is necessary to place limits on libertarian ideologies in this field and to stress with some energy the duty of the adult generations to 'mould' the new generations." (Unfashionable, perhaps, but surely correct, B.S.) Finally, in a perceptive paragraph, Gramsci states that "the active school is still in its romantic phase, in which elements of struggle

[1] *Ibid.*, p. 103, 94n.

against the mechanical and Jesuitical school have become unhealthily exaggerated—through a desire to distinguish themselves sharply from the latter, and for political reasons. It is necessary," he adds, "to enter the 'classical', rational phase, and to find in the ends to be attained the natural source for developing the appropriate methods and forms." This paragraph is, in my view, well worth pondering, since it is in that exercise, I suggest, that the left-progressive forces are now engaged in this country.

Like Lenin, Gramsci was sharply critical of what he also called "the old school". But he also denied that education should be based on a so-called specifically working-class culture. Both wanted to take what was best—what was essential—from the old school and to transform it, maintaining rigorous levels of study and achievement (Gramsci particularly warned against the temptation to let things slip with the wide extension of education). Teachers, who inevitably belonged to the middle strata, had the difficult and responsible task of inducting working-class children into knowledge, science and culture. Gramsci placed immense emphasis on their role, holding that the transformation of education, along these lines, was as much a matter of persons, of the teachers and who they were, and of the whole social complex, as of new curricula and methods—that is, of programmes and blueprints.

Finally, are these perspectives viable? Can we conceive of mass education for everyone—on this sort of level?

Obviously, not immediately—nor tomorrow, but in the long run, and finally under socialism—and through the transition to communism—yes. The fact that we live in a capitalist society does not mean that we should not fight for the humanist transformation of the school along these lines—indeed it renders it all the more urgent. The fight for comprehensive education, for the unification of the school, for participatory means of control, for clarification as regards the content of education, methodology and general ethos—all this is a start at least, and one of some significance in relation to this perspective—even if it is still necessary to find appropriate forms for such an education. And it is precisely in this area that intensive discussion among Marxists and others is necessary.

But, it is argued, the mass of the children are not capable of the levels of knowledge, skills, abilities, culture, that you predicate.

It is precisely here that Marxism should give confidence. Marxism stresses the educability of the normal child—the possibility, indeed inevitability of change, movement and development. It rejects the idea that the child is fatally conditioned by heredity or the so-called environment. This does not mean that Marxists hold that all children are equal, that there are no differences in the structure of the brain and higher nervous system at birth. Of course there are. The Marxist stand is that these anatomical-physiological peculiarities *condition*, but do not *determine* the child's development. That development is determined, rather, by the nature and form of the child's *activity*—in the home, at the school, and elsewhere.

The child is in no sense the passive subject of external stimuli. It is in his active interpenetration with his environment that specific characteristics are formed. Marxism sees the child's development as a matter of historical formation in the process of his education and upbringing. No child is born with given abilities or skills—only with the pre-requisites of their formation. In school this formation is a matter of systematic intervention—the school, and the teacher, has the responsibility of creating the optimum conditions in which this formation can take place. Education, therefore, is a process of active formation, and is seen as such by Marxists.

Mankind differs from the rest of the animal world primarily through the development of language, of speech, with its power of abstraction and generalisation. In his communication with adults through the use of language man (unlike the rest of the animal world which can only learn through the formation of conditional reflexes) is able potentially to grasp, assimilate, and finally appropriate that sum of knowledge to which Lenin referred.

Of course there are all sorts of difficulties in the way, both theoretical and practical—if we are thinking in terms of finding the correct educational procedures; more important, there are plenty of economic and political difficulties which must be overcome, while for the practising teacher in the classroom an immense variety of day-to-day problems have to be faced and overcome. It is clearly essential to find new forms for education—new solutions; to develop new types of pupil-teacher relations which will help to encourage and release the energies of the students; to learn how to use the familiar local environment of the child and its culture to induct him into universal aspects of knowledge, science and culture itself; to find the correct balance between flexibility and structure allowing both for the child's independent activity and the guidance necessary to facilitate and optimise learning. These are certainly crucial questions, and there are many more. But I suggest that the concept of mass, systematic, high-level education for all is not a pipe-dream. It is a conception that Marxists should hold firmly before them and attempt to realise, in spite of all the difficulties, even if its full achievement is possible only under socialism. In this sense the fight for education can be seen as an integral and crucially important aspect of the struggle for socialism.

INDEX

283